# Do You Believe in Magic?

# Do You Believe in Magic?

*Baseball and America in the Groundbreaking Year of 1966*

David Krell

ROWMAN & LITTLEFIELD
*Lanham • Boulder • New York • London*

Published by Rowman & Littlefield
An imprint of The Rowman & Littlefield Publishing Group, Inc.
4501 Forbes Boulevard, Suite 200, Lanham, Maryland 20706
www.rowman.com

86-90 Paul Street, London EC2A 4NE, United Kingdom

British Library Cataloguing in Publication Information available

**Library of Congress Cataloging-in-Publication Data**

Names: Krell, David, 1967– author.
Title: Do you believe in magic? : baseball and America in the
   groundbreaking year of 1966 / David Krell.
Other titles: Incredible story of baseball and America in 1966
Description: Lanham, MD : Rowman & Littlefield, [2022] | Includes
   bibliographical references and index. | Summary: "This book offers a
   unique look at a pivotal year in American history, tracing the
   significant events of 1966 by using the baseball season as its narrative
   arc but also examining the Space Race, television, film, politics,
   music, and more"—Provided by publisher.
Identifiers: LCCN 2022031584 (print) | LCCN 2022031585 (ebook) | ISBN
   9781538159439 (cloth) | ISBN 9781538159446 (epub)
Subjects: LCSH: Popular culture—United States—History—20th century. |
   United States—Social life and customs—1945–1970. | Baseball—United
   States—History—20th century.
Classification: LCC E169.12 .K728 2022  (print) | LCC E169.12  (ebook) |
   DDC 973.923—dc23/eng/20221021
LC record available at https://lccn.loc.gov/2022031584
LC ebook record available at https://lccn.loc.gov/2022031585

*For Mom.*
*Sheila Krell is the Sandy Koufax of moms.*

*For Debra Drabowsky*
*(August 4, 1959–October 5, 1959)*

# CONTENTS

# ACKNOWLEDGMENTS

LIBRARIANS AND ARCHIVISTS ARE THE UNSUNG SENTINELS PRESERVING history. I'm indebted to those who helped me on this extraordinary journey of chronicling a pivotal year in America.

Cassidy Lent at the National Baseball Hall of Fame and Museum's Giamatti Research Center provided files of news clippings that were invaluable for learning about the backgrounds of the players on the 1966 World Series teams—the Baltimore Orioles and Los Angeles Dodgers. Jon Kendle, her counterpart at the Pro Football Hall of Fame, sent similar information regarding the 1966 Miami Dolphins players and owners.

The New York Public Library's Main Branch at Fifth Avenue and 42nd Street, otherwise known as the Stephen A. Schwarzman Building, is a treasure for researchers. My deepest gratitude to the staff for obtaining the entire year of the *Los Angeles Herald Examiner* on microfilm from the Center for Research Libraries in Chicago through interlibrary loan (ILL).

Also, the NYPL accessed microfilm of the *Las Vegas Sun* and *Las Vegas Review-Journal* through the ILL process courtesy of the University of Nevada, Las Vegas. They were terrific resources for researching the debut of Caesars Palace.

The *Los Angeles Times* is digitized on ProQuest and newspapers.com. Baltimore's iconic newspaper, the *Sun*, is also available through these outlets.

Reba Pile and Meg Gers graciously guided me through the *Baltimore News-American* microfilm archives at the Enoch Pratt Free Library in Baltimore.

As always, I'm indebted to Martin Grams for the opportunity to give presentations at the annual Mid-Atlantic Nostalgia Convention in Hunt Valley, Maryland. Martin is the gold standard for historians, scholars, and authors in popular culture. During the trek that coincided with my research, I purchased some rare items in the MANC vendors room to examine for cultural context—a novel marketed in the *Batman* merchandising bonanza along with board games based on *I Spy* and *Thunderball*.

The University of Wisconsin archives staff helped me procure a transcript of the ruling in *State of Wisconsin v. Milwaukee Braves*. My deep appreciation goes to Abigail Nye and Jamee Pritchard at the university's Golda Meir Library in Milwaukee along with Cat Phan and Sarah Grimm in Madison. Lee Grady at the Wisconsin Historical Society was equally valuable in this quest.

Jenna De Graffenried at the Lyndon B. Johnson Presidential Library tracked down LBJ's remarks at the dedication of the Ellenville Community Hospital along with the president's diary for that date. They were extraordinarily helpful in reconstructing this important event for the Catskill Mountains region.

Lisa Bloomfield, Art Carine, Megan Purcell, and Marty Lessner deserve notice for their enduring friendships and insightful comments on the manuscript during the drafting stage.

Seema Kalia gave me editorial feedback and asked pointed questions about the book's story lines, themes, and events. Her editing suggestions were impeccable in tightening the narrative and improving its flow. Our conversations created several topic points that I hadn't considered. During a cold mid-Atlantic winter, she schlepped from Manhattan to Jersey City for editing sessions, always brought me a muffin for breakfast, and advocated for the cultural importance of Hallmark Christmas movies during our breaks, which were rare.

I've been fortunate to make great friends in the area of baseball scholarship at various Society for American Baseball Research conferences and the annual Cooperstown Symposium on Baseball and American Culture cosponsored by the State University of New York at Oneonta and the National Baseball Hall of Fame and Museum. They've been wonderfully supportive in my writing endeavors. I hope I've returned the favor in sufficient fashion.

Hal Lifson has been a terrific advocate for scholarship on 1960s popular culture ever since I met him 30 years ago. He encouraged me then to pursue writing about this area and gave me wonderful advice that I've passed to other writers when asked: put more of yourself and your point of view into the writing. His book *Hal Lifson's 1966! A Personal View of the Coolest Year in Pop Culture History* is an amazing visual chronicle of the year's cultural hallmarks. I'm proud to call him a friend.

Extraordinary interviews offered context not available in contemporary news accounts. Thanks to those who shared their insights: Barbara Bain, Bob Buege, Jason Culp, Cathy Dutton, Jim Gates, Paul Hefti, Johanna Herwitz, Kevin Jeffries, Jean Louisa Kelly, Melissa Ludtke, Barry Mednick, Mark Melonas, Joe Moeller, Beth Morris, James Nahigian, Kenn Olson, Wes Parker, Gregg Pericich, Annie Pilon, Deborah Potter, Rolando Pujol, Mark Racop, Marc Rayman, September Sarno, Rick Schabowski, Erika Scheimer, Bob Scherr, Lloyd Schwartz, Mary Sheldon, Bonnie Strangis, Sam Strangis, John Tilden, Jeff Torborg, Bob Trostler, Eddie Watt, and Lynette Winter.

Special recognition goes to Al Schallau, who generously provided an introduction to Eddie Watt, a rookie pitcher on the 1966 Orioles. Ditto Jon Goldberg, who connected me with Orioles bat boy Bob Scherr.

Photographs were crucial in complementing the narrative. My appreciation goes to the guardians of America's photographic legacy:

Kristen Brown, Laurie Judd, and Jody Lloyd Thompson at the Georgia Institute of Technology.

Sarah Cunningham at the LBJ Presidential Library.

Terri Garst at the Los Angeles Public Library.

Ken Cobb at the New York City Department of Records and Information.

William Halldin at Bank of America.

Andrea Felder, Maurice Klapwald, and Kiowa Hammons at the New York Public Library.

Matthew Lutts at Associated Press.

Becky La Roche at the city clerk's office in Riverside, Iowa.

Lynda Havard and Michael Pinckney at the Ronald Reagan Presidential Library.

Aimee Muller at the National Archives and Records Administration.

Su Kim Chung at the University of Nevada, Las Vegas. Su Kim also gave me access to oral histories of Stanley Mallin and Stuart Mason, who were integral to the construction and success of Caesars Palace.

Joel Kowsky at NASA.

The editorial team of Nicole Carty, Matt Evans, and Matt Seccombe was exemplary in helping me execute my vision.

Finally, my thanks to Christen Karniski at Rowman & Littlefield for her enthusiastic advocacy and editorial insight. Because of Christen, I got the chance to research one of America's forgotten but impactful years. It was quite a journey. I'm privileged to share it with you.

# INTRODUCTION

It was a very good year.

These six words comprise the title of a song that became a cornerstone of Frank Sinatra's sonic portfolio. The mournful, nostalgic rendition of a middle-aged man looking back on his life was a mid-1960s staple for fans of the Hoboken-born crooner.

The description can also apply to 1966.

My purpose in writing this book is to provide a detailed portrait of American life in 1966 as cultural revolutions changed standards, ignited trends, and erased traditions.

It was a year of visionaries who overcame improbability, impertinence, and pessimists. Jay Sarno unveiled Caesars Palace, which became a destination elevating the metrics of allure, opulence, and sexual charisma. This exemplar has since been modified and enhanced, leading to its flourishing decades after glitzy peers fell victim to a new breed of sleekness on the Las Vegas Strip.

It was a year of superheroes. *Batman* started a fad sending producers scurrying for scripts featuring costumed champions. Bright colors and tilted camera angles reflected a 1960s pop-art look in this immediately accepted parody of an iconic hero.

It was a year of spies. James Bond got some formidable competition in the espionage genre. Matt Helm and Derek Flint poked fun at 007.

It was a year of space voyagers. NASA's astronauts completed five successful missions in Project Gemini, which put America on track to land astronauts on the moon in Project Apollo.

It was a year of debuts for two ballparks in the major leagues, an exit for one of the game's greatest players, and a World Series pitting experience against youth.

It was a year of groundbreaking for civil rights. President Lyndon Johnson made a judicial appointment that caused controversy but turned a corner toward a more inclusive nomination process for minority judges.

It was a very good year for America.

Any one of these topics merits a book of its own, as do the others chronicled. The selected bibliography lists worthwhile entries.

Born in 1967, my initial exposure to the events, people, and culture of 1966 came largely through watching television, listening to music, and reading history during my Generation X childhood. I had learned about the space race permeating entertainment, the Monkees topping the record charts, Miranda warnings becoming the law of the land, and Sandy Koufax dominating National League opponents.

But writing a book requires amplification of research beyond decades-old memories.

I relied on first-person interviews, contemporary news accounts, best sellers, movies, and TV shows.

Until a time machine is invented, those strategies shall remain for authors, scholars, and historians.

But if that day ever happens, sign me up for a voyage to 1966!

# PROLOGUE

## *See You in September*

THE SCENE WAS FAMILIAR TO BALTIMOREANS WHO ATE BREAKFAST AT diners and delis in early September 1966.

A symphony emerges from the clinking of silverware used to stir coffee in cups on laminated Formica-covered tables, accompanied by waitresses with beehive hairdos, too much makeup, and thickened, regional accents underscored by their penchant for calling everyone "Hon."

A customer is asked if he wants a glass of "wawder" while waiting for the order to be filled. If he has dressed too quickly, she might tease with affection that he should look in the "mere" next time to make sure he doesn't miss a "budden."

Then there's the rustling of newspapers.

With their fingers blackened from the fresh newsprint, readers home in on the sports sections of the city's two major offerings—the *Baltimore News-American* and *Baltimore Sun* described the baseball fortunes that delighted Marylanders. As they shovel forks full of greasy, runny scrambled eggs into their hungry mouths, they absorb the latest news about the O's.

Smiles abounded in early September 1966.

A slight taste of tobacco remains on their tongues after finishing a post-breakfast cigarette; they pay their bills, leave a tip, and anticipate the day ahead.

Stock traders travel to Redwood Street. Dock workers, the port. Fells Point mechanics have garages full of cars waiting for tune ups after their customers' summer road trips to Ocean City had tested aging chassis, transmissions, and engines. Pikesville doctors predict an overflow of sunburned patients who squeezed in too much sunbathing during the last days of August.

It's a good bet that the Orioles and potential postseason success would enter into the conversation at some point.

Their kids await the beginning of the new school year. While summer's warmth begins to fade with the pace of an inchworm, students return to school enveloped in palpable excitement at seeing the transformations of their classmates. Some got taller. Some changed hairstyles. Some had funny vacation stories. After the customary greetings and exchanges of worries about their upcoming annum in education, baseball-minded students also talk about a World Series berth.

Younger folks were ecstatic. Older ones, nostalgic. "How about those O's? The last time this city's seen a championship nine was back during the war. The International League Orioles beat the Louisville Colonels from the American Association in the '44 Junior World Series."

Orioles fans anticipated a good season in 1966, coming off a 94–68 record in 1965. The team was formidable; Minnesota was dominant. The Twins' 102 wins outpaced the White Sox by 7 games and the Orioles by 8 to win the American League title and face the Dodgers in the '65 World Series. The AL champs pushed their counterparts to seven games, but they lost the final contest 2–0.

Winning the '66 AL pennant is a foregone conclusion for Baltimore's rooters. But anything can happen in baseball. Rainouts may result in makeup games and doubleheaders that sap ballplayers' energies. Losing streaks may emerge. Nothing is certain.

The National League team in the World Series is not determined either; three teams have a chance in the senior circuit. Pittsburgh and San Francisco are tied as the sun rises on September 1; Los Angeles trails by three games. Optimism and anxiety pair among the teams' followers in this pennant race, which inspire questions about the Dodgers' ability to repeat as NL champions.

When the NL pennant race sorts itself out, the league's representative in the World Series finds itself heavily favored by oddsmakers, pundits, and spouters of conventional baseball wisdom against a younger AL squad that is inexperienced but determined.

Surprises are about to happen.

CHAPTER ONE

# "Cannons at the Four Corners" (January)

"HAPPY NEW YEAR!"

When the clock struck midnight and 1965 faded into America's rearview mirror, there was the requisite sense of a clean slate that comes with the turning of the calendar to another annum.

Baseball fans experience something palpable on January 1; it's the unofficial beginning of the countdown to spring training. Declaring the number of days until pitchers and catchers report to Florida or Arizona invites debates, discussions, and questions about the upcoming season, a team's prospects, and offseason trades.

Denim-clad construction workers and their blue-collar brethren in South Boston grasped frosted mugs of Narragansett Beer with their hands roughened from years of working outdoors in fickle New England weather. Throughout pubs like Amrheins—the oldest bar in Southie, as locals call this part of the capital of Massachusetts—they clinked their mugs, sang "Auld Lang Syne," washed away regrets, and welcomed 1966.

To be a New Englander is to be a Red Sox fan, and to be a Red Sox fan is to be as devoted to the team as a bishop is to catechism. Conversation about Boston baseball is a year-round activity; discussions centered on Ted Williams and the upcoming vote by the Baseball Writers' Association of America for the annual Baseball Hall of Fame induction.

Three weeks later, the "Splendid Splinter" received a then-record 93 percent vote from the scribes. Red Sox fans might have been more surprised if Williams did not get the sufficient 75 percent vote than if the

Charles River froze in August. Williams had retired in 1960 with a .344 batting average, 521 home runs, and two MVP Awards.

Speculation abounded regarding his potential figures had he not given up three seasons to serve as a navy pilot during World War II and a majority of the 1952 and 1953 seasons during the Korean War.[1]

Baseball's aura presented wherever celebrations took place on this December–January cusp. The only things that changed were the beverages and the teams.

They drank from flutes of Dom Pérignon in the celebrity-owned mansions on North Roxbury Drive in Beverly Hills and talked about the Dodgers' heart-pounding World Series victory over the Minnesota Twins in seven games.

They sipped from whiskey glasses of 12-year-old Glenlivet scotch across Philadelphia's Main Line estates and wondered whether Bo Belinsky—famed for pitching a no-hitter as a rookie with the 1962 Los Angeles Angels—could improve on his 1965 performance of 4–9 with the Phillies.

They swallowed from martini glasses of vermouth and gin in Orange County's beach communities and anticipated the impending debut of Angels Stadium.

They gulped from bottles of Ballantine's ale in Bronx apartments and lamented the first losing season for the Yankees in 40 years.

As middle-class suburbanites gathered at parties from Westchester to Westwood, they made New Year's Eve small talk on shag carpets between eating fondue, finger sandwiches, and salty snacks like Nabisco's barbecue-flavored Chit Chat crackers. Entrance into the latter half of the '60s brought a sense of modernity to America. Among the traditional accoutrements like footwear—Charm Step for women, Florsheim for men—there were pockets of transformations happening with women's hemlines getting shorter and men's hair length getting longer.

In the background, Dave Brubeck's "Take Five" might be emerging from a Dual or Zenith hi-fi player while an RCA television aired NBC's *The Tonight Show*, starring Johnny Carson—a little more than three years into his 30-year reign as host—overseeing a celebration in his live New Year's Eve broadcast six stories above Rockefeller Center's iconic skating

2

rink. Studio 6B in 30 Rockefeller Plaza was Carson's home base until he left for Burbank, California, in 1972; when midnight approached, the Nebraska-born comedian introduced reporter Ben Grauer stationed seven blocks away in Times Square above thousands of people watching the traditional ball drop on top of the Allied Chemical Tower.

Grauer rattled off the highlights of 1965 with the speed of an auctioneer and the excitement of a ringmaster: the emerging conflict in Vietnam, expanded social programs like Medicare, controversy over the impending transit strike in New York City, and a record close for the Dow—just a few points shy of 1,000. Optimism made its annual appearance in the Times Square event; Grauer used the phrases "a sense of hope" and "a manifestation of the American spirit" to describe the scene.

Johnny Carson hosted NBC's *The Tonight Show* from 1962 to 1992. His live broadcast on New Year's Eve 1965 featured reporter Ben Grauer from the Hotel Astor in Times Square talking about events, including New York City's impending transit strike to begin 1966. COURTESY OF FRIEDMAN-ABELES PHOTOGRAPH COLLECTION/NEW YORK PUBLIC LIBRARY

A sense of hope boosted fans of the Baltimore Orioles anticipating another year rooting for a contender. Their third-place finish of 94–68 slotted them one game behind the White Sox and eight games behind the Twins in 1965. Maryland's largest metropolis—named for Cecil Calvert, 2nd Baron Baltimore—already had a rich baseball history when the St. Louis Browns left the Midwest in 1953, planted their flag in the Chesapeake Bay region, and changed the team moniker to Orioles. It was an endearment—Maryland's state bird is the oriole.

From 1882 to 1889, the Baltimore Orioles played in the American Association. In 1890, the team joined the Atlantic Association, then reverted to their former league to replace the Brooklyn Gladiators, who closed operations in late August.

Baltimore got one of the berths when the National League incorporated four teams from the AA in 1892 and topped the NL from 1894 to 1896. They also won the Temple Cup—a trophy for the winner of the NL playoffs—in 1896 and 1897.

The American League debuted in 1901 with another squad named the Orioles. This team lasted two seasons. From the wreckage caused by competitors raiding the roster for talent arose the New York Highlanders in 1903—later dubbed the Yankees—but it is not considered a predecessor by most baseball historians.

For Baltimore teenager Bob Scherr, the new year meant something more than celebrating with songs, parties, and TV specials. As the batboy for the Orioles, Scherr looked forward to his third—and what would be his last—season with his hometown team.

Scherr's after-school job gave him the best seat in the house for a magical season in 1966 and made him the envy of every schoolkid in the Baltimore area. But his tasks were more grunt than glamour. "We lived in Northwest Baltimore, close to Pikesville," explains Scherr.

> I had to get to the stadium four hours before the game. The clubhouse boy and I would clean the shoes and cleats, mop the floors, and clean the clubhouse. It took two buses and more than an hour to get to Memorial Stadium. When the game was over, I cleaned the spikes again, then polished and shined them. I would

take a cab home. For night games, sometimes I didn't get home until 2:00 A.M.

I got the job through Milt Pappas, who was a friend of the family. My father was a lawyer and he had represented a car dealership where a lot of the Orioles bought their cars. Whenever Milt would pitch, he would leave tickets. In 1964, there was a vacancy for a batboy, and I asked him if he would help me get the job. And he did.

At first I was the batboy for the visiting team. That lasted about a month. When the Orioles' batboy became one of the clubhouse boys, they moved me to his job starting in May 1964. Coincidentally, that's when I turned 15. I had that job for three years, then quit it and stayed with the Orioles for another three years as a statistician.

I still had to balance my schoolwork with my job, so I did homework in between innings in the tunnel leading to the dugout. It was a skill that lasted a lifetime. I could do 15 minutes of homework between innings and then do my job in the dugout. I learned how to work in short segments.

———⊙⊛⊙———

During the offseason, Scherr's benefactor had lost his slot with the Orioles when the front office traded Pappas, Dick Simpson, and Jack Baldschun for Frank Robinson. "Cannons at the four corners!" exclaimed Orioles general manager Harry Dalton in describing Baltimore's new defensive alignment: third baseman Brooks Robinson, first baseman Boog Powell, left fielder Curt Blefary, and right fielder Frank Robinson.[2] Pappas acknowledged the pragmatism of the exchange: "It's a good trade both ways. Cincinnati needed a starting pitcher and the Orioles have needed another big guy to drive in runs. Robinson has proved he can do that."[3]

Indeed. The Cincinnati import was a template for supremacy at the plate, leading the NL in slugging percentage three consecutive years and twice leading the major leagues, Rookie of the Year in 1956, MVP in 1961, MLB leader in runs scored and doubles in 1962, and a six-time All-Star when he arrived in Baltimore.

By late 1966, he would add a few more honors to his résumé.

Though he understood front-office fickleness and Robinson's value, the situation mystified Pappas because there was another member of the Orioles who would have sprinted to Friendship Airport for the next flight to Cincinnati.

"As a matter of fact, I never asked to go," said Pappas in a 1992 interview.

Steve Barber was the guy who was really anxious to be traded at the end of the 1965 season. He wanted to get out of Baltimore and asked to be traded, and we thought that if anybody was going to be traded, it would've been Steve Barber, because he had voiced his dissatisfaction with the city of Baltimore, the Baltimore Orioles organization, and so on and so forth. He was very vocal about it. But here it turned out to be me, and obviously it was quite a shock. Then getting to Cincinnati, and being traded for Frank Robinson, who was very popular—every time I took the mound I got booed. So it was not a very good situation for me in Cincinnati. I hated every minute I was there. Didn't like it at all.[4]

Robinson was not exactly fond of the decision either.

To exchange him seemed unthinkable to Reds fans unless Fort Knox was included in the deal. "All of those trade rumors I had been reading kind of died down after the baseball meetings," recalled Robinson later that December. "I sort of forgot about them."[5] It was an unpleasant surprise for the former Rookie of the Year and MVP who had found adoration in Cincinnati. "And I just asked myself—why? Why? And I was shocked, and I was hurt."[6]

For Reds general manager Bill DeWitt, the decision to send the slugger to Baltimore came down to age instead of ability. "We hated to give up Robby, but to get something good, you've got to give up something good and we would rather sacrifice an older player than a younger one,"[7] said DeWitt. There was a question about a trade involving Roger Maris and the Yankees, but DeWitt dismissed it and confirmed that the only other deal proffered with any concreteness came from Houston—a swap for Bob Aspromonte and Dick Farrell.[8]

Robinson's skills were unquestionable. But there was some baggage.

In 1961, Robinson was arrested for carrying a concealed .25 caliber automatic that he pulled out during an argument at a Cincinnati restaurant. A plea deal resulted in a $250 fine. It beat the alternative—a sentence of 1–3 years.[9]

"I try to get along with all the guys but, even though he's my teammate, I can't take Robinson," said Don Newcombe in a 1963 *Sports Illustrated* profile. "That guy is out there trying to maim people."[10]

When the 1966 baseball season ended, Robinson had become synonymous with Baltimore. If someone had posited that the city should have its own Mount Rushmore, the suggestions for candidates might have overwhelmingly been Robinson, along with Cecil Calvert, Francis Scott Key, and Edgar Allan Poe.

Even though Robinson's star power brought anticipation for the fan base, it was upsetting for Scherr because of his family's relationship with Pappas. Plus, the job's luster had evaporated. "By that time, being the Orioles batboy was no longer a dream job," reveals Scherr.

It got old and I was tired. It was a lot of manual labor. I almost didn't stay when they traded Milt because I was upset. But I thought about it, and Frank was such a great player, he could make a difference. In 1964, I had experienced a pennant race. Going into the last week, any one of three teams could have won: Chicago, New York, Baltimore.

In 1966, the regular second baseman was Jerry Adair. In spring training, Davey Johnson beat him out for the job. Adair was upset because he was only being used for pinch hitting. He stopped coming into the dugout during the games.

Near the All-Star break, Palmer was getting ready to bat when Bauer called for Adair to pinch hit. He wasn't there, so Palmer had to go up and hit. When the inning was over, I had to go to the bathroom. There I am in the stall with the door closed when I hear Bauer coming up the tunnel shouting for Adair.

He hears Bauer screaming and runs into the bathroom. Bauer storms in and grabs Adair. I see them through the opening of the door. Bauer has him against the wall, but they don't know I'm in the bathroom. The fight ended soon after that. During the All-Star break, Adair was traded.[11]

Standing at six feet, Scherr towered among his friends and some of the Orioles. So, instead of calling him the Bat Boy, they dubbed him the Bat Man.[12] A similarly named comic-book icon made his television debut that January, inspiring a superhero craze that dominated popular culture in 1966.

———— ✎ ————

The exterior of a Pasadena house on South San Rafael Avenue became known as "stately Wayne Manor" in the establishing shots of *Batman*. This new take on an old hero premiered on January 12, 1966, starring Adam West in the title role and Burt Ward as Robin the Boy Wonder. It was full of satire, camp, ultrafamous guest stars, and celebrity cameos.

Millionaire Bruce Wayne lives in his mansion with his teenage ward, Dick Grayson. As Batman and Robin, also known as the Dynamic Duo, they battle crime in Gotham City and conduct brainstorming sessions that take place in their inner sanctum beneath the mansion—the Batcave.

Although it had been used by filmmakers dating back to the silent films era, Bronson Canyon is most famous for supplying the Batcave's exterior. The opening at Bronson Cave—somewhat misnamed because it's a 50-foot, man-made tunnel through rock—is what viewers saw as the egress for the Batmobile. Set dressing included brush. Each week, the Batmobile emerges from the opening as the heroes begin their 14-mile voyage to Gotham City for a meeting with Police Commissioner Gordon and Police Chief O'Hara about that week's criminal crisis.

Debuting in *Detective Comics* #27 in 1939, Batman was cemented in the culture by the time that 20th Century Fox head of production Bill Self ran his idea for a TV show by William Dozier, a prominent producer and executive. Success was immediate. "I think we were surprised by the enormity of it," remembers Bonnie Strangis, who worked as Dozier's secretary for 16 years. "The test numbers were really, really low."[13]

Dozier used his secretary's first name for Gotham City police commissioner Gordon's offscreen secretary. Sam Strangis hadn't yet married

Bonnie when he worked as Dozier's production manager. "He was probably the best executive in the business," remembers Strangis. "He knew who to hire, how to put a package together, how to sell a show. He could sell anything."[14]

Dozier's daughter Deborah Potter recalled,

My father was in the used-car business before show business. He had an arrangement with a local car dealer where he would rent a Lincoln Continental. He was at a difficult spot in his career in the film business when Self gave him a bunch of Batman comics. There was my father sitting in the first-class section on an airplane reading comic books! It was my father's idea to do the show just like the stories with the Biff! Pop! Bam! Wham! in the fight scenes that you saw on the comic-book pages. He invented the show's camp style, but he didn't want to do it live in front of an audience. He was a very hands-on producer. When they created the logo, he showed it to me. I said that it should be a little longer, like a real bat. He listened to my idea and changed it.

The show had a meteoric rise and fall. It was successful immediately and actors wanted to do guest spots. It was like The Soupy Sales Show in that regard because Soupy had a recurring bit about a pie getting thrown in someone's face. Famous actors wanted to get the pie just like they wanted to be the guest villain or villainess on Batman.

My father's production company was called Greenway Productions, after the Beverly Hills street where we lived. My stepmother had life tenancy in the house from her late husband, David May of the May Company department stores.[15]

In August 1965, Dozier had analyzed the show's structural possibilities for ABC executive Douglas Cramer. One idea was to have the show air five days a week with each installment lasting 15 minutes, but Dozier favored a one-hour show in two 30-minute segments with a cliffhanger between them.[16]

With rare exceptions, every *Batman* story consisted of two half-hour episodes. The first begins with that story's special guest villain or villainess raising hell and havoc in Gotham City, forcing Gordon to call Batman and Robin for reinforcements. He does not know that the Bat-Phone actually rings at "stately Wayne Manor," where Bruce and Dick live with Bruce's aunt, Harriet Cooper, and the manor's butler, Alfred Pennyworth. Alfred is the only other person who knows that Bruce and Dick are Batman and Robin.

The format is simple. Alfred picks up the Bat-Phone in the study and notifies "Master Bruce" about an urgent matter. After a briefing from the commissioner, Bruce turns a knob hidden in a Shakespeare bust causing a bookcase to slide and reveal the Bat-Poles leading to the Batcave. Off go the heroes in the Batmobile to solve the latest crime threatening Gotham City. When the Batmobile exits the Batcave, a sign says that Gotham City is 14 miles away.

The Doziers had a beach house near Topanga Beach, where the former used-car salesman could be found pulling his latest Lincoln Continental into the driveway and soon meeting with *Batman*'s head writer, Lorenzo Semple, on the deck. In the Malibu sunshine, they hashed out the show's look, tone, and stories for what would become a popular-culture phenomenon. When Semple returned to his Old Spanish house at 765 Kingman Avenue in Santa Monica, it was a good bet that he would have three Carlton cigarettes lit in his downstairs office underneath the living room while he planned story lines for *Batman*.

After being injured as a volunteer ambulance driver in Libya during World War II, Semple served as an intelligence officer in Europe. His writing career launched as a short-story scribe for the *Saturday Evening Post* and *Collier's Weekly*. Two Broadway plays followed, along with scripts that established him as a TV writer; one script became a feature film starring Steve McQueen, one of his early works after *Wanted: Dead or Alive*.

When Dozier asked Semple to help him on the challenge of bringing a satirical version of the Dark Knight to television, the writer was living in Spain. It was a natural fit for Semple, whose curiosity helped him build an encyclopedic knowledge.

Semple's daughter Johanna Herwitz recalled,

My parents were in Mexico because they were novelty seekers. They liked to take off and do something just for fun, just to have a change. One year, they moved to Aspen. My parents gave dinner parties where my father would hold court, but he didn't really like to talk about writing. He was self-deprecating about it. He recognized that Batman was a special thing, though his interests went beyond writing scripts—he made model steam engines![17]

Semple began his *Batman* tenure with a script about the Riddler, played with a maniacal giggle by Frank Gorshin. A nightclub comedian and impressionist who looked like he could have been film actor Richard Widmark's younger brother, Gorshin had gained national fame with a dozen appearances on *The Ed Sullivan Show*.

"Lorenzo's pilot for *Batman* was so excruciatingly funny to me and fresh and different, I had never seen anything like it on television or even in the movies," remembered West.

And so, I said to my agent, "Okay, if they want me, don't leave the studio. Sign me up now because I want to do this. I really think I've got a handle on it." Sure enough, that was it. And I signed on and then they said, "However, would you test with a young man to see whether the chemistry's right." And I said of course I would.[18]

The model steam-engine maker with a curiosity as deep as Coldwater Canyon became a 1970s fixture in Hollywood storytelling, penning *The Parallax View*, *The Drowning Pool*, *Three Days of the Condor*, *King Kong*, *Papillon*, and *The Marriage of a Young Stockbroker*.

Dozier and Semple congregated with other writers and directors on how to distinguish *Batman* with tilted angles, bright colors, and a straight rather than exaggerated portrayal of the characters. Humor came from the absurdity. In the pilot, a full-costumed Batman enters the What a Way to Go-Go club and tells the owner that he doesn't wish to draw attention.

During preproduction, *Batman* earned the endorsement of Bob Kane, the comic-book artist who created the title character. In a letter to Dozier from November 1965, Kane said that he looked forward to seeing the Batmobile and comparing the costumes on the TV show to those in the comic books. Having looked at the scripts, he also said that he would have produced the show with the same "tongue-in-cheek" approach and pop-art visuals that Dozier envisioned.[19]

George Barris got the assignment to design the Batmobile. It stands alone as a marvel of automotive engineering, artistic modification, and popular-culture legend.

The Batmobile is a converted 1955 Lincoln Futura, a concept car that Ford unveiled at the 1955 Chicago Auto Show. With fins, a bubble windshield in the front, and a rocket-like exhaust of flame out the back, the Batmobile was a perfect blend for the space age. Barris introduced various gadgets and made adjustments, including the Bat-Phone, a TV screen named the Batscope, and a truncated steering wheel at the 10 and 2 positions resembling an airplane's control. Barris made three fiberglass replicas but used the chassis of the 1966 Ford Galaxie.

Mark Racop makes fiberglass replicas for nearly $300,000 each. With an array that would rival the Great Library of Alexandria, Racop has more than 93,000 photos and videos in addition to an encyclopedic knowledge about the show's 120 episodes. Licensed by DC Comics, Racop's team at Fiberglass Freaks in Indiana proves that the Batmobile is timeless. "You can park a 1966 Batmobile next to a $300,000 Rolls Royce, a million dollar Lamborghini, or a Ferrari, and nobody cares about the other cars at all,"[20] says Racop.

Adam West's portrayal earned him the affection of baby boomers who saw *Batman* on ABC and Generation Xers who found it in syndication during the 1970s. His competition was Lyle Waggoner; Dozier favored West. On September 13, 1965, Dozier wrote a letter to West explaining that Waggoner's audition resulted from a prior deal to screen-test for a role. Waggoner's *Batman* test was therefore pro forma. Plus, ABC had been considering Waggoner for another show, so it was a two-birds-with-one-stone situation. Additionally, Dozier revealed to West that Ward—whose real name was Gervis—would be the probable choice for Robin.[21]

West prepared for the role with literature. "I decided to read novels that scraped around inside the heads of characters who maintained dual identities, such as *The Scarlet Pimpernel* and *Scaramouche*," said the actor, whose prior television credits included *Maverick*, *77 Sunset Strip*, *Hawaiian Eye*, and *The Rifleman*. "I was a bit alarmed when I found the villain of [*Scaramouche*], the Marquis de la Tour D'Azyr, more interesting than the hero, due to his clever repartee and icy cruelness. I began to realize that whatever I did on the show, the villains were invariably going to be more interesting."[22]

Indeed, every episode's special guest villain or villainess balanced outlandish schemes against the righteousness of the Dynamic Duo; audiences rejoiced at seeing that week's ploy to dominate Gotham City and the ultimate defeat at the hands of Batman and Robin. Guest stars provided over-the-top portrayals that would have been flat in the hands of actors with lesser skills; their résumés had enough awards to fill a couple of trophy cases. David Wayne, Maurice Evans, Victor Slezak, Burgess Meredith, Julie Newmar, and Ethel Merman were Tony Award winners. Shelley Winters had two Oscars. Anne Baxter had one, plus a Golden Globe. Cliff Robertson and Art Carney had Emmys.

*Batman*'s absurdity has no greater example than Cesar Romero portraying the Joker. Romero's refusal to shave his trademark mustache—which the white makeup on his face could not obscure—showed the comic appeal of this Gotham City universe. Villainy was inspired not only by characters like the Joker, who had existed in the comic books, but also by the writers creating their own contributions either from imagination or from well-known pop-culture figures.

They based Ma Parker on the criminal matriarch Ma Barker, who was killed with one of her sons in a shootout with the FBI in central Florida in 1935. Winters played the fictional version in *Batman* and the real counterpart in the 1970 movie *Bloody Mama*.

The title character of *Shane*, a 1953 movie starring Alan Ladd, inspired Shame, a western-themed villain. The Clock King, the Penguin, the Riddler, and Catwoman came from the Batman comic books. Writers also had fun with naming the henchmen of that week's villain or villainess.

The Minstrel strummed his lute, taunting Batman and Robin with rhymes as he sought to take over the Gotham City Stock Exchange with the help of Treble and Bass. Inspired by Robin Hood, the Archer disrupts

Gotham City with Maid Marilyn, Crier Tuck, and Big John. Gotham City mayor Linseed is a play on the name of New York City mayor John Lindsay, who presided when *Batman* aired on ABC.

Burgess Meredith's interpretation of the Penguin included a quacking noise when he got excited; it became a hallmark along with those already established by the comic-book stories—purple top hat, cigarette holder, and monocle. There have been reports that Dozier first offered the role to Spencer Tracy and Mickey Rooney, but it's difficult to imagine anyone but Meredith. The Rooney story was stated again in the 2003 TV movie *Return to the Batcave: The Misadventures of Adam and Burt*, which recreated the genesis, production, and cancellation of the series.

Meredith was the epitome of a working actor ever since 1935, when Maxwell Anderson's *The Winterset* established him in a leading role. A year later, he appeared in the film version. In 1939, he costarred in *Of Mice and Men* with Lon Chaney Jr. But a patriotic country seeing World War II depicted in the movie theaters identified him as famed war correspondent Ernie Pyle in 1945's *The Story of G.I. Joe*.

It was a glorious time to be an actor. Meredith had been roommates with Jimmy Stewart in Coldwater Canyon; his acting clique also included Charles Laughton and Henry Fonda. But Meredith suffered when the House Committee on Un-American Activities pursued the slightest whiff of communism in Hollywood beginning in the late 1940s, even if an actor went to a couple of communist group meetings more than a decade before. Meredith found himself on the Hollywood blacklist. His highly significant career deflated.

By the early 1960s, he had rebounded; Rod Serling cast him in what became one of the signature episodes of *The Twilight Zone*: a librarian who survives a nuclear holocaust and joyfully assembles the books that he finally has time to read, then suffers a breakdown when his glasses break. Otto Preminger, primarily a director and one of three actors to play Mr. Freeze on *Batman*, had cast Meredith in several of his films, including the Washington, DC–based *Advise and Consent* in 1962.

Meredith's granddaughter Annie Pilon recalled,

He thought that Batman would be a one-shot deal. He didn't expect it to be so big. But he loved that the villains were such over-the-top characters. There was a theatrical quality that you don't see on TV. When Danny DeVito played the Penguin in *Batman Returns*, my grandfather appreciated that the movie introduced a new generation to the characters. Plus, the TV series enjoyed a renaissance because of the movies.

*Batman* was his first true commercial success after his career was almost annihilated by McCarthyism. It was sweet revenge to play a victim of communist hunting in *Advise and Consent* and Army lawyer Joseph Welch in the 1977 TV movie *Tail Gunner Joe* about Joe McCarthy. It was Welch who asked, "Have you no sense of decency, sir?" That was the beginning of the end for McCarthy. My grandfather won an Emmy for that role.

His success began a new part of his career and proved that it's never too late to follow your dream.[23]

Meredith's career could have stayed in the theater. But his desire to explore different facets of the human condition provided a roster of credits exemplifying the life of a character actor. To Meredith, the Penguin "had a Dickensian quality—or a spoof of one. It was fun to act."[24]

It's to the credit of Meredith and his fellow portrayers of villainy that their acting is recognized and admired decades after *Batman* was canceled in 1968. "Of all the roles I've ever done, this is the first time my own kids have wanted to watch me," said Meredith. "If I spent all my time in Shakespearean companies and only did art movies like Olivier, my position would be more dignified and more serious, I might even be a better actor. But this is America, and I'm a man moved by the rhythms of his time, so I'll just take amusement at being a paradox."[25]

Robert Butler directed the first two story lines featuring the Riddler and the Penguin. "I remember consciously thinking this guy knows most of the answers about performing and has been most of the places one performs," said Butler of Meredith in an interview for the Archive of American Television.[26]

Although the Penguin became his most famous role, Meredith solidified his popular-culture status with his portrayal of Mickey Gold-mill in the 1976 movie *Rocky*. Sylvester Stallone created the characters of the gruff boxing trainer and his protégé, heavyweight boxer and oft-underdog Rocky Balboa in the first three movies and the fifth of the *Rocky* franchise. Meredith's performance earned him kudos from his costar, who called the actor "an irreplaceable legend, a craftsman who rarely comes along, not in one generation but in several generations."[27]

There's a park in Pomona, New York, where Meredith had a home beginning in the 1930s; he stayed there when he traveled back and forth from New York to Los Angeles. But there's nary a mention of his distinguished acting career on the signs of this Rockland County green space. If kids create scenes based on Batman characters while they're playing in Burgess Meredith Park, it's quite possible that they're unaware of the namesake's rich legacy in theater, film, and television.

─────❦─────

Gotham City's real-life mayoral counterpart began his first term as the clock struck midnight on New Year's Eve and faced his first crisis when New York City's transit workers went on strike; it was resolved 12 days later. John Lindsay had been elected to Congress in 1958, but the handsome, personable Republican broke with party lines by backing liberal policies, including the Department of Housing and Urban Development. President Lyndon Johnson appointed Robert Weaver, who he described as "a deep thinker and a quiet but articulate man of action,"[28] to be his first HUD secretary. Four days later, the Senate confirmed him. It took less than three hours.[29]

President Lyndon Johnson appointed Robert Weaver to be the secretary of housing and urban development in January 1966. Here are Weaver and Johnson at the president's signing of the act that created the HUD Department a few months before he got the appointment. COURTESY OF LYNDON B. JOHNSON PRESIDENTIAL LIBRARY

Weaver—who headed the Housing and Home Financing Agency, which got overtaken by HUD—was the first Black member of the cabinet. His great-grandfather had been a slave.[30]

It was another breakthrough in a year of terrific change.

CHAPTER TWO

# Hollywood's Other Dynamic Duo (February)

LESBIANS. CUNNILINGUS. ORGASMS. DRUG ADDICTION. BODY IMAGE. Virgins. Sex. Suicide. Autism.

These subjects were taboo for mainstream entertainment until Jacqueline Susann wrote *Valley of the Dolls*. Not merely a work of titillation, it focuses on a troika of women who suffer epic tragedies as their journeys of success and strife intertwine to underscore the phrase "All that glitters is not gold."

Susann combined events, people, and personalities from her real life and those learned through the show-business grapevine to create her narrative. It pulled back the curtain of glamour to reveal the emotional, mental, and physical burdens of success in show business with details that left readers in 1966 turning the pages so fast they risked getting paper cuts.

In the book, Jennifer North is a beautiful actress with breasts that men crave to nuzzle and women envy to have. She keeps her three-year lesbian affair in Europe secret from the public and rises to the top of Hollywood's inconstant roster of stars. When Jennifer gets diagnosed with breast cancer, she overdoses on pills—described by Susann as "dolls"—rather than get a mastectomy to save her life. Her reason is selfless; Jennifer's husband, a United States senator, worships her body. So she believes the removal of a breast would amount to failure in his eyes.

Anne Welles has natural beauty. A friend of Jennifer's, she is the proverbial "good girl" that men want to marry. While living in a boarding house with aspiring teenage actress Ethel O'Neill—later renamed Neely O'Hara—Anne begins working as a secretary for a talent agency. Anne suggests that Neely take over a small part in a Broadway show starring legendary actress Helen Lawson and implores her boss to represent Neely.

Though she begins as a wide-eyed novice entertainer who only wants a break, Neely becomes a living example of the seven deadly sins. She lusts after Anne's husband, gains weight from her gluttony, gets greedy for more success even though she becomes a famous singer and Oscar-winning actress, acts like a sloth because of the tiring effect of the "dolls," gets fired from studios for not showing up on time to film her scenes, demeans people who only want to help her succeed, expresses envy of younger entertainers who she believes are a threat, and embodies selfish pride by refusing to believe in her drug addiction when sent to a facility to conquer it.

Lyon Burke, Anne's husband, reluctantly manages Neely's career and at first abhors her egotism, greed, and Vesuvian temper. When Anne learns that Neely is bedding Lyon, the realization stuns her emotionally with the force of a rocket thrust.

*Valley of the Dolls* set a new standard for publishers. Where they might have been afraid to showcase certain authors, Susann changed the paradigm.

———— ∞ ————

While adults devoured the tales in Susann's fictional but plausible universe, their children watched moderate fare like *Gilligan's Island* in 1966. Airing on CBS from 1964 to 1967, this sitcom featured seven characters from different walks of life forced to work together to survive.

The sitcom's theme song explained the premise: the SS *Minnow*, a Honolulu tour boat, encounters a vicious storm and shipwrecks on an island 300 miles from Hawaii with five passengers and a crew of two.

Through three seasons, three TV movie reunions, and two animated series, it's never known whether Gilligan is a first name or last name.

Real-life references were rare. One exception was the February 24, 1966 episode "Ship Ahoax," when Ginger claims that she has psychic powers and says, "In five minutes, I can convince him he's President Johnson. In ten that he's Lady Bird."

There was an undercurrent to the appeal of *Gilligan's Island*. While the castaways survived a calamity, so did America. The opening scenes accompanying the theme song take place in Honolulu Harbor; they were filmed after the assassination of President John F. Kennedy on November 22, 1963. Flags at half-staff can be seen in the background.

Bob Denver starred as the title character. Alan Hale Jr., namesake and son of movie star Alan Hale, played Jonas Grumby, referred to as Skipper. Jim Backus played stuffy and snobby Thurston Howell III, paired with Natalie Schaefer as the somewhat ditzy but never judgmental

In 1966, CBS stars shone brightly on the TV landscape. Tina Louise of *Gilligan's Island* poses with her fellow actors at the ribbon cutting to inaugurate CBS Studio Center the year before. Joining her are Clint Eastwood and Paul Brinegar of *Rawhide* and Robert Conrad and Ross Martin of *Wild, Wild West*. COURTESY OF VALLEY TIMES PHOTO COLLECTION/LOS ANGELES PUBLIC LIBRARY

Lovey Howell. Redheaded sex bomb Tina Louise played Hollywood actress Ginger Grant; brunette Dawn Wells had the role of fresh-off-the-farm Mary Ann Summers. Russell Johnson played Roy Hinkley, aka Professor, who always had an explanation of scientific principles involved in their attempts to be rescued.

*Gilligan's Island* combined slapstick, well-crafted characters, and guest stars for episodes that had the castaways close to being rescued, only to have an obstacle prevent it. Usually it was well-meaning but absent-minded Gilligan who did something that triggered the obstacle.

Their only link to civilization is a radio for news reports, and visitors who never disclose the island's location when they return.

*Gilligan's Island* creator Sherwood Schwartz was a 48-year-old writer with radio credits including *The Bob Hope Show*, *The Adventures of Ozzie and Harriet*, and *The Alan Young Show*. Like many radio scribes, he moved to TV in the early 1950s: *I Married Joan* and *The Red Skelton Show*. *Gilligan's Island* began from Schwartz wanting to separate from the pedantic but proven foundations for TV stories. "One day the idea of a group of diverse characters being forced to live together began to take shape. They would be a 'family,' but of a very different sort. But what brings them together? And why are they forced to stay together?

Maybe a desert island, I thought, there's little likelihood they would be found. And if their boat were wrecked, they couldn't escape.

A great many comic possibilities came to mind immediately, based on two major themes: the problems of modern man dealing with primitive life on an uninhabited island, and the conflicts among people as they are forced to adjust to each other.[1]

Sherwood Schwartz's son Lloyd recalled his father's work on the show:

My dad and Jim Backus did radio together and *I Married Joan*. My dad expanded the part of Thurston Howell III because he knew what Jim could do with the character. He invented the combination of jutting your jaw out and talking in a Harvard way. Alan had a couple of failed shows and lived in the shadow of his father. Skipper gave him an identity and he almost never took the captain's hat off. Great guy. Very warm.

Tina didn't really know how to play Ginger until dad told her the character's creation was influenced by Marilyn Monroe. Dawn was a former Miss Nevada, sweet as could be. Natalie Schaefer was oddly enough exactly like Mrs. Howell. Oblivious to the world. Dad was at her house and she said that she had problems with the radio because she only got the news. He had to explain that she could get other channels.

Russell Johnson was a very warm, very funny guy. He only had one requirement from my father—he wanted to know that he wasn't saying nonsense when he talked about science. Bob was very interesting. He was a much more talented actor than he got credit for. One of the great reactors of all time.[2]

⎯⎯∞⎯⎯

When February began, imagining the 1966 Los Angeles Dodgers without Sandy Koufax and Don Drysdale was like imagining a hot fudge sundae without hot fudge.

California's baseball versions of Zeus and Jupiter dominated forecasts of Dodgers fans anticipating a season of joy. Winning had become a probable result; Los Angeles had added two World Series championships in the last three years by sweeping the New York Yankees in 1963 and prevailing against the Minnesota Twins in 1965's seven-game contest.

This recent pedigree combined with the duo's awe-inspiring performance in the '65 regular season—49 victories, a shade more than half of the team's 97 tallies in the W column—to instill a sense of destiny in the citizens of Dodger Nation awaiting dispatches from Dodgertown, the team's spring training complex in Vero Beach, Florida. Faster than the newly released Shelby Mustang could get from 0 to 60 miles per hour on an open stretch of Pacific Coast Highway, they conjured visions of Koufax, Drysdale, et al. notching a second consecutive World Series title.

Success was not inevitable. But it felt close.

Dynastic pride was eminent. Beachgoers relaxing in Santa Monica, millionaires shopping for wedding anniversary gifts in Beverly Hills, elementary school students trading baseball cards in Sherman Oaks, campers hiking in Malibu Creek State Park, real estate agents selling split-level homes in Woodland Hills, college professors creating syllabi in Westwood, and restaurateurs welcoming customers in Boyle Heights discussed the Dodgers.

On February 23, their chests-out saunter turned into a shoulders-slumped shuffle.

Whether by news reports or word of mouth, they learned of possibly losing the duo if a salary demand went unfulfilled by Dodgers owner Walter O'Malley and general manager Buzzie Bavasi.

Drysdale underscored—and Bavasi agreed—that the friendship shared between the hurlers and the front-office executives would continue. But there was no mistaking that he and his left-handed counterpart left emotions out of the equation for three-year deals, which differed in LA press reports. The *San Bernardino Sun* gave the amounts as $450,000 for Drysdale and $600,000 for Koufax. Bavasi claimed that he didn't know about the $600,000 figure until he learned about it through the press. Bob Hunter cited the same figures in the *Los Angeles Herald Examiner*.[3]

But the *Los Angeles Times* cited an annual salary of "approximately $167,000" for each hurler.[4]

"However, Sandy and I are grown up and this is a business affair," said Drysdale. "We want to handle it the way we feel is right, and in a proper manner for all concerned. . . . It's not up to me what the terms are, or to comment on the position of our attorney."[5]

If completed, each deal would exceed Willie Mays's annual income significantly—the Say Hey Kid drew $125,000 from the coffers of San Francisco Giants owner Horace Stoneham.[6]

The following day, Koufax clarified that the press reports were incorrect regarding the salary imbalance; each pitcher wanted the same amount of money. But they reserved specifics to keep the negotiations private. Drysdale emphasized, "I will not comment on the figures, because this would put me in the position of negotiating through the papers."[7]

The Associated Press stated that the 1965 salaries were $75,000 for Drysdale and $74,000 for Koufax.[8] According to Drysdale, the Dodgers paid him $80,000 in 1965; Koufax's salary was $85,000.[9]

In his autobiography published after the 1966 season, Koufax disclosed that the Dodgers first proposed $100,000 for him and $85,000 for Drysdale at the beginning of the holdout.[10]

But there was another factor for O'Malley and Bavasi to consider—and their gold-star track record of success implies that they did—along with the siphoning from the Dodgers' bank account for salaries. Koufax and Drysdale in the starting lineup translated into marquee value of Ruthian proportions for Dodgers home games. In 1965, the Dodgers led the major leagues in attendance, exceeding 2.55 million. The next highest figure belonged to the Astros. But the team's new domed stadium was the attraction, not the team's ninth-place finish with a 65–97 record. In its rookie season, the Astrodome—officially named the Harris County Domed Stadium—drew more than 2.15 million.

Besides ticket sales, O'Malley added concessions and parking fees to the financial cushion for a boon that would make Jack Benny, Scrooge McDuck, and Monopoly's Rich Uncle Pennybags applaud. So Koufax and Drysdale knew their importance. They wanted compensation in accordance with their exploits, which were already the stuff of legend.

Twice, Koufax had won the Cy Young Award. Drysdale, once.

Each had led the major leagues in strikeouts three times. Drysdale in 1959, 1960, and 1962. Koufax in 1961, 1963, and 1965.

Koufax's output also counted four no-hitters, including his perfect game in 1965, the lowest ERA in the National League for each of the last four seasons, the lowest ERA in the majors twice, and the highest number of wins in the majors for two of the last three seasons.

With stamina that seemed kryptonian, Drysdale led the majors in games started for the last four seasons.

Their combined World Series performances in the championship seasons of 1959, 1963, and 1965 amounted to a 7–3 record.

Koufax made a personal decision that has long enjoyed religious prominence in the '65 fall classic. His decision to sit out the first game because it fell on the Jewish holiday of Yom Kippur has been a cultural touchstone reflected in scores of bar mitzvah speeches, rabbis' sermons, and op-ed columns in Jewish newspapers from Malibu to Montauk. Moses receiving the Ten Commandments on Mount Sinai, King David marrying Bathsheba, and Sandy Koufax refusing to play on the holiest day of the Jewish calendar are stories that Jewish children can usually recite by the time their age reaches double digits.

"I tried to deflect questions about my intentions through the last couple of weeks of the season by saying that I was praying for rain," wrote the fireballer in his 1966 autobiography. "There was never any decision to make, though, because there was never any possibility that I would pitch. ... Yom Kippur is the holiest day of the Jewish religion. The club knows that I don't work that day. When Yom Kippur falls during the season, as it usually does, it has always been a simple matter of pitching a day earlier, with two days' rest, when my turn happened to be coming up."[11]

Drysdale and Koufax figured on a united front thanks to Drysdale's first wife, Ginger, when they met Koufax for dinner in the offseason. According to Drysdale, a conversation about their contracts led them to conclude that Bavasi was using psychology laced with subterfuge. When Koufax had gone to Bavasi earlier that day, he told the pitcher that Drysdale was asking for a lower amount in salary. Drysdale went in the day before and got the same blarney regarding Koufax.[12]

In addition to the salary demand that would secure the duo in the upper echelon of ballplayers, the length of the contract would break the O'Malley edict of one-year agreements. Bavasi tried to separate the two players by giving them the option of breaking down the money 50–50 but offering different contracts. Bavasi was concerned, rightfully so, about a precedent of other players joining together. He mused about a trio of outfielders combining for a negotiation.[13]

There were other possibilities that could create headaches requiring Excedrin delivered by the truckload to 1000 Elysian Avenue.

What if a pitcher-catcher duo showed up in the Chavez Ravine front office with a demand for salary increases and multiyear contracts? What if a reliable double-play combination refused to play under the current contract?

There was also the nuclear option—Drysdale and Koufax not playing in '66.

It would be heresy to fans. But Bavasi acknowledged the possibility, perhaps as a bluff: "I'm not saying they have to play baseball. They've made big money in-and-out of baseball and have invested it wisely. They may be financially independent. I don't know."[14]

When the Dodgers plane took off from Los Angeles International Airport on February 26, the absence of Koufax and Drysdale was considerable, frightening, and genuine. It seemed that both sides were entrenched, forcing the Dodgers to begin their annual spring training exodus to Vero Beach without the boost from their star pitchers. But theirs was not the only absence impacting the team's morale. Base-running threat Maury Wills—who had broken the single-season stolen-base record in 1962 with 104 steals—had a "nightclub engagement" in Tokyo.[15]

Bavasi clarified that the pitchers were not a holdout in technical terms because that only applied if they refused to show up at the beginning of the regular season.[16] Still, it was a moot point.

Spring training's usual mantra consists of managers and coaches relying on optimism for the upcoming season as long as the players stay healthy. But an ominousness increasing in strength hovered for the '66 Dodgers. Bavasi underlined his stance with a declaration against the sought-after figure now reported as $1 million for the pair. He leveraged fear against greed when he spoke to the Dodgers congregating in the Indian River County complex created when his predecessor, Branch Rickey, converted a navy housing base into Dodgertown in the late 1940s. "No amount of pressure will make me meet their demands," declared Bavasi. "If I did, I would have to tear up all your contracts and give you new ones to make things equitable."[17]

Though unified, Drysdale and Koufax were opposites in how they came through the ranks of the Dodgers organization.

Koufax gave Dodgers fans a sense of invincibility during the 1960s, but his tenure during the team's last years in Brooklyn showed no signs of excellence. An ascendance seemed about as likely as Nathan's changing its trademark offering from hot dogs to hamburgers. His combined record from his rookie year of 1955 to 1960 was 36–40. Control, or lack of it, was evident.

In 1958—the Dodgers' first year in Los Angeles—he led the majors in wild pitches with 17. For the first three years, Koufax compiled 486 innings and 297 walks. But he added to his strikeouts: 131 in 158⅔ innings, 173 in 153⅓ innings, and 197 in 175 innings, respectively.

Dodgers catcher Norm Sherry unlocked the secret to Koufax's excellence—hold back.

Koufax threw hard every time. Sherry surmised that if he focused on accuracy rather than speed for each batter, his control would improve. And it did. In 1961, Koufax led the majors in strikeouts with 269 and had an 18–13 season.[18]

Drysdale's trajectory had a straighter path.

He was heralded as an ace at the beginning of his first major-league season in 1956.

After he went 8–5 for the Bakersfield Indians in the Class C California League in 1954 and 11–11 for the AAA Montreal Royals in 1955, the Dodgers gave the 19-year-old his shot. Bill Roeder of the *New York World-Telegram* and the *Sun* praised Drysdale but cautioned that the 19-year-old's lack of experience likely made him a strong candidate to remain with Montreal for some seasoning rather than join the Brooklyn squad.[19]

When the Dodgers okayed the right-hander, Roeder hedged. Drysdale will be in a Brooklyn uniform "at least as far as the early season is concerned," wrote Roeder. But he noted, "Every time this kid pitches, you see experienced hitters acting confused. He has them checking their swings or letting obvious strikes go by or lunging at the last minute that they hit to the wrong field."[20]

On April 23, 1956, Drysdale got his first taste of a major-league game that wasn't an exhibition. He did not disappoint: nine strikeouts for a 6–1 victory over the Phillies at Connie Mack Stadium. It began when he struck out the top of the lineup—Richie Ashburn, Bobby Morgan, and Granny Hamner. The last two struck out looking.

Ashburn was an offensive threat, underscored by an NL-leading .338 batting average and MLB-leading on-base percentage of .449 in 1955. His .441 OBP in 1954 led the NL.

Drysdale had given up five hits and allowed the game's only run in the eighth inning when Frank Baumholtz pinch-hit for Murry Dickson and singled. After Ashburn got out, Morgan singled and sent Baumholtz to third base. Hamner's sacrifice fly to Dodgers right fielder Carl Furillo scored him for the home team's only run.

In his sophomore year, Drysdale notched two two-hitters, one three-hitter, and four shutouts. Though the young phenom was from the sun-soaked environs of Southern California, he assimilated into the Borough of Churches and formed an emotional bond with Brooklynites, as did fellow LA natives Duke Snider and Jackie Robinson.

When the Dodgers announced their move to Los Angeles after the 1957 season, Drysdale, despite heading back to his hometown, questioned the effect on the team and the fan base that had enjoyed a connection since 1883. "What about all those people who lived and died with the Dodgers? How were they going to feel about this? And all those friends I'd made in Brooklyn. I might never see them again. It was a very emotional time for me. It was an emotional time for all of us. But I don't think it really sunk in until the next year when we didn't go back to Brooklyn. Maybe I didn't want it to sink in. Maybe that's what it was."[21]

Los Angelenos felt similar twinges when Koufax and Drysdale leaving the team inched from possibility toward reality. The fans found succor in considering the other players in the lineup.

---

Wes Parker entered 1966 with an unglamorous but noteworthy achievement. He ended the '65 season atop the major leagues in sacrifice hits with 19. Parker played for the Dodgers from 1964 to 1972.

A child of Southern California privilege, Parker grew up in Brentwood with a private-school education, his material needs met, and a natural athletic ability in several sports besides baseball. Money, though it bestowed abundant opportunity, did not generate airs, snobbery, or a feeling of entitlement in him. They were shunned in the Parker household, where the raison d´être was the pursuit of excellence based on decorum and learning.

Parker spoke of his time with the Dodgers:

We were not interested in individual statistics. When you're at bat or in the field, you don't want to let your teammates down. We didn't care who was at the plate if the game was on the line.

Pittsburgh, Cincinnati, Milwaukee, and San Francisco were superior offensively in 1965. But we were a better team in 1966. We had better pitching when we picked up Don Sutton and Phil Regan. Jim Lefebvre and I had more experience. But we also had a culture of winning. That's underrated. We went on the field expecting to win. We talked in the clubhouse about how to win. The fans expected us to win. We did it with pitching, defense, and timely hitting.

I really liked playing for Walter Alston. He just expected you to do your job and I was really good at self-motivating. He didn't have private meetings very often. He never gave pep talks. Danny Ozark was as fine a man as I ever met. He knew the game real well. He was wonderful at giving signs as a third base coach. He had special signs just for me.

Jim Gilliam was underrated. He could do anything to help us win, whether it was getting a clutch hit or laying down a bunt. Gilliam and Wills were the most intelligent ballplayers I ever played with.

Buzzie Bavasi was a good baseball man. Very decisive. He was very sure of everything that he did. He treated each player individually. He could be tough with us but he had a tender spot. Occasionally, in the clubhouse he chewed everyone out. When you went into his office to negotiate, he was fair and he'd have fun with it. He was really involved. You knew that he cared about the players.[22]

---

When Joe Moeller put on a Dodgers uniform for the first time in 1962, he already knew what it meant to be a winner. The 6'6" right-hander was a member of the 1961 Reno Silver Sox—California League champions. It was one of three minor-league teams that he played on that year.

Moeller went 6–5 in '62 and got sent to the triple-A Omaha Dodgers in the American Association in late July. He notched a 2–1 record for Omaha but found his groove in 1963 with the Spokane Indians in the Pacific Coast League: 16–11 with a 3.61 ERA. In 1964, Moeller took a slot in the pitching rotation when Johnny Podres had to sit out because his elbow surgery in the offseason continued to plague him.

Dodgers manager Walter Alston used Moeller mostly in relief for the 1966 season. During that summer, he went to El Camino College and studied philosophy and U.S. history because he was working toward a BA degree. Moeller played in 29 games but only started eight because the LA rotation was already strong with the quartet of Drysdale, Koufax, Osteen, and Sutton. His record was 2–4.

Moeller remembers,

> They [Drysdale, Koufax, Osteen, and Sutton] started except for those eight games. I usually pitched the second game of a double-header. Our pitching knowledge was the oral history that developed from [John] Roseboro and [Jeff] Torborg studying the hitters.
>
> When I was pitching, I'd look down from the mound, and in the dugout boxes, there'd be Joey Bishop, Cary Grant, Frank Sinatra, and Doris Day. Players could sit behind home plate and take notes. Right in front of me were Cary Grant and Dyan Cannon. He asked if he could go in the clubhouse. He stood at the door like a little boy. Baseball brought him back to being a little kid. He was the nicest guy.
>
> Leo Durocher was a coach, and he'd have his entourage of reporters. He'd say [to me], "Let's get a drink. Oh, you're not old enough. Get a milkshake." The reporters would laugh. Durocher didn't like that I was young and had a good bonus. Davis told him to "lay off the kid."[23]

—⚬⚬⚬—

Jeff Torborg had the best seat in the house.

His 10-year career as a major-league catcher included two games affirming the greatness of two legendary hurlers. Torborg was the backstop for Koufax's perfect game in 1965. Eight years later, during his tenure with the Angels, he caught Nolan Ryan's first of seven no-hitters.

When the Westfield, New Jersey, native entered the Dodgertown complex in 1966, he wondered what the prospects were for the returning World Series champs without the blink-and-you-missed-it fastballs of his perfect-game battery mate and the 6'6" pitcher whose physical presence was so formidable he could have played the heroic character in any one of the westerns dominating the prime-time TV lineup.

The Dodgers' continuum of excellence was in peril.

Torborg caught 56 games for the Dodgers in 1965. But a '66 season without the game's dominant southpaw and right-hander would be like sitting on a two-legged stool. Although spring is a time of renewal, every day that passed without a détente meant an increased chance that the end of a reign was approaching. Fast.

Torborg recalled,

It was a difficult spring. We were the defending world champions, but an average team without Koufax and Drysdale. We knew Sandy was in pain. He couldn't throw between starts. His elbow exploded. He had the best curveball I've ever seen. But in Minnesota, he pitched a three-hitter on two days' rest without it. Even in the perfect game, he didn't have a good curveball early. There were two curves; one was tighter and harder. He could really pull down on it. Call it 12 to 6, like the hands on a clock. I had to get closer to the hitter because it had a big spin and a big break. You got the feeling it could hit the dirt and be a strike.

When you think of the Dodger bullpen, there was Jim Brewer, Ron Perranoski, and Bob Miller. When the phone would ring, it was usually for Perranoski or Miller; Brewer had a screwball that he learned to throw in the bullpen when we were in Milwaukee. His best pitch was a screwball.

We had advance scouts who gave us written reports. To prepare, John Roseboro and I would know the lineup and how we would approach it. We met with the pitchers, but Don and Sandy didn't need any help. Osteen was a crafty pitcher.

Those Dodger teams were very close. Walt relied on meetings, but not in-depth technical meetings, more team and family attitude types of meetings. Rosey was a mentor for me. He was a unique guy, and the pitchers respected him. I was lucky to be in it—they started platooning the catchers. In 1965, we clinched against the Braves at Dodger Stadium on Friday night. Saturday, Walt said, "I'm going with Rosey the rest of the way." In the game, somebody bunted and Rosey threw it away. He joked, "It's your fault. You're supposed to be in here."

Walt was not overly hands-on with pitchers and catchers. We'd explain our decisions during the game. "Skip, he moved in the batter's box." Walt would respond, "You have a better view than I do."

Gilliam was a magician at the plate. He could work the count, which allowed Wills to run. Parker could also run. Jim Lefebvre came through the Dodgers system. We believed in ourselves. Everyone had their role. The veterans made sure that if someone didn't look like they were putting out, which wasn't often, that player would raise his game. Don would say, "You're messing with my World Series money."

Johnny Podres was a pistol. He lived above the apartment that my wife Suzie and our toddler Doug were renting that season.

Bavasi had a great personality. I didn't have much in the way of stats. I made $7,500 in each of the first two years. I got the World Series check, which was $12,000. By the next negotiating period between year two and year three, I asked for more money. When you hit like I was hitting, you don't get more. He said, "You got World Series money."

He called the house and he could be intimidating and clever. He'd leave a fake contract on his desk where a player could see what other players were "making." He said, "I have to have you sign or it doesn't look good."

I told him, "Buzzie, I can't sign for that."

"I already announced that you signed. Don't worry, what do you want?"

I told him, and he gave it to me.

He was legendary with his tricks, but he was a good guy.

Danny Ozark I knew from the instructional league, when I went from Rutgers and signed with the Albuquerque Dukes. He would take a bucket of balls, an infielder, and a fungo bat, then stand on the mound and hit balls at me as hard as he could while I had my catching gear on. He would challenge you. I liked Danny a lot.

Preston Gomez was one of the smartest coaches around. He would have a different sign for each player.[24]

—————⊗⊗⊗⊗—————

While Dodgers fans scanned headlines for news of the team's brightest stars reconciling with the front office, NASA scanned the stars in the sky. Its mission to land a man on the moon before the end of the 1960s—following President Kennedy's proclamation at Rice University in 1962—took a leap forward on February 26, 1966. An unmanned space-

NASA launched the new *Saturn 1B* rocket in late February 1966. It was a crucial test to see how the rocket would perform with the command and service modules for Project Apollo, the three-man missions that sent astronauts to the moon. COURTESY OF NASA

craft completed a suborbital flight to test the performance of the *Saturn 1B* rocket and Apollo command and service modules.

The 37-minute flight took the rocket 5,264 miles from the launch site at Cape Canaveral, Florida. It was a welcome success after launch delays that lasted more than three hours.[25]

Another advance for NASA. It wouldn't be the last in 1966.

## CHAPTER THREE

# "Back in the Fold" (March)

WHEN A MAJORITY OF PLAYER REPRESENTATIVES IN THE MAJOR LEAGUE Baseball Players Association (MLBPA) nominated Marvin Miller, a steel industry labor executive, to be their mouthpiece and strategist in March 1966, he sought to strengthen the players' bond. Unified, they stood a chance at changing the status quo, which bound a player to a team through the reserve clause in player contracts. Owners had the power to treat players as property to be traded or dismissed with little to no chance of appeal, negotiation, or argument.

Miller disrupted this foundation of baseball.

With appreciation for Robin Roberts and Bob Friend as stout endorsers, Miller acknowledged years later that 16 of the 20 representatives provided the ballast for the first steps toward a union guided by, but not ruled by, him. "Despite tremendous pressure from their clubs to desert the union before it even got started, all of them supported me fully."[1]

Miller eclipsed Judge Robert Cannon, who had been an informal adviser to the players for seven years. The Wisconsin jurist never took a salary, instead settling for reimbursement of expenses. But the position of executive director of the MLBPA would be salaried at nearly $1,000 a week.

Cannon was selected; 13 of 20 teams endorsed him. He didn't need unanimous approval, but he wanted a higher approval number.[2] So he stepped aside.

Input was critical. Miller's approach was one of learning rather than lecturing. After getting the position, he said, "I'm very anxious to get the views of the players and find out what they would like this association to become. I'll have to feel my way and I'll be dependent on what they think."[3]

This strategy became his hallmark.

Players' frustrations, challenges, and goals informed Miller in his function as a shield drawing heat from the commissioner, owners, and media regarding bargaining strategies, salary disputes, and long-term projections. He went to each of the 20 ballparks for introductions to the players who he hoped to consult on bringing them out of the valley of servitude to a peak of strength, confidence, and leverage.

In a conversation with former owner and showman Bill Veeck, Miller recalled his first impressions and the weighty problems existing beyond the reserve clause and salaries. "I did anticipate that there was a lot of room for progress, that the conditions of the players was such that you almost . . . it was not an exaggeration to say it could only go up from there."[4]

Schedule adjustments were also needed. Players didn't fly around Metropolis in blue tights with a red cape and an "S" emblazoned on their chests. They needed off days, particularly after a road trip.

Miller's bona fides included 14 years with the United Steelworkers; the last six were spent as assistant to the union's president. Previously, he worked in research. But the union experience did not affect his selection.

Or so the players stated.

Bob Allison represented the Twins and ensured that Miller's other attributes were factors. "It just so happens he is a union man," stated the 1959 American League Rookie of the Year and three-time All-Star. "We considered candidates from various fields. We chose him because he qualified as an outstanding co-ordinator. The fact he is a union man is out. We didn't buy it and Miller, himself, didn't buy it. The players will still have the power. He will be under us."[5]

During the World Series, a nationally syndicated article cited the new union chief's vision of representing the players as one entity rather than person-by-person. "The players see their association as dealing with anything but their own individual salaries, but on anything affecting the players as a group there will be negotiations on a broad base."[6]

But there was a resilient faction conscious and wary of upsetting the ownership base. Complaints, though valid, could be perceived and portrayed as noisy bravado and unparalleled selfishness. Owners could tire of players who proved to be against baseball tradition, which had worked pretty well for the front office. "Roberts had warned me to expect resistance among the players, but I also suspected that the owners had had a hand in stirring up opposition," recalled Miller in his 1991 autobiography. "Baseball's owners had had their way too long to accept any loss of control to a union without a struggle. And I hadn't even met any of the owners!"[7]

The former steelworkers' union man got elected in April with a nearly 80 percent vote of the players. His spring training listening tour in 1966 set the tone for his relationship with the players. He earned their trust; they prized his command of the issues.

Miller's tenure at the MLBPA lasted nearly 20 years, coinciding with five American presidencies, the expansion of four teams in 1969 and two teams in 1977, the introduction of cable television, and the escalation of commercial endorsements for players.

When Curt Flood challenged the reserve clause in the early 1970s, Miller did not initially want the ballplayer to do it. But he saw the argument's importance and the need for backing by the MLBPA. Owners had benefited from this quirk in contracts, which gave them a powerful domain; players did not have a voice in choosing another employer. A player on the Braves could be traded to the Giants with no recourse.

Flood's pursuit failed in the courts, but Andy Messersmith and Dave McNally later cleared the path.

Messersmith, a Dodgers pitcher, played in the 1975 season absent a signed contract between him and the club. It was a bountiful year for the right-hander who had come off a 20–6 record in 1974, leading the National League in wins. In 1975, he went 19–14 and led the senior circuit in games started, complete games, innings pitched, batters faced, and shutouts. His 2.29 ERA was second, following Randy Jones. Defense prospered with his second consecutive Gold Glove.

Messersmith and McNally took on decades of history and challenged the owners at arbitration. Peter Seitz ruled that the reserve clause was unfair. And so, 10 years after he began his quest during 1966 spring training to improve players' well-being—financial and otherwise—Miller scored a major success with this victory in the players' favor.

Free agency was born.

———— ∞∞∞ ————

Miller changed players' lives off the field. Roy Hofheinz changed the field itself.

A symbol of the Houston Astros (né Colt .45's) since the team's inaugural season of 1962, Hofheinz, a part owner and the face of the front office, championed the building of the Astrodome. After it debuted in 1965, a dilemma emerged. The Lucite panels installed to allow light became obstacles when players couldn't see fly balls. It was decided to paint the panels black, but the field's natural grass died without light.

Monsanto's ChemGrass solved the problem. "I hereby dub thee Astroturf," declared Hofheinz in March 1966 regarding the futuristic stadium's new signature.[8]

It was not a simple journey to find a replacement for natural grass. Hofheinz tested the material with horses, elephants, cars, and the University of Houston Cougars football team.[9] On March 19–20, the Astros introduced the new playing surface in two exhibition games against the Dodgers. LA won both games, 8–3 and 4–1.

Dodgers first baseman Wes Parker observed, "The difficult thing is the ball bounces one way on the grass and one way on the dirt part of the infield. It almost gathers speed. You have to either play in to get the ball before it hits the dirt, or way back to get it after it bounces a couple of times on the dirt. . . . I got caught in between twice."[10]

"The ball picks up spin on the grass part and when it hits the dirt, really kicks off that—quick," said fellow infielder Jim Lefebvre.[11]

Astros shortstop Sonny Jackson identified a problem for bunters: "For some reason, maybe the grain, the ball gets pulled toward the pitcher's mound when you bunt. If you lay one down right on the rim where the infield meets the dirt, it won't run off and go foul."[12]

Artificial turf became a standard in many ballparks and stadiums, alleviating the worry of a grounds crew responsible for maintaining a playing surface against weather's fickleness. Without the ambition of Hofheinz, it might never have leapt from concept to execution. It was another victory for the former Harris County judge who kept an apartment in the Astrodome and represented a Texan swagger that was catnip to journalists and fuel for Houstonians' pride.

The Astros did not play .500 ball until 1969. But every sports fan knew that Houston's dome and turf created a new standard. Fenway Park, Wrigley Field, and Yankee Stadium had been renowned for decades, but they reflected past glories. The Astrodome was the future.

—⚬⚬⚬—

Spring is a time of renewal.

Trees get lush with leaves after winter left the branches bare.

Passover and Easter are the Judeo-Christian cornerstones of the season, inducing extended families to gather, pray, and eat together. The last time that happened was likely December, combined with lighting the menorah for Chanukah and decorating a pine-needle tree for Christmas.

Baseball fans rekindle their hopes in springtime, express nostalgic yearnings for yore, and talk about the potential of past glories being repeated. While fans turned to the sports pages during spring training, conversations had plenty of fodder.

"Can the Dodgers repeat as World Series champions?"

"What's the story on this new pitcher, Jim Palmer, working the hill for the Orioles?"

"The A's are perpetually in the cellar ever since they moved from Philadelphia to Kansas City in 1955. Do you think they'll ever move again?"

"Watch out for the Reds. This kid Pete Rose led the majors in hits last year. His Rookie of the Year Award in '63 was no fluke, huh?"

"Yastrzemski had another great season. He led the major leagues in doubles and the American League in slugging percentage. I wonder if this means that the Red Sox will be competitive."

"Leo's back. I guess his Hollywood career is over."

The Cubs' front office tapped Leo Durocher to helm the ball club that only played home games in the daytime. When he last managed a ball club—the New York Giants—in 1955, Elvis Presley made his television debut on *Louisiana Hayride*; Ray Kroc built his first McDonald's restaurant; Jim Henson introduced Kermit the Frog on a Washington, DC, television station; Disneyland opened; *Blackboard Jungle* escalated the popularity of rock and roll with the hit "Rock Around the Clock" by Bill Haley and the Comets; and President Dwight Eisenhower pushed for the legislation that would pass in Congress the following year and create the Interstate Highway System.

After leaving the Giants, Durocher's activities were mostly baseball related: TV commentator and coach with the Dodgers in addition to a stint hosting *Jackpot Bowling*.

Having an affinity for show business, Durocher basked in the aura of glamour existing because of the team's geographic proximity to TV studios. Guest appearances as himself included *The Beverly Hillbillies*, *The Donna Reed Show*, *The Munsters*, and *Mr. Ed*.

But being a coach under Walter Alston, who was the Dodgers' manager from 1954 to 1976, discomfited Durocher because people would seek his counsel after Alston gave his opinion. "No two people have the same opinion on everything. What could I do? I had to be quiet and walk away."[13]

Once a teammate of Babe Ruth and Lou Gehrig on the vaunted Yankees of the late 1920s and a member of the Cardinals' "Gashouse Gang" in the 1930s, Durocher had solid experience as a leader. Braves manager Bobby Bragan—who had also skippered the Pirates and the Indians—praised Durocher, for whom he played during his tenure with the Brooklyn Dodgers. "Leo was the best manager I played under. If anybody in this baseball business can help the Cubs, Leo is the man."[14]

Durocher began his managerial career as a player-manager with the Dodgers from 1939 to 1945, excepting 1944 when he didn't play at all. He did not capture any NL pennants in Brooklyn, but he nipped at the heels of Stan Musial and his fellow Cardinals in 1942 and 1946. The sons of St. Louis edged the boys of Brooklyn by two games each season and later won the World Series. From the middle of the 1948 season through 1955, Durocher managed the Giants.

When "Leo the Lip" returned to helming in '66, he brought a pedigree of passion matched by a ferocity that earned him his nickname. Arguments with umpires were showcases; his description of an opposing team as "nice guys, finish last" had morphed into a signature declaration without the comma.

Chicago's new hire restored the team to a sense of normalcy in addition to invoking baseball nostalgia. Since 1960, the NL club had employed a "College of Coaches" concept revolving around a group of eight leaders. There was no clear authority. Durocher also had the burden of lifting the Cubs from their 1965 finish in eighth place, 25 games behind the Dodgers.

During spring training, Wes Covington saw Durocher's value in a no-nonsense approach.

A 10-year veteran, Covington had come to the Cubs after stays with the Braves, White Sox, Athletics, and Phillies. "Durocher is different," offered the slugger who ended his MLB livelihood in 1966 with a .279 career batting average. "You goof, and he kicks you right now. Once he does that he washes his hands of the situation, and it's completely forgotten. The next day or the next game everybody starts all even again because he doesn't lock anybody in a permanent doghouse."[15]

Durocher's asset was his experience in how to handle ballplayers, both as a group and individually. Some managers are statisticians. Others, strategists. Durocher belonged with the latter, knowing which buttons to push for each player to contribute value to the ball club. Winning mattered; everything else was secondary.

Durocher barked to the Dodgers during spring training in 1947 that Jackie Robinson was going to break the color line and anybody who had a problem with that reality better work harder for their jobs or leave the team.

After Willie Mays got promoted from the Giants' triple-A Minneapolis Millers and went 1-for-26 to start his major-league career in 1951, Durocher consoled the future star and assured him of a place in the lineup. It prompted Mays to finish the season at .274.

But there was notoriety surrounding Durocher.

Commissioner Happy Chandler suspended him for the '47 season because he allegedly consorted with gamblers.

The 1951 Giants overcame a deficit of 13½ games behind the Dodgers in mid-August to tie for first place in the NL. A three-game playoff ended when Bobby Thomson hit a three-run homer to win the deciding game in the bottom of the ninth inning. The Giants won, 5–4.

Decades later, controversy erupted when Joshua Prager penned a 2001 article for the *Wall Street Journal* revealing that the Durocher-led Giants had somebody manning a spyglass in a room behind the center field bleachers of the Polo Grounds. Prager's book, *The Echoing Green*, added new context to the comeback and Thomson's home run off Ralph Branca.

Durocher's mission to get the Cubs out of the bottom of the senior circuit was no easy task considering the competition throughout the NL squads: Hank Aaron, Eddie Mathews, Don Drysdale, Sandy Koufax, Maury Wills, Juan Marichal, Willie Mays, Willie McCovey, Vada Pinson, Pete Rose, Jim Maloney, and Roberto Clemente.

The Cubs fared worse in Durocher's inaugural year of leadership with the team. They went from 72–90 in 1965 to 59–103 in 1966. But things turned around in '67 with an 87–74 record followed by an 84–78 finish in 1968. The '69 Cubs won 92 games. Durocher finished his stretch with the Cubs in 1972, leaving in midseason after a 46–44 record. He joined the Astros toward the end of the '72 campaign, compiling 16 wins and 15 losses. After an 82–80 finish in '73, Durocher retired from managing.

Working for the Cubs stood apart from his other jobs because of his relationship with the owner. In his autobiography, Durocher lauded Phil Wrigley, calling him "simply the finest man to work for in the world. The most decent man, probably, I have ever met." Where other managers avoid talking about negative performances, Durocher debriefed his boss on all aspects. According to Durocher, Wrigley said, "You're the only manager I ever had who keeps coming by when we lose."[16]

---

While Durocher represented a back-to-the-past aura, Commissioner William Eckert's ruling on a prospect in March 1966 changed the destiny of the Mets.

Had Tom Seaver stayed with his original team, Durocher and his Cubs would likely have been battling the Atlanta Braves in the '69 NL playoff. But Atlanta's contract with the University of Southern California pitcher was ruled invalid.

Because Seaver had taken the mound for USC during the '66 college baseball season, he could not sign a professional contract. Eckert designated the Braves' $50,000 offer as the figure for a club to sign Seaver; a lottery would decide the right-hander's fate. Mets president George Weiss was initially against signing Seaver, but he allowed his staff to move forward.

"So we went into the draft, and we were one of three clubs, Cleveland, Philadelphia, and the Mets," recalled Mets front-office executive Bing Devine. "And we were the one who won the drawing. I got a call from Lee MacPhail, the deputy commissioner, saying, 'You just won Tom Seaver in the draft.' I thought it was good. More than anything else, I was thinking that George was feeling, [if] we were as high as we were on Seaver, there would be more clubs interested in him. He thought, I wonder now just how good Seaver is."[17]

Seaver bonded to the Mets fan base immediately. He won the 1967 NL Rookie of the Year Award, followed by three Cy Young Awards, two NL pennants, and a World Series championship with the Mets. He twice led both leagues in ERA and struck out at least 200 batters seven years in a row. Five times he led the NL in strikeouts.

In 1977, a trade that became known as the "Midnight Massacre" sent Seaver to the Cincinnati Reds in exchange for Dan Norman, Pat Zachry, Doug Flynn, and Steve Henderson. "Tom Terrific" pitched a no-hitter with the Reds, then played for the White Sox and the Red Sox. He ended his career with a 311–205 record. In 1992, the Baseball Hall of Fame inducted Seaver with 98.84 percent of the vote, the highest percentage until Ken Griffey Jr. got 99.32 percent in 2016.[18]

Seaver was known as "the Franchise" during his time with the Mets. But Casey Stengel was the first icon for the team. The Mets hired him to be their first manager in 1962.

Stengel had more lines on his face than a New York City subway map. It was more evident when he smiled. On March 8, 1966, the man responsible for the second half of the moniker at Huggins-Stengel Field in St. Petersburg, Florida, had reason to do so. Accompanied by Ford Frick—former baseball commissioner and the sport's éminence grise—Stengel walked before the crowd and learned that he had been elected to the Baseball Hall of Fame.

The vote of the 11-man Old Timers' Committee was unanimous.

Frick's announcement humbled Stengel under the Florida sky. "It's nice to know you've done something in your life that people thought was worthwhile. . . . So many men done amazing things it makes you feel regret that four or five others are not in it. I feel sorry for the others that didn't get in."[19]

It was a special election. Connie Mack and Lou Gehrig had similar paths; former commissioner Kenesaw Mountain Landis was elected posthumously a couple of weeks after he died in 1944.

Considering Stengel's résumé, the news did not shock the crowd at the St. Petersburg ballpark.

Older attendees clapping for Cooperstown's latest electee might have remembered Stengel's playing days in the major leagues, including a career average of .284 with the Dodgers, Pirates, Phillies, Giants, and Braves from 1912 to 1925. He played in three World Series and did quite well, batting .364 in four games with the 1916 Brooklyn Robins; .400 in two games with the 1922 New York Giants; and .417 in six games with the 1923 Giants. The '22 Giants won the title against the Yankees.

Stengel left the Dodgers after playing 12 games in 1925 and began working as a manager with the Worcester Panthers in the Eastern League. A six-year stint followed with the Toledo Mud Hens in the American Association. He began helming Brooklyn in 1934 and stayed for three seasons. "I want my players to enjoy themselves on the field by getting a big kick out of playing winning baseball," said Stengel when the Dodgers hired him.[20]

Boston had him from 1938 to 1942. He left and then came back to replace Bob Coleman after 46 games. In eight full seasons and most of a ninth, Stengel had nary a winning record.

That changed when he took over the Oakland Oaks, managing for three seasons and winning the Pacific Coast League championship in 1948.

During his reign as the Yankees' manager from 1949 to 1960, he brought five World Series championships to the Bronx in his first five seasons. There were two more titles in addition to three appearances resulting in losses to the Dodgers, Braves, and Pirates.

Stengel's position as the manager of the expansion Mets in 1962 led to his presence in advertisements for Rheingold, the team's first beer sponsor. Leading the Mets from 1962 to August 1965—when he retired after falling and breaking a hip—earned Stengel a place in Mets lore. Although the team had an abominable record of 40–120 in its inaugural year and no winning season during his reign, Stengel's celebrity status brought fans to the ballpark.

He had come to spring training in 1966 as a front-office adviser. Three years before they earned the nickname "Miracle Mets" for an upset victory over the Baltimore Orioles in the 1969 World Series, *Newsday*'s Mets beat reporter Steve Jacobson used the term in a feature describing Stengel's appearance at spring training: "Bed sheets painted with 'Amazin' Mets' are out this year. The slick sign painter this year will be the first in his neighborhood to call them the 'Miracle Mets.' Casey Stengel says so."[21]

Rookie skipper Wes Westrum had hopes for the Mets to not only climb from their 10th-place domain but also be competitive. "I was trying to get to ninth place and he's talking about the first division," said Stengel. "I saw it done once [by the Boston Braves in 1914], but I didn't think it could be done."[22]

---

There were reasons to celebrate in other corners of America. NASA had entered 1966 with *Gemini 8* slated as the year's first manned launch after seven successful missions in 1965. Two were unmanned.

*Gemini 8* would be the first time that two spacecrafts docked in orbit, a key part of sending men to the moon for Project Apollo. At the beginning of the month, Russia hit a milestone when its *Venera 3* spacecraft became the first to impact another planet's surface—Venus. Again, Russia had outpaced America in the space race.

President Kennedy's vow in 1962 to land a man on the moon by 1970 and return him safely to Earth further amplified each Russian success. Launched on March 16, *Gemini 8* provided a welcome sight and a needed adrenaline boost to America's standing. But the voyage for Dave Scott and Neil Armstrong was anything but a smooth ride.

While celebrants looked forward to the next day's parades and visits to bars named O'Reilly's, Callahan's, and Doyle's along with thousands of establishments boasting Irish names to celebrate St. Patrick's Day, they watched TV news accounts with furrowed brows about a truncated flight, and exhalations of relief that the astronauts splashed down safely.

What had been scheduled as a three-day flight ended nearly 11 hours after its launch. Up to the point of unforeseen danger, it was uneventful. Armstrong and Scott had executed their flight but were one step above Marcel Marceau in their vocal description. "At one point, as the spacecraft neared the docking operation, the Gemini crew was asked to be a little more expansive in its comments aloft," wrote *Los Angeles Times* aerospace editor Marvin Miles.[23]

Docking the capsule with the Agena target vehicle caused smiles and handshakes in NASA's Mission Control. It was a short-lived celebration. The two craft—now joined as one—spun around during *Gemini 8*'s fifth orbit. Armstrong separated the two, but the capsule continued its spinning and forced the astronaut to use the thruster system designed for reentry to correct the problem. That meant scrubbing the rest of the flight, including Scott's scheduled space walk.

What author Tom Wolfe described as "the right stuff" was evident in the capsule. In his 2004 dual memoir *Two Sides of the Moon* with cosmonaut Alexei Leonov, Scott revealed, "I have often been asked since how I felt during those moments of high tension. Was I afraid? Did I realize I might never see the Earth at our highest peak in such situations? Emotion did not come into it. Everything was happening so fast and we

NASA astronauts Dave Scott and Neil Armstrong faced a perilous situation during their *Gemini 8* mission when they couldn't get the capsule and target vehicle that were joined to stop spinning. Scott later wrote, "That took every ounce of our energy, every effort of concentration." COURTESY OF NASA

had to find a solution. That took every ounce of our energy, every effort of concentration."[24]

Three days after the *Gemini 8* flight, NASA said that a short circuit in the rocket's wiring was the likely cause for the violent spinning.[25]

Armstrong had been in the U.S. Air Force's Man in Space Soonest program (MISS), a predecessor to NASA, which overtook space exploration priorities upon its formation in 1958 beginning with Project Mercury, which consisted of seven astronauts selected to make solo missions in a capsule.[26] During Project Mercury's life span, NASA recruited new astronauts for Project Gemini.

Unlike the single-man Mercury capsules, Gemini capsules held two men. On September 17, 1962, NASA announced Armstrong and eight other pilots as the "New Nine" to follow the "Mercury Seven" in America's space chronicles. The others were Frank Borman, Pete Conrad, Jim Lovell, James McDivitt, Elliot See, Tom Stafford, Ed White, and John Young. Armstrong and See were test pilots in the civilian sector; Conrad et al. were from the navy and air force.[27]

Armstrong's parents were equally famous on the night of September 17 through their appearance on *I've Got a Secret*, with the secret being NASA's selection of their son. Betsy Palmer deduced it.

After *Gemini 8* launched, Vice President Hubert Humphrey underscored the nation's commitment to land an astronaut on the moon before the hourglass of the 1960s ran out of sand. He bolstered the view that space exploration not only has a tangible benefit for scientific knowledge but is also an asset that cannot be quantified by slide rules, medical analysis, or flight evaluations.

Inspiration and imagination ruled from the rockets piercing blue skies toward blackness, circling the globe, and bringing mankind one flight closer to planting the Stars and Stripes on the moon before Russia could get there with the ominous flag of a hammer and sickle in yellow against a red background. "What we do in space affects man's spirit, mind, brain power, commitment and performance," declared the vice president.

NASA had endured nicks and cuts to its budget; lofty goals did not create a prophylactic around the money and allow expenses to expand without some oversight. The escalating situation in the Vietnam War had also interfered with the national budget and "required postponement of our objectives."[28]

Three days after Armstrong and Scott's splashdown, NASA carved new territory with an announcement: the first three-man mission of Project Apollo.[29]

---

Meanwhile, there was no sign of resolution in the Koufax-Drysdale holdout. The 1966 baseball season looked gloomy not only for the LA squad but also for their competitors, who relied on the hurlers' marquee value to boost attendance on Dodgers road trips. The Astros front office estimated a loss in the neighborhood of $200,000 if the aces did not play in Houston.[30]

Koufax and Drysdale had remained as steadfast as a statue in their salary demands of O'Malley and Bavasi, who were equally adamant.

By mid-March, Bavasi had made one offer. It was met with silence, which frustrated the executive. "I could get Maloney, Marichal and Jim Grant for what I offered. Maloney is asking only $50,000 isn't he? Is Koufax worth four Jim Maloneys?"[31]

Probably not.

San Francisco had Juan Marichal. Cincinnati, Maloney. In the previous season, Marichal had a 22–13 record. Maloney went 20–9. Twins hurler Grant led the AL in wins: 21–7.[32]

Koufax led in strikeouts; Maloney and Marichal placed sixth and seventh, respectively. Koufax had the lowest ERA. Marichal, the second lowest. Maloney was fourth.

Any one of the three pitchers would have been formidable additions to the Dodgers had they been available, but the Koufax-Drysdale pairing had Dodger DNA. Both had worn blue and white since their big-league debuts.

In the last week of March, Bavasi increased his proposal to $112,500 for Koufax and $97,500 for Drysdale. The pitchers dismissed Bavasi's figures; O'Malley underscored the status as a "final offer" and declared that "the incident is being closed."[33]

Bleakness prevailed over Dodger Nation.

Koufax and Drysdale employed a novel method in the negotiations by using a lawyer named J. William Hayes to be their intermediary. Dealing with players directly had been the norm for owners and general managers. Hayes leveraged a ruling by a California court that limited personal service contracts in the state to seven years.

Olivia de Havilland had sued Warner Bros. in the 1940s, and her success motivated the state legislature to codify the ruling. The actress best known for playing Melanie Hamilton in *Gone with the Wind* became a figure of courage for standing up to studios in this ultracritical scenario challenging Hollywood's status quo.

Hayes readied to attack baseball's reserve clause under the de Havilland paradigm.

Then some light penetrated the darkness—Bavasi raised the offers to $120,000 and $105,000 for Koufax and Drysdale, respectively, cited as "authoritative estimates" in the March 31 edition of the *Los Angeles Times*.[34]

Drysdale's salary was reported as $110,000 in the *Los Angeles Herald Examiner* on March 30, the day that the players joined Bavasi in a press conference to announce the compromise, but without specifics.[35] The following day, the *Herald Examiner*'s reporting showed "an estimated $105,000" for Drysdale but tagged Koufax with a figure of "approxi-

Dodgers general manager Buzzie Bavasi flanked by Don Drysdale (left) and Sandy Koufax (right) while actor Chuck Connors looks on. Connors, a former ballplayer in the Dodgers organization, was a key factor in the compromise that ended the pitchers' salary holdout during spring training. COURTESY OF LOS ANGELES HERALD EXAMINER COLLECTION/LOS ANGELES PUBLIC LIBRARY

mately $132,500." It eclipsed Willie Mays's $125,000 paycheck to make the southpaw the game's highest-paid player.[36]

"I'm convinced that was the major reason why the Dodgers moved, because we knew they had found out about Bill Hayes's little discovery," said Drysdale in his 1990 autobiography. "I can't prove it, but my guess is that the Dodgers realized they were playing with fire and that if we went to court, they might lose us both and get nothing in return."[37]

The unsung hero in the resolution was a member of both the sports and entertainment worlds—Chuck Connors. Having known O'Malley and Bavasi from his time as a player with the Dodgers organization, Connors had a unique value to offer as a go-between.[38] He persuaded the general manager to meet with the right-hander; Koufax rejected an invitation to attend but gave Drysdale his proxy. At the time, it was reported that Hayes made the call to Bavasi and urged him to meet with Drysdale.[39]

Dodgers fans breathed easier and slept heavier once Bavasi and O'Malley secured the fireballers for '66. No longer would REM phases be interrupted by nightmares of taking on Roberto Clemente, Willie Mays, et al. without Koufax and Drysdale.

"I'm just happy to be back in the fold," stated Drysdale at the news conference. "This is the most trying thing that ever happened to me."[40]

Southern California's other fan base in the national pastime also had a reason to rejoice. It was one in a series of changes causing a cultural revolution in 1966. Baseball would never be the same.

America, neither.

## CHAPTER FOUR

# Is This Heaven? No, It's Anaheim (April)

THE LOS ANGELES ANGELS HAD THEIR OWN HOME. FINALLY.

LA's Wrigley Field—at the intersection of Avalon Boulevard and East 42nd Place—provided a home base for the major-league Angels during their inaugural year of 1961. They became tenants at Dodger Stadium when Dodgers owner Walter O'Malley unveiled his Chavez Ravine masterpiece in 1962. For the next four seasons, the American League squad—redubbed the California Angels in September 1965—anticipated playing in their own ballpark.

On April 19, 1966, Angel Stadium in Anaheim hosted its first regular-season game. Pride reigned. Players basked. It was a welcome event to Angels fans, who had tired of feeling overshadowed by the Dodgers.

"The whole ball club is looking forward to a season in OUR park," said infielder Jim Fregosi. "Baseball is a game of runs and hits, but I don't care what anybody says—it's tough to play in a ball park that belongs to somebody else. You can't even run the organization correctly. In Orange County, the people seem enthusiastic and behind us 100%."

Joe Adcock had a similar outlook. His last season would be in 1966, which ended a career including two National League pennants and one World Series title with the Braves. Adcock had been through the adrenaline-laced phase of getting a new ballpark during his tenure with the Braves, so he knew the psychological boost that comes with a new home.

"This is going to be a different year," said the veteran who had begun playing in the major leagues in 1952. "We moved down the freeway to

Anaheim and we're no longer in a borrowed ball park. It's our own. I went through the same thing at Milwaukee and whoever heard of the Braves before they left Boston? We've got too many good, young kids on this club to be in the second division."[1]

Though he likely wasn't known to most of the 31,660 patrons attending the Angels–White Sox game on this April evening, city councilman Jack Dutton was the driving force behind this civic project of epic proportions. As the 52-year-old Dutton folded his 5'11" frame into his Cadillac for the drive to the stadium, he had the satisfaction of seeing a vision realized through glad-handing to boost confidence and hand-holding to lessen worry.

An early riser, Dutton had already had a long day that began with his familiar routine of drinking coffee and reading the newspaper. On this date, the Orange County media splashed stories and commentaries about the ballpark's official debut that evening.

Dutton's appearance resulted from his duty as a political functionary playing a key role in getting the financing approved for the stadium. A lifelong Anaheimian, he probably would have been there even if he had nothing to do with the beginning of a new era for the Angels.

Love for his hometown ran as deep as the waters a few hundred yards off Anaheim Bay. Even his social calendar was filled with events related to the community. Dutton was married twice. If Dutton and either wife had a night out, it's likely they were headed to a fund-raiser for a civic project. Or a Man of the Year testimonial. Or a Christmas party at City Hall. Or a dinner with a colleague where the city's business was often the main topic of conversation.

Dutton had succeeded in business with enough money to retire in his 40s; an asset portfolio included a restaurant with a luau theme. But he saw politics as an avenue to blend his commercial pragmatism with a sense of civic obligation, adding a touch of blarney in his boasts to Anaheim's power brokers about the impact of a stadium on the city.

Foremost, Dutton knew that a stadium had immeasurable marketing value; bylines of every sports reporter covering their teams on California road trips would feature Anaheim below the reporters' names. The Angels had 81 home games a year, which meant 81 opportunities for the city to be promoted in newspaper, radio, and TV coverage. But the ballpark idea was not immune from criticism, particularly because of news reports involving tax money to build the ballpark.

When Disneyland debuted in 1955, Anaheim became a household word. Dutton, along with the city's inner circle of influencers, saw an opportunity to leverage that notoriety and compete with Los Angeles and San Francisco as prime destinations for residents, businesses, and tourists in the Golden State.

Dutton's path was quite literally a rags-to-riches story. He began his business career as a kid "selling wiping rags" to clients who dealt with oil spillover as a daily occurrence. If someone worked at a gas station, shipyard, or oil refinery in Southern California in the 1920s and 1930s, there's a good chance that worker used his product.

Dutton's tenure as a city councilman lasted from 1962 to 1970. After that, he served one term as Anaheim's mayor.

Cathy Dutton recalled her father's impact:

Long Beach was lobbying to build a stadium for the Angels. He and a few other council members understood the optics of having a team in Anaheim, broadcasts from Anaheim, and how that would make Anaheim a recognizable destination. He knew that with the momentum Disneyland had given Anaheim, a baseball team would build off that vision. And he loved baseball. It was a perfect project.

Those were magical years that started with pixie dust. The Anaheim Stadium, the Anaheim Convention Center, the development of the Canyon area that was envisioned by the prior council and leadership and the subsequent population growth of the city were all things he was proud of.

He never looked at the stadium or the convention center as his achievements. He always felt that it was a team made up of the council and the city manager. He was most proud of being part of that team of visionaries.

From the time the Angels arrived in 1966, he would attend at least 50 games a year until his later years. Then he'd listen on the radio or watch on TV. That is until he got mad at them in 2002 when they were threatening to go on strike. Then he stopped watching in protest. Unfortunately, he died before he got to see them win the World Series that year. I'm quite confident that it took him passing and his nudging God to make the win happen (along with "The Cowboy"—Gene Autry). In fact, when he got sick, they had had a lousy start to the season. He eventually fell into a coma. We would put the TV on so he could hear the game.

After the Angels had won 19 of 20 games, I went to visit him at the hospital. I turned on the TV and told him about their winning streak. He hadn't been conscious for weeks and, miraculously, he woke up and said, "You've got to be kidding." And he went back into his coma. Those were the last words he ever spoke.

He really is a perfect example of the American dream. Start small, become an entrepreneur, and make money on your own terms. He was raised by his grandmother on a ranch and had a lot of responsibility. I think his ability to persuade was intuitive.

He loved serving. He hated politics. For him, the toughest part of the job was the politics and the inaccurate information that could be disseminated. Putting Anaheim on the map was personal and civic pride from his love of the city he was born and raised in. He was a strong believer that those who can should do.

He was a glad-hander for sure, but he also had clear beliefs and ethics and was never afraid to say exactly what he thought and believed. He always focused on the issues and never made it personal. The city manager who served Anaheim from 1950 to 1976 told me once, "We didn't always agree on everything, but I always knew where he stood." As a city manager, you can work with that.

———✖———

Angels owner Gene Autry had the good fortune of Dutton's political savvy, which complemented the entertainer's business abilities. There was a mutual respect and admiration between the duo fostered by Dutton's interest in horses and rodeos. Autry grew up in rural Texas and Oklahoma, got discovered by Will Rogers, and began recording songs in 1929.

His repertoire reached sales exceeding 100 million copies. Autry's success in western movies, radio, and TV made him an A-list performer.

Autry was not one to settle for fame and fortune through his entertainment career, though. He added TV and radio stations to his ledger of investments, consolidating the outlets as Golden West Broadcasters. Autry's journey to inaugurating the new ballpark began in the wake of the Pacific Coast League removing the predecessor-in-name Angels and the Hollywood Stars from Southern California when the Dodgers

The California Angels got their own stadium in 1966 after spending a season at LA's Wrigley Field and three seasons sharing Dodger Stadium. COURTESY OF SECURITY PACIFIC NATIONAL BANK COLLECTION/LOS ANGELES PUBLIC LIBRARY

transplanted from Brooklyn in 1958 and gained the territorial baseball rights to the region.

Autry based his purchase of the rights to an AL franchise in the region on neither folly nor passion. It was shrewd business planning.

When the Dodgers left Autry's radio station KMPC for KFI in 1959, Autry confronted a void of sports programming to fill; AL expansion created a fantastic opportunity to be the exclusive radio broadcaster for the nascent team.[2]

AL president Joe Cronin had a different idea—invite Autry to be an owner. Autry secured the deal on December 7, 1960. Later he bought television station KTLA, which broadcast the team's games. The "Angels" moniker was a logical choice to honor the history, lore, and excitement of the PCL squad.

Coming into Angel Stadium's debut, Anaheim's team had won three of their first four games on the road to begin their 1966 baseball season. There was every reason to be optimistic for the first home game. But the White Sox soured the night with a 3–1 defeat of Mr. Autry's team.

---

Georgia's pride was evident.

During the first month of the 1966 baseball season, Atlanta amplified its already strong notoriety given its place in American culture as the home of Coca-Cola. After 13 years as a midwestern club, the Braves moved from Milwaukee to Atlanta.

For Peachtree State residents who still winced at the Civil War's outcome—referred to as the War of Northern Aggression in some quarters—Atlanta's ball club provided an outlet for their heritage-filled pride. "Nothing since we lost the Civil War has meant more to us than bringing the Braves here," said Governor Carl Sanders. NL president Warren Giles, a non-Southerner, further emphasized the legacy of the Deep South by reminding a reporter that the song "Dixie" prompted him to "stand and cheer."[3]

It was not a smooth transition, though. There were legal arguments in addition to moral questions following team emigrations. Fans were stunned that their beloved players would leave. In addition to the Braves moving from Boston to Milwaukee in 1953, shifts had occurred for teams from Brooklyn, Manhattan, Philadelphia, and St. Louis. Fans called them abandonments.

On April 11, smiles and handshakes abounded at a celebration dinner held at the Atlanta Marriott underscoring the importance of the moment. Conversations about the upcoming baseball season and the Braves' competition dominated conversations as the attendees clinked glasses for toasts. It's likely that they talked of the social progress being made earlier that day when Emmett Ashford became the first Black umpire in the major leagues, officiating behind the plate for the Indians–Senators game in the nation's capital. The Indians won 5–2.

Mayor Ivan Allen beamed like a father of the bride. And rightfully so. He savored the moment with the confidence that his leadership maintained through the administrative, financial, and legal obstacles that might have intimidated a politico with lesser stamina. As Dutton did with Anaheim, Allen saw his city's future, and it involved a major-league team.

There were bumps and bruises accompanying politics, a profession of pie-in-the-sky promises, jaw-dropping taunts, and extortion-like threats behind the scenes. But on this night when the anticipation ran as thick as a Southern live oak tree, the benefit surpassed the cost. Like Anaheim, Atlanta would be known in datelines throughout the country—the *Atlanta Constitution* reported that the number of writers to cover the Braves' inaugural game exceeded 130.[4]

Atlanta kicked off the season at their new home the following day.

The opening of a new ballpark is no different than the debut of a casino, airline, restaurant, or amusement park. Dedication to customer service is paramount and must be emphasized upon the entrance of the first patron. Braves president John McHale called attention to this philosophy for the press. Winning was important, but the team's brand had to stand for more than excellent ballplaying. "A baseball man never fails to get those butterflies on opening night, no matter what his job," said McHale. "I worry about everything, but mostly about the impression our workers all over the park make on the customer.

"We want every man who comes into the Stadium to feel we want to make him happy. We don't want him to have any problems and we're trying to train our [staff] to keep that uppermost in their minds and deal with fans accordingly."[5]

Any doubts about the tenants of Atlanta Stadium drawing a crowd were immediately extinguished by the attendance for the first game: 50,671.

The first official major-league game in the Deep South was a 13-inning affair against the Pittsburgh Pirates ending in a 3–2 loss for the hosts. Atlanta's Tony Cloninger pitched the entire game; Pittsburgh used three pitchers.

Atlanta's mayor Ivan Allen throws out the first ball to inaugurate the Braves in their new city. The first regular-season game was a 3–2 loss in 13 innings to the Pittsburgh Pirates. COURTESY OF WSB RADIO RECORDS, POPULAR MUSIC AND CULTURE COLLECTION, SPECIAL COLLECTIONS AND ARCHIVES, GEORGIA STATE UNIVERSITY

Fans saw a pitching duel between Cloninger and Bob Veale for the first four innings. Cloninger kept the Pirates scoreless in the top of the fifth; Atlanta drew first blood with Joe Torre's solo blast.

Veale evaded further damage an inning later after walking Cloninger with one out and giving up a single to Felipe Alou. Facing 35-year-old slugger Eddie Mathews—coming off a .251 season in '65 with tremendous power that notched 512 career home runs—and Hank Aaron, who exemplified consistency at the plate, Veale had baseball's angels on his side. With Cloninger on second and Alou on first, the Pittsburgh southpaw dispatched the two power hitters. Mathews whiffed. Aaron, a career .305 hitter who went yard 755 times, grounded to third baseman Bob Bailey.

Jim Pagliaroni, Pittsburgh's backstop, tagged Cloninger for a solo homer to lead off the Pirates' half of the eighth and tie the score at 1–1. He did not praise the site as a hitter's ballpark despite his blast. "This is a beautiful park, but our guys complain the ball doesn't [carry] well here. I'd say that's right."[6]

It looked like the Braves were destined for a Hollywood ending to begin this new chapter in Georgia baseball history. Veale loaded the bases with two outs in the bottom of the ninth by walking Joe Torre, Denis Menke, and Lee Thomas. Pirates skipper Harry Walker sent Elroy Face to relieve the left-hander; Frank Bolling flied to Willie Stargell in left field and sent the game into extra innings.

In the bottom of the 11th, the hosts loaded the bases again. Aaron singled and stole second; Rico Carty walked, and both runners advanced on Torre's sacrifice bunt to Don Schwall, who had replaced Face to begin the bottom of the 10th.

Menke drew an intentional walk, likely to increase the chances of a double-play grounder to end the inning. Schwall struck out Thomas, and Bolling's grounder to third base forced out Menke at second. "But I hated to see that Thomas come up with the bases loaded and done out in the 11th," said Schwall after the game. "He usually hits me pretty good. This time I got him out."[7]

Stargell broke the tie with a two-run homer in the top of the 13th. He had gone 0-for-5 already against Cloninger, who had the stamina of a marathoner. Stargell, a left-handed batter, revealed that he wanted to wait on a pitch and try to smack it to the opposite field. "But he threw me a high curve and I leaped on it. When I connected I didn't think it would go out but it just did clear the fence and I believe I danced around those bases. It sure helps when you win the opener, especially away from home."[8]

Atlanta got a boost when Torre cracked his second homer of the night, a solo home run in the bottom of the 13th with one out. But Menke followed with a strikeout, and Thomas's grounder to Pittsburgh shortstop Gene Alley ended the game.

Despite the loss, Atlantans celebrated their team; Milwaukeeans frowned. They had lured the Braves from Boston in 1953 with great fanfare, including a new stadium. Now they were on the other side of the equation as the baseball community accustomed itself to the Atlanta moniker. Milwaukee's hopes in restoring the team to the Badger State rested on the analysis of circuit court judge Elmer Roller, whose decision was the latest controversy on a legal trek that Braves ownership never wanted to make.

It had begun in January, when Roller mandated that Wisconsin's lawsuit against the NL and the Braves organization go to trial rather than be dismissed.[9] Georgia's court system defied the Wisconsin jurist— Fulton County Superior Court judge Sam McKenzie issued a permanent injunction declaring that the Braves must play baseball in Atlanta.[10]

Roller instead went forward with the case in his courtroom, heard the arguments from both sides, and made his decision a day after the Braves' first game.

Wisconsin won its biggest victory since the Black Hawk War: Braves ownership along with the NL broke the state's antitrust laws.[11]

Roller's ruling included the provision that Milwaukee get an expansion team in 1967. It was the legal equivalent of a bottom-of-the-ninth, game-winning grand slam for Milwaukee's baseball fans. Or so they believed. The Braves et al. appealed, but it wouldn't be decided until July. Meanwhile, the team stayed in Atlanta.

The Baltimore Orioles aimed to break into the upper ranks of the AL after two straight seasons of 90-plus wins and third-place finishes—two games behind the Yankees in 1964 and nine games behind the Twins in 1965. An extra-innings contest against an inferior Red Sox team—62–100 record and ninth-place finish in 1965—tested Baltimore's stamina on Opening Day.

The temperature was in the mid-40s, unusual for a baseball game. More so was the ending: a bases-loaded balk by Boston right-hander Jim Lonborg in the top of the 13th gave the Orioles the first notch in their 1966 W column as the game headed toward the four-hour mark.

Designed to prevent deceit, a balk can be called only if at least one runner is on base, and it advances each runner one base. Lonborg's mistake happened because of Hamlet-like hesitancy. "It was a moment of indecision," said the right-hander. "I was supposed to throw a curve and just as I started my windup a thought flashed through my mind: Nope. I'm going to throw a fastball. Then it was too late."[12]

It was one of two balks Lonborg made in 1966 (the second came on July 29); his career number is nine. Baltimore's victory set the team on a path toward a 97-win season and a World Series berth. Opening Day was a forerunner for their season—the Orioles won 13 of their 20 games that went into extra innings; they never fell below .500.

—— ∞∞∞ ——

Baltimore's extra-innings victory was a nice way to start '66. The Dodgers also had an Opening Day win with a 3–2 victory over the Houston Astros at Dodger Stadium. Ron Fairly twice banged a single to score Maury Wills and hit a sacrifice fly that gave Wes Parker a chance to cross the plate. It was probably no surprise because Fairly led the home team in RBIs for 1965. But what may have been surprising—maybe shocking—was the lack of attendance for the World Series champs in this game that lasted a little more than two hours. Drawing a crowd of 34,520 disappointed those who expected the stature of a championship to inspire fans to attend. Instead, it was the lowest Opening Day attendance for the Dodgers since they began playing in LA in 1958.[13]

Los Angeles only notched one strikeout and achieved 10 hits off veteran hurler Robin Roberts and reliever Frank Carpin.

The Dodgers had moved to LA after the 1957 season; their West Coast presence was fixed in American popular culture by the mid-1960s. The national pastime was just one identifier of the Southern California lifestyle. Thanks to the Beach Boys, surf culture became a prized fantasy for landlocked teenagers from Bismarck to Buffalo suffering brutal chills in winters and settling for lakes, rivers, and community pools as their aquatic recreation in summers. *Gidget* starred Sally Field and featured the surfing genre on a weekly basis during the 1965–1966 TV season. There were 32 episodes. The last aired on April 21, 1966.

The title character debuted in the 1957 novel *Gidget: The Little Girl with Big Ideas* by Frederick Kohner, who based the character on his daughter Kathy's Malibu surfing and dating escapades. Five novels and three movies cemented Gidget as a household name before the TV version.

Field possessed the girl-next-door looks and eager personality necessary to carry this prime-time interpretation, which was her first acting job. "I only remember joyous things about *Gidget*," said Field. "I don't remember a single day that I didn't want to be there. It was simply glee. Absolute, total, exhausting glee."

At its core, *Gidget* is about a teenage girl and her father.

Gidget's mom is deceased, which leaves Russ Lawrence (played by Don Porter), a college professor, alone to help his daughter navigate around her mistakes, disappointments, and misunderstandings toward adulthood.

"That was really a wonderful time for me to explore something I didn't really feel that I had ever had," revealed Field. "I wasn't really close like that with either of my fathers for various reasons. And so, Don Porter kind of became that for me. He was just wonderful. He really took care of me. First of all, he respected me and he didn't treat me like 'Who are you, you newcomer?' But more than that, he was just such a loving, gentle, sweet caring man."[14]

There was also the well-intentioned though often uninvited advice from Gidget's sister and brother-in-law, Anne and John.

*Gidget* has a familiar dynamic between the title character and her friend, Larue Wilson. One is a noble-minded dreamer with schemes requiring counsel from a grounded confidant. Hamlet and Horatio. Lucy and Ethel. The Lone Ranger and Tonto. Tony Soprano and Silvio Dante.

Larue was after the same things Gidget wanted, mostly attention from boys. Where Gidget was cute and affable, Larue was gawky and plain. But that made the latter girl more identifiable to the typical teenager who strived for acceptance in a peer group obsessed with looks, personality, and status.

Lynette Winter played Larue. She recalled,

Sally and I hit it off the first time we met for my film test. She read off screen, me on. We cracked each other up like the two teenage girls we were. And those antics continued on through the filming. When one of us was off camera we would make faces at the other much to the consternation of several of the directors we had.

I hung out in Sally's trailer. We'd go over lines or gossip. We got fan mail, Sally much more than I did. My fans were those who were like my character, slight misfits that recognized themselves in me. I got those letters long after the show closed, saying they missed someone on screen they could identify with.

I loved working on the show. It was such a shock to everyone when we were canceled. Not just the cast but crew and execs alike. I think there are many reasons the show resonated. Don was the perfect father, understanding and loving. I, of course, as the comic relief who everyone still roots for. And Sally who could cry at the drop of a hat—I always envied her that trick—and was as endearing as her character. And of course, all the cast who truly cared for each other. Fond memories.[15]

———⊶⊷———

James Michener's number-one best seller *The Source* challenged readers to take a literary odyssey through the history of Israel framed by an archaeological dig at the fictional site Makor in the present day with three main characters: a Jew, an Arab, and an American.

Michener's work was a literary groundbreaker, no pun intended. This wondrous chronicle elevated the history of Israel to a wide audience less than 20 years after the land had been restored to historic Jewish governance in the late 1940s through a United Nations charter. Michener begins his saga with an affirmation of Judaism's openness toward others in Israel: "Just like the Jews. Denied religious liberty by all, they extend it to everyone."[16]

In the post–World War II era, Michener's task was daunting. Making a region's story come alive demanded more than diligent scribbling. Known for his exceptional research, Michener authored detailed novels that taught more about the topic than an upper-level college seminar.

For his narrative about Israel, he chose *The Source* for the title to reflect the water well described in the beginning of the novel and uncovered at the end.

Michener described the customs of Judaism in a compelling way for a readership wanting to read more sophisticated literary fare in the 1950s and 1960s. What Jews knew and embraced for generations became fodder for tolerance by gentiles as they began to learn the wondrous traditions set in the five books of the Torah.[17]

*The Source* frames the narrative through artifacts discovered at the well and an explanation of their corresponding eras. Israel's hallmarks are described in great detail, including King David's reign, the ritual of circumcision, the birth of Christianity, and the evolution of worship rules for Jews.

After saying the blessings over the wine and challah at Shabbat dinners, Jewish families talking about *The Source* might have added Hollywood's look at a recent slice of Jewish history to the conversation—the story of Colonel David "Mickey" Marcus in *Cast a Giant Shadow*, which premiered that same year. An American Jew, Marcus got his release from the army after World War II and helped the Israeli paramilitary organization named Haganah to establish Israel.

It's a story of rediscovery for Marcus, who gets a comeuppance of sorts when General Mike Randolph employs reverse psychology and says that the United States has no reason to assist Jews in the Middle East because the Arabs have the oil. Then Randolph reveals that Marcus needs to aid his own people because it's the right thing to do.

Though Marcus is doubtful, Randolph underscores the horrors of Dachau and the moral importance of the historic homeland. "What about you? Are you too big to go back and help your own people unless they bow down and kiss your West Point ring? What happened to that insubordinate S-O-B that jumped out of one of my planes over Normandy? Won the Distinguished Service Medal? Are you proud of that medal and ashamed you might win the Star of David? Stand up and be counted, Mickey. There's a lot of us that'll stand up with you. L'chaim."[18]

It's a powerful speech reminding American Jews of the struggles and triumphs that created the modern state of Israel. Although the movie business was founded and largely run by Jewish executives, writers, and producers, there was a fantastic dearth of Jewish-themed stories.

Kirk Douglas plays Marcus, and John Wayne plays Randolph.[19]

———————

When Americans turned the calendar at the end of April, they could point with pride to progress. A Black umpire made a terrific leap toward equality when he took his position behind home plate. American Jews enjoyed thoughtful portrayals in popular culture. Television portrayed female characters as powerful rather than secondary.

But America's groundbreaking wasn't finished. Not by a long shot.

CHAPTER FIVE

# Spies and Dolls (May)

THE ST. LOUIS CARDINALS HAD A NEW NEST.

Busch Stadium debuted on May 12, replacing the team's ballpark with the same moniker.[1] That storied site had seen six World Series championships for the Redbirds, ending its tenure with a 10–5 loss to the San Francisco Giants on May 8.

Cardinals fans celebrated their new refuge with a 4–3 victory over the Atlanta Braves on a cold night hardly representing springtime. St. Louis finished 1966 with an 83–79 record, placing sixth out of eight teams. Bob Gibson had a 21–12 record with 225 strikeouts. Orlando Cepeda hit .303. Lou Brock led the major leagues with 74 stolen bases. It was the first of a string of seasons where he topped his brethren in thefts: In nine years, he led the National League eight times and the majors six times.

The first Busch Stadium ended its tenure as a baseball cornerstone of the Midwest on the same day that Frank Robinson entered the annals of baseball rarities in Baltimore. On May 8, he crushed a Luis Tiant pitch in an Orioles–Indians game and sent it out of Memorial Stadium to the delight of Baltimore's baseball fans. Power, thy name is Robinson.

The epic blast happened in the second game of a doubleheader; Baltimore won both contests. Decisively. The scores were 8–2 and 8–3. Robinson's dinger went 451 feet till it hit the ground and ended an estimated 540 feet from home plate. The slugger with Samsonesque strength could not recall smacking a pitch as solidly, but he acknowledged that he did hit one that went farther—503 feet in Cincinnati in 1965. What made

The St. Louis Cardinals moved from Busch Stadium to a new home with the same name in 1966. The moniker reflected the team's Anheuser-Busch ownership.
COURTESY OF THELMA BLUMBERG COLLECTION, THE STATE HISTORICAL SOCIETY OF MISSOURI

the feat more delicious than usual was his opposition; Tiant had three consecutive shutouts when he took the hill in Baltimore.

Luis Aparicio had led off the first inning with a single and sprinted to second base when Tiant threw a wild pitch. Russ Snyder grounded out, then Robinson went stratospheric with a home run to give Baltimore a 2–0 lead. Boog Powell singled, then scored on Curt Blefary's double to increase the padding to three runs.

In recent days, Robinson neared .440 when a 2-for-14 output plummeted his average to .371. It was outstanding by any measurement for a mortal ballplayer. Still, the sudden drop caused concern; it abated when Robinson deduced the reason—an injured left shoulder suffered when he stole third base during a 3–0 loss to the Senators on May 3.

The right-handed batsman figured that the injury prevented him from lifting his left arm to its normal position during an at-bat. Measures were implemented. "Then in batting practice today before the first game, I told several of the guys, 'I think I've found what I'm doing wrong.' I wasn't getting my bat out in front," explained Robinson. "Now, I've got my arms and hands back up where they belong despite the discomfort—forcing myself. I struck out my first turn against [Sonny] Siebert, but I knew I was on the right track. I felt better and got a good rip. I had been pulling my head out, too, so with the change, I was also seeing the ball better."[2]

Orioles fans had been cautiously optimistic at the beginning of the month when their team stood atop the American League with a half game separating them from Cleveland. Now they were in second place and three games behind.

An orange flag with the word "Here" in black marked the spot where the ball landed outside the stadium. F. W. Haxel, a family-owned Maryland flag company, manufactured it; when Memorial Stadium was demolished in the 1980s and the Orioles moved to Camden Yards, the team gave the flag to a fan whose name has been lost to history.

Mark Melonas restored this history for the 50th anniversary of Robinson's home run. As a furniture maker who went to art school, he understands the artistic, communal, and cultural importance of the "Here" flag.

My dad was a teenager who lived in Hamilton, a neighborhood that's a little north of Memorial Stadium. Baseball was the king of sports in the 1950s and 1960s. They had recreation leagues, kids played stickball in the street, there were softball games in the city parks after Sunday mass at Annunciation Church on Preston Street or St. Nicholas in Highlandtown.

I was reading a book about the Orioles when the 49th anniversary of the home run came around. I wanted to get a 'Here' flag made to mark the spot again. As I did more research about the Orioles, I got the sense that a lot of older Baltimore people had left the city during the 1960s and a changing of the guard took place regarding fans. But a new flag would be emblematic that people are still here. It's a way of reclaiming the neighborhood and showing how the site connects to the history of the city. Robinson was a heroic Black ballplayer who had some of the highlights of his career at Memorial Stadium in addition to the home run.

The more history I read, I could only imagine how segregated it was in Baltimore in the mid-1960s. It was a hopeful thing that a baseball team that had been successful with core players traded for Frank Robinson. He has this arrival where he ignites this team and the fan base to cheer for a Black man. He is the guy who helped put the Orioles over the Yankees and everyone else. The people who donated to pay for the 'Here' flag is a classic Baltimore story. They wanted to memorialize the home run so this story would be told.

I called F. W. Haxel and asked if the company made the "Here" flag in 1966. They confirmed it, so I had them make an exact replica. The YMCA is the steward of the playing field. I told them about my idea to place a flag in left field along the chain link fence that is the border. They were okay with it. On the 50th anniversary, we raised the flag.[3]

---

By 1966, the spy genre governed popular culture.

It was Ian Fleming's fault. Or John F. Kennedy's. Or maybe Barry Nelson's. Or Sean Connery's. Or Cubby Broccoli's and Harry Saltzman's in tandem.

When President Kennedy endorsed Ian Fleming as his favorite author, interest in the James Bond franchise accelerated. Espionage tales seemed to be abundant, if not omnipresent.

Fleming had penned stories featuring the British spy also known as 007 beginning with the 1953 novel *Casino Royale*; the anthology TV show *Climax!* used it as the basis for an episode the following year starring Barry Nelson.

Sean Connery's portrayal in the first Bond film—*Dr. No* in 1962— formed the template. He had dangerous gadgets and cutting-edge cars, thanks to Major Boothroyd in the first two films and Quartermaster—

informally labeled Q—beginning with *Goldfinger* in 1964; Fleming's tales did not feature such a character.

Bond partnered with women who could rival *Playboy* centerfold models for beauty, a Princeton doctoral candidate for intelligence, and Dick Butkus for toughness. Their prey: a villain usually set on destruction for greed set against exotic locations that titillated moviegoers.

There were three Bond movies over the next three years: *From Russia with Love, Goldfinger*, and *Thunderball*.

A Cold War aura formed a through line in the spy-laden popular culture of the 1960s. Blofeld's Kruschevian appearance as the title character in *Goldfinger* was an avatar for Russians who stood on the other side of freedom. *Get Smart* parodied the KGB and CIA with the cleverly named KAOS and CONTROL.

Animators got involved too.

Boris and Natasha delighted children with their hilarious yet unfulfilled schemes to defeat a squirrel and moose named Rocky and Bullwinkle. Secret Squirrel's 000 designation paid homage to Bond; Morocco Mole was his partner in crime fighting. Tom of T.H.U.M.B. had Swinging Jack.

*The Man Called Flintstone*, a film premiering in 1966 after *The Flintstones* finished its six-year run on ABC, relied on the premise of Fred Flintstone being identical to secret agent Rock Slag and replacing him on a vital mission to defeat the villainous Green Goose. The *Post-Standard* of Syracuse called it "handsomely done."[4] The *Los Angeles Times* credited the production aspects: "Charles A. Nichols, director of animation, and his crew of technical artists have wrought inventively to give these characters life in this spy comedy with music."[5] On the soundtrack is Louis Prima's interpretation of a romantic ballad "Pensate Amore" during a Rome sequence. Pebbles and Bamm-Bamm sing about what they will be when they grow up.

If audiences worried about Russia in a post-JFK world, they could immerse themselves in espionage tales on film where square-jawed heroes commit acts of derring-do accompanied by gorgeous love interests.

In *The Silencers*, Dean Martin plays Matt Helm, a former agent with ICE—Intelligence Counter Espionage—turned photographer. When we first see Helm, he's resting in his circular bed, enjoying slumber, and dreaming about the models he's photographed for the covers of outdoors magazines.

A phone call from his former boss, MacDonald, wakes Helm from his reverie. MacDonald needs him to defeat a plan by the Big O organization, but the specifics are not yet known. He uses a beautiful blonde to entice the ace agent back into the spy game. She's actually a double agent for Big O; Helm's spy compadre Tina arrives and shoots the villainess in the back, revealing a dagger in the blonde's hand.

Big O's scheme is called Operation Fallout. A test missile launched from White Sands, New Mexico, headed for a target in the Pacific Ocean will be sabotaged and turned toward a new target—Alamogordo, New Mexico. Russia will be blamed for attacking a key part of America's nuclear arsenal, war will begin, and Big O will emerge as the preeminent body while the two superpowers destroy each other. The story's twist is the identity of the chief operative with the code name Cowboy. It's Tina.

Other spy-themed fare at the movies included fodder provided by NBC's *The Man from U.N.C.L.E.* Both *To Trap a Spy* and *The Spy with My Face* were culled from episodes of the show featuring two agents working for the United Network Command for Law and Enforcement, a fictional union of nations committed to geopolitical stability. Illya Kuryakin and Napoleon Solo represented a Russian-American détente in their pursuit of villainous activity across the globe. Where Maxwell Smart and Agent 99 had to deal with KAOS, Kuryakin and Solo targeted THRUSH—Technological Hierarchy for the Removal of Undesirables and Subjugation of Humanity.

Robert Vaughn played Solo; David McCallum played Kuryakin. Leo G. Carroll played their supervisor, Alexander Waverly.

Del Floria's Tailor Shop in Manhattan's East 40s, presumably near the United Nations building, masks U.N.C.L.E.'s headquarters. To continue the illusion of U.N.C.L.E. being a real entity, the closing credits thanked the men and women of the United Network Command for Law and Enforcement.

*The Man from U.N.C.L.E.* ran from 1964 to 1968 on NBC. "At one point in 1966, we were receiving between the two of us 70,000 fan let-

New York City has an allure unlike any other metropolis. This photo of the Manhattan skyline from 1956 exemplifies the city's post–World War II construction. By 1966, it would be even more crowded. The headquarters for the agents in NBC's *The Man from U.N.C.L.E.* were located behind a tailor shop in the East 40s, near the United Nations building approximately in the center of the photo. COURTESY OF NEW YORK CITY DEPARTMENT OF RECORDS AND INFORMATION SERVICES

ters a month," said Vaughn in an interview for the Archive of American Television.[6] Nostalgia for the show resurfaced in the early 1980s when Vaughn and McCallum reteamed in the TV movie *Return of the Man from U.N.C.L.E.*

Derek Flint is an ultrasuave, parodic version of the debonair spy template cultivated by Sean Connery as James Bond. In *Our Man Flint*, he has no interest in returning to the field. He prefers instead to relax in his tricked-out Manhattan apartment—by visual evidence, it appears to be in the San Remo on Central Park West—with a foursome of beautiful women tending to his physical needs, two-sided artwork that can flip

77

by electronic control, and other accoutrements allowing him to pursue gourmet cooking and relax after teaching ballet in Moscow.

007 never had it so good.

Zonal Organization World Intelligence Espionage recruits its top operative to defeat Galaxy, an association gearing to control the world's weather and claim that it will help mankind. No extreme weather means no catastrophes. But all that power in the hands of one group can lead to enslavement in a totalitarian society.

Flint refuses to use the gadgets and weaponry offered, including a Walther gun. Instead, he has a cigarette lighter with 83 uses. When he's trapped in a vault, Flint employs the miniature blowtorch function.

Spies emblemized culture, sophistication, and intelligence for men. Women did not have such role models in abundance. Flint's *ménage à cinq* framework treated women with adoration, respect, and kindness, yet it was clear that they were servile. When Gila Golan's character submits to Flint by the end of the movie and makes the group a *ménage à six*, Flint is neither condescending nor mocking. It's simply accepted that women orbit around his gravitational pull sexually, intellectually, and emotionally.

James Coburn's portrayal of American spy Derek Flint was a comedic turn, prompting Harry Haun of the *Nashville Tennessean* to declare, "[It] offers the ultimate in cloak-and-dagger derring-do, suspending credibility altogether and pushing flamboyant exploits to the point of becoming the screen's first live-action comic strip."[7]

During a promotional trip across the Midwest, Coburn compared his spy to the British counterpart. "Flint is a vulnerable person, which always draws out audience sympathy. That's how he differs from James Bond. Flint has the possibility of evolution. He's not a machine. Bond's tragedy is that he's locked into an organization, whereas Flint is an individual who can shrug off others' demands."[8]

Coburn starred in a sequel, 1967's *In Like Flint*. But the actor's attitude toward this hip, mod spy was frustration rather than fascination. "Jim Coburn was by no means an unknown actor when he went into *Flint*, but he was not widely considered to be a leading man," explained producer Saul David. "*Flint* changed all that for him, but he was never very proud of the role and by the time the sequel rolled around he had expressed his restlessness in several public appearances."[9]

The sequel ended the Flint series.

———— ∞∞ ————

Hollywood's trove of espionage-themed tales inspired Milton Bradley to follow suit with a string of board games. Parents could choose from *James Bond Secret Agent 007* or games inspired by *Goldfinger* and *Thunderball* for gifts on birthdays, Christmas, or any of Chanukah's eight nights.

Targeted to kids upwards of age 10, the games exemplified the spy genre's pervasiveness in the mid-1960s. Kids looked forward to getting together with friends and avoiding homework for a couple of hours when they could imagine being spies through rolling dice and moving pieces around a board while adhering to a series of rules.

While Coca-Cola and Pepsi dominated the soft-drink market, it would not be unusual for the kids to consume Patio, Fresca, or Tab along with salty offerings like Nabisco's barbecue chicken–flavored snack Pik Chicks, Humpty Dumpty potato chips, or Quaker's Dippy Canoes corn chips shaped like the water vessels in the name.

For a break from game playing, they gorged themselves on Archie Comics' spy series *The Man from R.I.V.E.R.D.A.L.E.*, which ran in 1966 and 1967.[10]

Whether the playing surface was a bedroom floor in Waukegan, a kitchen table in Omaha, a lounge chair in La Jolla, a recreation room couch in Bethesda, or a beach in Fort Lauderdale, the games prompted relaxation and casual discussions about varying topics pertinent to their existence. Which teacher was the strictest? Which athlete was the school's best? What's the funniest sitcom?

Conversations could turn quickly to more sobering topics. In the mid-1960s, the country was not as united, and cornerstones were not as strong as in decades past. Intermarriage between religions was not dominant but certainly more evident. Divorce, too. One couldn't read the front page of the newspaper or watch the evening news without getting frightened of the increasingly volatile situation in the Vietnam War, which eventually killed more than 50,000 servicemen.

Questions arose. Whose parents were getting divorced? Which member of the synagogue had married a shiksa? Whose older brother had gotten drafted and was potentially heading to serve his country in Southeast Asia?

Fathers experienced similar conversational dynamics in their card games.

Complaints about bosses, clients, and underlings yielded to observations about a secretary's sex appeal that could only be discussed out of the wives' hearing radius. They bragged about their latest business deal, but they were more boastful about buying Cuban cigars from a connection despite the embargo against Cuban imports that began during the Kennedy presidency.

Laughter punctuated the smoke-filled air of ill-gotten stogies and nicotine-laden cigarettes complemented by scotch, martinis, or beer if the men preferred alcohol over soft drinks. As the wisps caused by exhalation drifted toward stucco ceilings and recessed lights, men discussed their teenagers approaching draft age and offered sighs and winces emphasizing the worry lines on their faces. Parents with kids serving in Vietnam had the empathy of their friends.

Where suburban fathers had gin rummy, poker, and pinochle, suburban mothers had mahjong. This tile game that originated in 19th-century China became a 20th-century staple for community pools, country clubs, and suburban homes. In between statements of "one bam," "two crack," and other terms of the game, the women drank watered-down martinis, smoked unfiltered cigarettes, and shared richly sourced gossip.

No matter the topic of conversation or the participants, music provided the soundtrack. In mid-1960s middle-class America, kids tuned their transistor radios to the local market's Top 40 station. The latest roster included "Wouldn't It Be Nice" from the Beach Boys' new album *Pet Sounds* and Nancy Sinatra's anthem "These Boots Are Made for Walkin'."

Adults had high-fidelity stereos forbidden to offspring lest they unintentionally break a needle, scratch a record, or raise the volume to a decibel level that could be heard two blocks away.

Companies branded their stereo products as state of the art with words, slogans, and phrases created by Madison Avenue to manufacture desire, fulfillment, and envy. Color television was not fully saturated—*The Dick Van Dyke Show*, *Perry Mason*, *The Munsters*, and *The Addams Family* were among the remaining shows still filmed in black and white—so advertisers determined to gain the loyalty of consumers. Admiral had "the most scientifically advanced" color television; Maganavox's stereo sound for music and television was "Astro-Sonic," whatever that meant.

Sounds that sprang from speakers told tales of love, an evergreen topic for songwriters and composers.

The Walker Brothers lamented heartbreak with "The Sun Ain't Gonna Shine Anymore"; Petula Clark declared her bottomless capacity for adoration in "My Love"; The Lovin' Spoonful echoed the fickleness of males with "Did You Ever Have to Make Up Your Mind?"; and Percy Sledge underscored the power of emotions in "When a Man Loves a Woman."

There was a simplicity bordering on naïveté revealing an evolving sensitivity in 1960s songwriting. When it tapped an emotional nerve, that was largely because all elements of the song resulted in a piece that made the listener believe it was performed just for him or her. Motown excelled at this. "You Can't Hurry Love" by the Supremes; "Reach Out, I'll Be There" by the Four Tops; and "My Guy" by Mary Wells gave listeners hopefulness contrasted by the mourning in "What Becomes of the Brokenhearted?," desperation in "You Don't Have to Say You Love Me" by Dusty Springfield, and resilience in "Red Rubber Ball" by the Cyrkle.

<hr>

Bill Cosby was a comedian emerging against the backdrop of the civil rights battles capturing America's attention in newspaper headlines and TV news footage. With peers Flip Wilson and Richard Pryor, they gained national exposure on *The Ed Sullivan Show* and *The Tonight Show*. But the next level, whether a TV show or movie, seemed to be out of reach for Black comedians.

Rob Reiner changed that.

His father, Carl, had honed his comedy chops as a writer and performer for *Your Show of Shows* and worked alongside Sid Caesar, Howie Morris, Imogene Coca, and Mel Brooks. That experience inspired him to create *The Dick Van Dyke Show* and name the main character after his teenaged son. After his parents returned to their Beverly Hills home from a night out, Rob told them about the hysterical comedian that he had watched on TV earlier that night.

Reiner invited the young comedian to the set at Desilu-Cahuenga Studios, where his producing partner Sheldon Leonard laughed along with the cast and crew as Cosby entertained them with tales from his routine. Leonard hired Cosby for *I Spy*, and Reiner also may be credited with the casting of Robert Culp. He had starred in *Trackdown*, which lasted two seasons. But he wanted to break into the writing end of show business and requested that Reiner critique a script. Reiner, a symbol of TV's comedy excellence, sent it to Leonard, who had more experience with dramatic material.

And so, Leonard now had his duo; Culp penned seven episodes for *I Spy*. NBC aired it for three seasons from 1965 to 1968.[11]

The Culp–Cosby pairing had chemistry that was necessary, palpable, and compelling. That Cosby was a Black actor on a prime-time show caused a stir among stations, particularly in the South where civil rights activists were sentinels in a social justice war against an entrenched bigotry. There was fear among stations who balked at carrying the show, according to Culp in a 2007 interview.

Alexander Scott was Kelly Robinson's equal, not a cookie-cutter character lacking depth and providing comic relief. It was a deliberate approach. Forty years after the show went off the air, Culp emphasized Cosby's attitude toward underplaying the race issue in the stories. "He said, 'Our statement is a non-statement.'"[12]

In an interview a couple of months before production started for the first season, Cosby said, "Bob and I discouraged the writers from making it a major point that a Negro was there in a starring role. First I'm a guy, then I'm a Negro."[13]

Cosby won the Emmy for Lead Actor all three years that *I Spy* was on the air. A comedian on the rise, Cosby had the endorsement of his costar regarding the humor. "He trusted me totally with regard to story and all that that entails and all that that embodies whether it's my writing or somebody else's writing. And I trusted him utterly, obviously about the comedy."[14]

Culp's success on *I Spy* made him a household name, but the journey to success was hardly brief. Jason Culp, Robert Culp's son, recalled,

Dad became an actor when he was about 14 years old after having desperately wanted to become a cartoonist. He was talented. He adored *Terry and the Pirates*, which exemplified the kind of thing he was attracted to—action adventure and comedy based in reality. Not so much Superman and Batman, but stories that could plausibly happen.

He went to New York for theater but found his way into live TV from 1951 onward and built a résumé of leads in anthology drama shows. But he was always writing.

He did an episode of *Zane Grey Theatre* as Hobie Gilman but didn't know it was a pilot for *Trackdown*. He didn't even know what a pilot was. His agent told him, he went to California, and he never came back. The series did remarkably well considering there were so many westerns.

After that, he was blackballed as being flinty because he had a bad time with the producer. But then eventually he started doing guest shots. By the time *I Spy* came around, he had been the highest paid special guest star on other people's shows and almost priced himself out of the business. He played a lot of heavies and brought style and panache to these roles, but he also did comedy.

For *I Spy*, he was secretly writing scripts that he planned to lay on the desks of Sheldon and the producers. He subversively created the tone and paradigm without being asked to. And it worked. As much as they resisted him, they recognized how good the scripts were and took them all. He wrote seven episodes of *I Spy* and directed one.

The phone was not always ringing with offers after the show ended. But he could be relied on to bring a spark and style to his guest appearances. There was a charm to his characters. He did a lot of guest-starring roles on situation comedies including *The Golden Girls*. Until *The Greatest American Hero* came along, he had resisted doing a series again. It ran for 45 episodes.

He loved working with Katherine Helmond as Ray Romano's in laws on *Everybody Loves Raymond*. I don't think they expected to come back so often after the first appearance. They were on 10 more times.

My dad had an independent spirit. There was no father presence in the home after he was 13 years old. He was raised by his maternal grandparents in Berkeley. His grandfather was like a character out of a Louis L'Amour story. Jack of all trades. Gold miner. Trapper. Western man. He could build anything and shoot anything. He was my dad's true and only idol.[15]

———— ∞ ————

Culp died in 2010. During a performance in Clearwater, Florida, Cosby recalled that the press compared him to Jackie Robinson, which is a well-worn semblance often made when a Black man achieves a breakthrough in any industry. In an analogy that could only be appreciated by baseball fans with an inkling of historical knowledge, Cosby said that Culp was Eddie Stanky, Pee Wee Reese, and other members of the Brooklyn Dodgers who accepted Robinson as a ballplayer who happened to be Black rather than a Black ballplayer.[16]

Sheldon Leonard's vision had paid off. Cosby's success and the treatment of Kelly Robinson and Alexander Scott as equals contributed to great strides in civil rights during the 1960s. Marches and boycotts get news coverage, but a prime-time show reaching 30 million people has unparalleled power to persuade.[17]

Leonard and his Hollywood brethren had profited from the espionage trend, producing highly significant stories ranging from pun-filled parodies to location-rich dramas. Sexual innuendo was blatant. Espionage was a category ripe for exploitation in the 1960s; villains were avatars for real-life Russian foes. Audiences could laugh at the antics and cheer at the victories. Either way, they got emotional, mental, and physical releases from newspaper headlines provoking conversation at best and fear at worst during the Cold War.

As NBC finished airing the first season of *I Spy*, Leonard readied to end the life span of another show in his production stable. The last episode of this innovative show aired in June; it disrupted television's accepted norms, creating a new baseline for situation comedies. Humorous dialogue, realistic scenarios, and a stellar cast combined for an Emmy-winning show revolving around the personal and professional lives of a TV comedy writer.

He resided at 148 Bonnie Meadow Road in New Rochelle.

CHAPTER SIX

# The Life and Times of
# Robert Simpson Petrie (June)

CARL REINER WAS TELEVISION'S EXEMPLAR IN CREATING STORIES BASED on realistic situations.

On June 1, 1966, Reiner's fictional universe of *The Dick Van Dyke Show* ended after 158 episodes.

It had all begun back in 1958. Reiner wrote a pilot for *Head of the Family*, which aired in the summer of 1960 and starred Reiner as Rob Petrie, a TV comedy writer for *The Alan Sturdy Show*. CBS did not pick the show up for its prime-time lineup.

Several months later, Sheldon Leonard revived the idea. But Leonard offered to get somebody else to play the lead role. He suggested Dick Van Dyke.

Reiner changed the boss's name to Alan Brady and played him in 20 episodes, sometimes only appearing by voice. He made appearances as other characters and also wrote 40 of the first 60 episodes.

Before starring as Rob Petrie, Van Dyke had tremendous success on Broadway with *Bye Bye Birdie*. But casting him for Reiner's revamped version of an autobiographical idea was not automatic. "Over the years, I have heard and read about other actors they considered, including Johnny Carson," explained Van Dyke. "I have also heard and read various accounts of why they liked me. My favorites? I wasn't too good-looking, I walked a little funny, and I was basically kind of average and ordinary."[1]

Van Dyke's supporting cast was a murderers' row of comedy.

Mary Tyler Moore as capri pants–wearing Laura Petrie, Rob's wife; Rose Marie as husband-seeking comedy writer Sally Rogers; Morey Amsterdam as Rob's other cowriter and king of the one-liners Buddy Sorrell; Richard Deacon as the frustrated producer of *The Alan Brady Show* and brother-in-law of its egotistical star; and Jerry Paris and Ann Morgan Guilbert as Jerry and Millie Helper, the Petries' neighbors, populated Rob Petrie's world. Rob and Laura had a young son, Ritchie, played by Larry Mathews.

*The Dick Van Dyke Show* premiered on CBS on October 3, 1961.

The final episode—aptly titled "The Last Chapter"—consists of clips complementing a story line featuring Rob seeking to publish his memoir. It ties up the series with a resolution, which was a rare occurrence in the 1960s.[2] A publisher claims that Rob's book is unoriginal; Alan sees its potential and wants to star in a TV series based on the book. He will play Rob, and his trio of scribes will write it. An unseen but apparently powerful producer named Leonard Bershad will produce it. Reiner paid homage to his partner—Sheldon Leonard's real name is Sheldon Leonard Bershad.

This story parallels the show's genesis of CBS rejecting *Head of the Family* and Leonard reviving it.[3]

"Sheldon Leonard, who was a master of story and structure and Carl, who was the master of comedy would get into some very interesting arguments about what would work and what wouldn't," said Van Dyke. "I think my best education came from listening to those two brilliant people argue with one another. Nobody ever got angry. They just argued about the philosophy of the whole thing. It was wonderful."[4]

The Leonard-Reiner pairing was unbeatable to the cast. CBS thought otherwise.

After the first season, *The Dick Van Dyke Show* got a pink slip from CBS. With the combined zeal of a cheerleader at a USC football game and an attorney arguing before the United States Supreme Court, Leonard advocated his case to the show's sponsor, Procter & Gamble.

P&G's executive responsible for advertising on the show submitted to Leonard's enthusiasm. "I'm glad that you believe in the show as I do," said the producer. "No, I don't believe in the show," responded the executive. "I think it should be canceled. But I believe in your belief in it."[5]

P&G agreed to pay for half of the advertising time available for a national sponsor. Lorillard Tobacco Company picked up the other half.

Reiner fueled the show's stories with plausibility. They included Rob being persuaded to help produce the PTA show, explaining the events of the night his son Ritchie was born, dog sitting for Buddy's German shepherd, getting called for jury duty, recalling his first day at *The Alan Brady Show*, and reconnecting with army buddies. "If it didn't happen to one of us, it's not in the show," said Reiner after the show had been on the air for three months.[6]

*The Dick Van Dyke Show* also contributed an entry to the spy genre in the 1966 episode "The Man from My Uncle." Rob and Laura let the FBI use their home for a stakeout to monitor a suspicious neighbor; Godfrey Cambridge guest stars as an agent named Harry Bond who dissuades the couple from making jokes about his moniker being the same as that of 007.

Rob fulfills his fantasy of being a part of the subterfuge, which results in an arrest of the criminal—the neighbor's nephew. There's a nod to the era's spy culture in the episode's tag—the final scene before the closing credits—when Rob uses a walkie-talkie, jokes that he's agent 009, and demands that THRUSH release his fellow agents.[7]

There are other 1960s hallmarks in the stories of the talented comedy writer who, like his portrayer, hailed from Danville, Illinois.

Sally discovers a teenage singing sensation at a bowling alley, which underlines the episode "The Twizzle." Randy Eisenbauer combines the dances "the twist" and "the sizzle" and accompanies his creation with a song clearly influenced by Chubby Checker's popular incarnation of "The Twist."

*The Twilight Zone* influenced the episode "It Looks Like a Walnut," where Rob dreams he's on the planet Twilo and finds Laura emerging from a closet full of walnuts.

"The Redcoats Are Coming" celebrates the British Invasion of rock and roll begun when the Beatles appeared on *The Ed Sullivan Show* on February 9, 1964. The popular singing duo Chad and Jeremy play Ernie and Fred, aka the Redcoats, who have traveled across the Atlantic Ocean to appear on *The Alan Brady Show*. Like the lads from Liverpool, they cause a frenzy among teenage girls during the days before the broadcast.[8]

Bill Persky and Sam Denoff broke ground in the 1963 episode "That's My Boy??" With their scripting panache, Reiner's producing oversight, and John Rich's direction, the story line joins race and comedy with hysterical results.

After hosting dinner for the Helpers and Mel, Rob recounts the events after Ritchie's birth. His belief that the baby was switched at birth—with evidence including a birth certificate of Baby Boy Peters—causes him to invite the Peterses to the Petrie abode to resolve the problem. When the couple arrives, the audience responds with gasps, laughter, and applause lasting nearly 30 seconds. They're Black.

The day after Mary Tyler Moore died in 2017, CBS aired a one-hour special titled *Love Is All Around* honoring her career. Persky revealed to national correspondent Jim Axelrod that Reiner confronted CBS executives about their hypersensitivity to the story, even though the subject matter wasn't controversial. "When Carl brought the premise to the network, they said, 'You can't do that.'"

When Axelrod asks why, Persky explains, "Because it was right at the beginning of the civil rights movement. There was a lot of unrest. So they weren't going to let him do it, and Carl said that he would quit the show if they didn't."[9]

Reiner's comedy instincts were not just brilliant; they were insightful. He respected the audience's sophistication to decipher the premise—Rob was the well-meaning fool. Plus, the Peterses were suburbanites just like the Petries. A Black husband and wife portrayed as a generous, compassionate couple on par with Rob and Laura spoke volumes about integration, acceptance, and tolerance.

Persky said that the laughs interrupted the actors for 20 minutes. "Every time we tried to start the scene again, the laughter would start anew."[10]

Moore lit the torch of style for a new generation of housewives, with fashion adding to the show's realism. It was a choice that would have caused June Cleaver, Margaret Anderson, and Alice Mitchell to blanche and blush. "I immediately caused a stir in my style of dress," said Moore. "I wore pants. TV wives didn't do that. They wore full-skirted, floral-print dresses with high heels, even while vacuuming! My comedic insecurities pushed me to take a stand on something, and this seemed a reasonable issue. I may not have known jokes, but I knew what young wives were wearing. I was a young wife, and I wore pants."[11]

So, why did *The Dick Van Dyke Show* end in 1966 after five years if it still had formidable ratings and remarkable quality?

In its last season, the show won the Emmy for Outstanding Comedy Series. Van Dyke and Moore took home statues for Lead Actor and Actress in a Comedy Series; Persky and Denoff won the Outstanding Achievement in Comedy Emmy Award for the episode "Coast to Coast Big Mouth."[12]

In 1968, Leonard explained the reason in a lecture at UCLA. Money.

During the show's run, Van Dyke hit the jackpot with his role as street artist turned chimney sweeper Bert in *Mary Poppins*. "*Dick Van Dyke* went off the air because everybody was much too successful," said Leonard to the next generation of TV programmers, advertisers, writers, and producers. He then explains that Van Dyke's popularity stimulated interest from movie studios, particularly Disney. Moore and Reiner also received lucrative deals elsewhere. When a TV star finds success on film, it's very difficult, if not impossible, for TV production companies and networks to match the offers, financially or otherwise.[13]

After *The Dick Van Dyke Show* went off the air, the titular star continued his film career with seven additional movies released before the end of the 1960s.

Moore's career suffered an immediate blow. This, despite her popularity, talent, and presence. Cast as the star in a musical based on the novel and movie *Breakfast at Tiffany's*, Moore never hit the boards on Broadway as Holly Golightly. At least not officially. The genius of producer David Merrick couldn't save it; he closed the show after four previews in December 1966.

Moore found no shortage of offers, though. She starred in four movies and one TV movie after her Emmy-winning stint as America's sexiest housewife ended. Her credits include a role as a nun in *Change of Habit* with costar Elvis Presley.[14]

Audiences could look forward to a healthy life for Rob Petrie et al. in syndication. But the chance of Van Dyke and Moore working together on anything substantive again didn't seem possible once they were immersed in other projects.

And then *Dick Van Dyke and the Other Woman* happened in 1969.

Van Dyke had returned to CBS for two prime-time specials; Moore rebuffed opportunities to join her former costar but changed her mind for the third special. "I didn't want to do any television after the series ended," said Moore. "When they asked me to appear with Dick I just didn't want to be a guest and do things I'd already done. And I thought it was too soon after the end of our show to come back and do the kind of show we now have done. I think timing is right on this one."[15]

But a TV series was not on Moore's wish list. "No chance, no! I don't think there's another Carl Reiner and Dick Van Dyke around, and once you've done the best it's foolish to go back and do second best."[16]

Things didn't go exactly as planned.

Moore returned to prime time on the fall 1970 schedule with a situation comedy set around Mary Richards, a Minneapolis TV news producer. *Mary Tyler Moore*—known also as *The Mary Tyler Moore Show*—aired for seven seasons on the Tiffany Network, earning 29 Emmy Awards. Moore's TV influence did not stop at the soundstage, though. She and her then husband, Grant Tinker, formed MTM Productions to produce the show. It became a powerhouse responsible for quality programming in the 1970s and 1980s, including *WKRP in Cincinnati*; *The White Shadow*; and the spinoffs *Rhoda*, *Phyllis*, and *Lou Grant* from her show.

In an episode of *The Mary Tyler Moore Hour*—the second of two short-lived comedy-variety shows following Moore's sitcom—Van Dyke guest starred. One sketch showed them parodying the Petries as an elderly couple. It would be 25 years before they played Rob and Laura again. In 2004, CBS aired *The Dick Van Dyke Show Revisited*, a one-hour special starring Van Dyke, Moore, Marie, Guilbert, Van Dyke's brother

Jerry, and Reiner reprising their roles around the idea of Alan Brady asking Rob and Sally to write a eulogy while he's alive.[17]

———— ✺ ————

*The Dick Van Dyke Show* made the stars household names thanks to an audience of millions. Ernesto Miranda became a household name thanks to an audience of nine—the justices of the U.S. Supreme Court.

Whether in comedy or drama, it's a matter of course for the "Miranda warning" to be spoken in a scene portraying an arrest. Authenticity so requires. On June 13, 1966, the Supreme Court ruled that once arrested, a suspect must be notified of the right to remain silent and the right to an attorney. Neglecting to follow these parameters may lead to a judge dismissing the prosecution's case.

*Miranda v. Arizona* considered the circumstances surrounding the arrest and confession of Ernesto Miranda, a 23-year-old suspect in a case of kidnapping and rape. The Fifth Amendment of the U.S. Constitution mandates, in part, "No person shall be compelled in any criminal case to be a witness against himself, nor be deprived of life, liberty, or property, without due process of law."

Chief Justice Earl Warren explained that law enforcement must uphold this constitutional precept during "custodial interrogation." There is the option of a waiver for a suspect or defendant, but it cannot be made without knowledge, understanding, and lack of coercion.

Detectives trying to elicit information face a substantial barrier if the legal counsel card is played. Its potency is steadfast. Warren wrote, "If, however, he indicates in any manner and at any stage of the process that he wishes to consult with an attorney before speaking, there can be no questioning."

The notice of the right against self-incrimination was not enough for the majority, which emphasized that there must also be a statement explaining the ramifications of speaking. Utterances may be used as evidence in a trial. For these warnings to have any value, the defendant must not only be aware of them but also understand the implications of exercising or dismissing the rights.

The U.S. Supreme Court's decision in *Miranda v. Arizona* required that a person be apprised of the right to remain silent and the right to counsel upon arrest. Ernesto Miranda had been arrested for the kidnapping and rape of an 18-year-old woman. COURTESY OF ARIZONA DEPARTMENT OF CORRECTIONS, REHABILITATION, AND REENTRY

Miranda was identified by his alleged kidnapping and rape victim in a Phoenix police station. After two hours of interrogation, which was not preceded by a warning of the right to an attorney, Miranda signed a confession. A jury found him guilty on the kidnapping and rape charges; his sentence was 20–30 years for each count, running concurrently.

The U.S. Supreme Court's ruling reversed the Supreme Court of Arizona's decision that the police did not violate Miranda's rights. The written confession had a typed statement on top indicating lack of coercion combined with knowledge and awareness of his rights.

Warren found that the absence of warnings vitiated the confession signed by Miranda: "Without these warnings, the statements were inadmissible. The mere fact that he signed a statement which contained a typed-in clause stating that he had 'full knowledge' of his 'legal rights' does not approach the knowing and intelligent waiver required to relinquish constitutional rights."

Arizona prosecutors retried Miranda and got a conviction in 1967.[18]

---

"We're on our way!"

Astronaut Tom Stafford's exclamation was a welcome relief to NASA staff, who had endured three delays before *Gemini 9* launched. Project Gemini required its astronauts to execute tasks as a kind of dress rehearsal for the Project Apollo moon landing missions. Here, Stafford and his fellow pilot Gene Cernan had three major assignments: a space walk, docking with another spacecraft, and landing the capsule on target in the splashdown.[19]

The target vehicle—the augmented target docking adaptor—had been launched on June 1; Stafford and Cernan went up two days later. When they neared the 11-foot-vehicle, they found it resembled an "angry alligator" with open jaws. When fired, explosive bolts were supposed to remove this part of the craft that was a "fiberglass shroud" to protect from volcanic-like temperatures during the launch. NASA's consensus was that the bolts fired but didn't shake the shroud loose. This failure prevented the duo from maneuvering the nose of their capsule into the target area for docking.

NASA's Mission Control dismissed Stafford's idea to bump the shroud loose. Another brainstorm involved Cernan cutting the tether linking it to the vehicle during his space walk. These were simply too dangerous for experimenting.[20]

More than 30 years later, Cernan chronicled the *Gemini 9* flight in his autobiography and mentioned with his signature, outspoken humor that the latter scheme when first presented might have made him a permanent space voyager because it hadn't factored the target vehicle's spinning, his rookie status for a space walk, and the possibility "that the band,

Thomas Stafford and Gene Cernan piloted NASA's *Gemini 9*
mission. It was burdened with complications, including Cernan's
visor fogging up during his space walk. Three years later, Stafford
and Cernan reteamed for *Apollo 10*, joined by John Young, who
piloted the command module. COURTESY OF NASA

under tension from a spring, might snap apart, whip back and puncture
my suit. It was another recipe for turning me into Satellite Cernan."[21]

Instead, they executed their planned rendezvous with the alligator-
looking craft but adjusted their plan to do it three times. Docking was
no longer an option.

With one rendezvous completed, Stafford and Cernan tried again
but eyeballed the situation rather than use the capsule's radar. This was
a survival test. If a future mission were unable to use radar in midflight,
they could point to *Gemini 9* as a paradigm for how to handle it; Stafford
and Cernan had to be focused like surgeons. "Merely finding a dot in the
universe without the help of radar was an overwhelming problem with

millions of possibilities. Travel on the wrong path for just a little while, and you would never locate it."[22]

They were successful.

For their last rendezvous, they executed a scenario involving a lunar vehicle stagnating in "a lower orbit." The astronauts would need to pretend the "alligator" was the one in distress; data would be reported for Apollo astronauts to study. Project Apollo was designed for three-man crews, with two astronauts landing on the moon in a spacecraft that detached from the command module. They would later reconnect, move to the capsule for reentry into Earth's atmosphere, and splash down in the ocean.

If the command module pilot needed to save the lunar craft from further danger, NASA would already have created a procedure using Stafford and Cernan's analysis as the backbone. They didn't trust the computer's analysis at this point in the flight, so they used a manual approach. "When we looked for the target, the mental perception was that we were falling straight down to Earth, and we did not even see the gator until we were within three miles of it."

In less than 20 hours, *Gemini 9*'s astronauts and their counterparts at Mission Control in Houston adjusted the flight plan, added complex tasks, and gave the engineers a wealth of information to use in designing future missions. Stafford and Cernan needed rest and requested a delay for the space walk. Cernan executed the extravehicular activity (EVA) on the third and final day of the flight. It was exhausting but illuminating.[23]

This was the third space walk; Russian cosmonaut Alexei Leonov had preceded NASA astronaut Ed White in 1965.

But Cernan had a different task than his fellow NASA spacewalker during the two-hours-and-eight-minute trip outside the capsule. He had to find out if he could move and position his body "just by pulling on the long umbilical tether." It was a battle between the cord and the astronaut. "I felt as if I was wrestling an octopus," said Cernan. "The umbilical cavorted with a life of its own, twirling like a ribbon, trying to trap me like a cord winding around a window shade."[24]

Compared to the simulations in training, Cernan's venture was "four to five times more difficult." There were complications with the backpack designed for propulsion and a fogged helmet visor.[25]

Cernan suggested that an astronaut conducting an EVA needed more control, autonomy, and safeguards, not only for protection but also for the freedom to observe in calmness rather than fight in frustration with the cord connecting him to the capsule. White had a device that Cernan called a "sort of space gun for mobility." A similar gadget would be useful along with the addition of more opportunities—handholds and footholds—on the capsule's exterior for an astronaut to grip. Absent these changes, Cernan deduced that future astronauts "would flop around like a rag doll."[26]

*Gemini 9*'s capsule splashed down in a textbook execution. The USS *Wasp* was less than three miles away. Stafford and Cernan's landing target was less than a half mile from the location where their craft bobbed in the South Atlantic Ocean. When they arrived on the *Wasp*, the astronauts had a call from President Lyndon Johnson, who praised their "performance under pressure" and "smooth efficiency."[27]

———— ∞∞∞ ————

As the summer solstice beckoned, fans of the spy genre basked in the sunshine and absorbed the recently released *Octopussy and The Living Daylights*, an offering of two short stories by Ian Fleming, published posthumously in June 1966. Fleming penned 12 novels and nine short stories about the spy who ignited a cultural trend in the 1960s.

If those readers were baseball fans, conversations prospered during reading breaks. And there was plenty to talk about in this sixth month of the 66th year of the 20th century. The Twins bashed five home runs in one inning, Indians right-hander Sonny Siebert blanked the Senators 2–0 in a no-hitter, and the Orioles overpowered the American League with a 25–8 record for the month.

Their decisive 11–3 victory against the A's on June 30 capped an exhausting 17-game road trip to Washington, Boston, New York, Anaheim, and Kansas City. It was a master class in hitting: 8 doubles, 11 singles.

Hank Bauer praised his squad, which notched a 12–5 record on the road, for their resilience. "When things go bad nobody gripes, they just try a little harder," explained the Orioles manager, then in his third year of helming the team. "Look at Boog Powell. His batting average was down around .180 and in the span of one month he picked up more than 100 points. I see by the paper that he's just behind George Scott (Red Sox) in runs batted in. Now, I'd call that a pretty courageous comeback, wouldn't you?"[28]

Powell finished '66 with a .287 average, the fourth-highest in his career.[29]

The Orioles ended June with a four-game cushion against the second-place Tigers. Marylanders dared to think that Bauer's boys could outpace the AL for the rest of the season, causing optimism about the Birds from barbecues in Pikesville to beaches in Ocean City.

But a moment during baseball's most prestigious event the following month made followers of the national pastime forget about standings and statistics. A legend diverted attention from himself to spotlight the ugly side of baseball's heritage.

CHAPTER SEVEN

# A Great Speech in Cooperstown (July)

BASEBALL FANS TRAVEL TO UPSTATE NEW YORK BRIMMING WITH anticipation rivaling the moment when a roller coaster approaches the zenith of the tracks. Whether princes or paupers, their passion for baseball spurs them on their trek to the prominent repository guarding rare artifacts, records, and memorabilia: the National Baseball Hall of Fame and Museum in Cooperstown, New York.

It is this village that fans learn to synonymize with the elite of the national pastime around the time they learn to hit a ball off a tee. By road, it's about four hours from New York City. Travelers from farther points may need to fly into Albany and then trek an hour or so on the highway.

The Hall of Fame was founded in 1936 with the first class of inductees: Babe Ruth, Christy Mathewson, Honus Wagner, Ty Cobb, and Walter Johnson. The building was completed in 1939.

There are motels where visitors can lodge, but the prime real estate is occupied by bed-and-breakfast establishments about a 10-minute stroll from the brick-faced edifice at 25 Main Street. Dating back to the 19th century, these abodes ranging from quaint to grand are temporary dwellings for the world's baseball fans. As the sun climbs the sky over Otsego Lake, the aroma of a freshly cooked breakfast greets the lodgers in the morning. Over pancakes, biscuits, and freshly squeezed orange juice, they share stories with their fellow baseball aficionados about their travels to Cooperstown.

Memories of long-ago games and favorite players are recounted. There's an adage among baseball fans—the best players are the ones who played when you were 12 years old. A baby boomer from Minnesota delights in tales about Harmon Killebrew's power; a Generation Xer from Pittsburgh beams as he tells a story about meeting Willie Stargell; and a millennial from Mamaroneck shares his memories about the 9/11 attacks and the Diamondbacks–Yankees World Series that gave the country a few hours of escape from the tragedy's aftermath.

Bonds are forged in moments. Nowhere can you make faster friends than in a conversation about baseball.

It is here where you might catch a glimpse, overhear a conversation, or shake the hands of baseball's heroes during the one weekend every summer that ignites a mass pilgrimage to this sports mecca: the Hall of Fame induction.

Fans invade Cooperstown and its environs by the thousands, signifying their fealty to that year's inductees by donning symbolic accoutrements. Mets caps for Tom Seaver. Padres T-shirts for Dave Winfield. Yankees jerseys for Derek Jeter. Membership is certified in the Hall of Fame atrium with a plaque depicting an inductee's visage and a brief biography of accomplishments.

The path to Cooperstown is created by the Baseball Writers' Association of America, whose members vote on admission into the uppermost of baseball's upper echelons. On July 25, 1966, there were two inductees—Ted Williams and Casey Stengel.

A month shy of his 48th birthday and garbed in a sport jacket, slacks, and collared shirt with no tie, Williams looked like he could have been a middle-aged, gregarious boss of a midsized company hosting a summer brunch as he strode to the podium outside the Hall of Fame for his induction. Fans recalled a stellar career as they awaited his speech.

Williams, a San Diego native, began his professional baseball career with the Red Sox organization's minor-league structure. First he played for his hometown Padres of the Pacific Coast League in 1936 and 1937, then with the 1938 Minneapolis Millers in the American Association where he placed second in batting average with .366.

In 1939 the lanky outfielder with wrists of iron caused New England's baseball fans to gossip about this latest elevation to the major leagues. They were not disappointed. A story during spring training mentioned that the young slugger bashed a ball 500 feet.[1] In his first major-league at-bat, he knocked a double off Red Ruffing. It was the first of 2,654 hits—including 521 home runs.

Williams led the majors in RBIs in his rookie season. He did it twice more in his 22-year career. His batting average of .406 in 1941 was the last to break the .400 barrier.[2]

With an elegant swing, Williams projected an almost machinelike efficiency. Had he been a lumberjack, he likely would have felled a tree with fewer strokes than his axe-wielding brethren. New England's baseball fans revered Williams. The rest of the American League feared him.

His lifetime .344 batting average marks his excellence, which is underscored by an on-base percentage of .482—the highest ever in the major leagues.[3] By 1966, he had filled out somewhat, but he still looked fit enough to send the ball over the Fenway Park fences, at least during batting practice.

There are the obligatory speeches from players, managers, and executives receiving the honor of induction; they thank parents and coaches, wives and children, teammates and friends. At times, voices halt and eyes water. Induction is more than the recognition of an outstanding career; it's a rare opportunity for the honorees to publicly acknowledge their inner circles who are anonymous to the fans. An emotional response is natural.

Ted Williams went beyond the usual consideration. Way beyond.

He used the moment to shine a spotlight on baseball's past racism. Entrenched, it had prevented great players from competing in the major leagues until Jackie Robinson broke the modern-day (post-1900) barrier in 1947. But integration was not immediate. The Yankees did it in 1955 with Elston Howard. The Phillies had their first Black player in 1957. Pumpsie Green joined the Red Sox, the last team to integrate, in 1959.

When Williams spoke about anything involving baseball, he did it with a sense of authority. This time was no different: "Baseball gives every American boy a chance to excel. Not just to be as good as someone else, but to be better than someone else. This is the nature of man and the name of the game. And I've always been a very lucky guy. I hope some day Satchel Paige and Josh Gibson will be voted into the Hall of Fame as symbols of the great Negro players who are not here only because they weren't given the chance."

It needed to be said.

Gibson has been credited with hitting more than 800 home runs. He died at 35 years old in 1947 from a brain tumor, three months before Jackie Robinson broke the color line with the Brooklyn Dodgers.

Paige dominated his opposition, finally getting signed to a major-league contract at 42 years old by Cleveland Indians owner Bill Veeck in 1948. He had a 6–1 record; Cleveland won a one-game playoff against the Boston Red Sox and beat the other team from Boston in the '48 World Series, Indians over Braves in six games.

Paige and Gibson were rivals and friends known to all baseball followers. Gibson played for the Homestead Grays, who called Pittsburgh and Washington, DC, home. Each city had a major-league team, so it was logical that White fans of the Pirates and Senators would have heard about Gibson.

Paige played for the Kansas City Monarchs. Until the A's vacated Philadelphia after the 1954 season, Kansas City remained a minor-league city. But Paige's exploits were famous, especially when he pitched against Negro League teams in major-league cities.

Williams's plea was not answered immediately, though.

In 1971, the Hall of Fame inducted Paige. Gibson, the year after. Cool Papa Bell received the Cooperstown honors in 1974. Oscar Charleston was the lone Negro Leaguer in the bicentennial class, joining players Roger Connor, Bob Lemon, Freddie Lindstrom, and Robin Roberts along with umpire Cal Hubbard in 1976. Only Roberts had played his entire career after Robinson's breakthrough season. In 2006, the Hall of Fame inducted 17 players and executives from the Negro Leagues.

But even when the writers began honoring Negro Leaguers, prejudice laced the process. Williams did not offer a restriction in his statement; baseball commissioner Bowie Kuhn thought otherwise in early 1971.

At first, an exhibit and a wing were floated as ways to honor Negro Leaguers. There was a quirk in the Hall of Fame membership requirements—10 seasons in the major leagues. This "separate but equal" concept was a doubling down on prejudice. Players couldn't get in the

Hall of Fame because they didn't have the mandated playing time, which was a result of pre-1947 racial blocks. This idea of segregation in Cooperstown was dismissed, thankfully. Inductees get a plaque in the atrium no matter their race.[4] Justice for all.

Paige, Gibson, and Bell might not have been accepted into the Hall of Fame until the late 1970s had the prejudice remained against the Negro Leagues. Or even the 1980s. It took a sports legend to remind the world that not only had a great injustice been done by an unwritten code banning Black players, but also that the institution marking grandness had not honored them with admittance.

Acknowledgment of America's unequal treatment had been slow, sometimes stagnant. Until 1948, the armed forces were segregated. The landmark U.S. Supreme Court case *Brown v. Board of Education of Topeka* in 1954 dismissed the "separate but equal" paradigm that okayed separate schools for Black and White kids. Hamilton Holmes and Charlayne Hunter were the first Black students at the University of Georgia in 1961. James Meredith broke the higher-education barrier at the University of Mississippi a year later. The March on Washington led by Martin Luther King Jr. happened in 1963. Civil rights leader Medgar Evers was shot and killed in his driveway that year.

There had been a 1957 Civil Rights Act, but the historic 1964 legislation strengthened antidiscrimination laws regarding employment. President Lyndon Johnson signed the Voting Rights Act into law a year later, squashing the long-embedded template of discrimination in voting processes, including literacy tests. Also in 1965, the Black community suffered the Watts riots and the assassination of Malcolm X.

Williams's speech fit perfectly with the aura of change in the racial arena.

Following Williams at the induction ceremony, Casey Stengel—never known to suffer a shortage of words—recalled his early days of playing with the Brooklyn Dodgers when Charles Ebbets owned the team. Always a raconteur with a sense of humor, Stengel remarked on the changes in the financial structure of baseball: "I played my first year, I was transferred to Kentucky, and I always thought that would be great for me because I knew that's where they kept the gold in this country."[5]

Ted Williams and Casey Stengel share a laugh during their induction into the Baseball Hall of Fame. In his speech, Williams called for players from the Negro Leagues to be inducted in the future. COURTESY OF ASSOCIATED PRESS

Cooperstown represents baseball past. In 1966, Houston represented the future. NASA's headquarters city was known around the world as the place where America's astronauts lived and worked. The baseball team's name reflected the modern era when it changed from the Colt .45's to the Astros the year before. Good-bye, Old West. Hello, Space Age.

On July 19, the Astros introduced a new playing surface that replaced both the outfield and infield grass for the first time.[6] It was a revolutionary technology aptly named.

Astroturf.

An Astros–Phillies contest at the Astrodome inaugurated Astroturf with an 8–2 victory for the home team. Patience seemed to be the consensus in adjusting to a nylon field. But there was one detractor whose voice rang out, catching attention like a dinner bell for Texas farmhands after toiling in the sunshine for eight hours. Phillies outfielder Tony Gonzales revealed the intricacies posing problems for him: "The ball bounces like a rubber ball. You can't hold your footing. It's hard to stop when you charge the ball. They should have left it like it was."[7]

While Jim Bunning was on the losing side of Astroturf's initiation, he faced a more difficult task on July 27 when he squared off against Sandy Koufax in what proved to be an example of endurance for both hurlers. It was a 12-innning affair; LA won in the bottom of the 12th for the 2–1 victory.

If one also wanted an example of Koufax's power, this nighttime game at Dodger Stadium ranked with his four no-hitters, which included a perfect game. The Dodgers southpaw whiffed 16 and allowed four hits. Bunning was also authoritative—12 strikeouts, six hits.

It was one of the last times that Koufax would take the mound.

---

Another battle of endurance and worry culminated in a Wisconsin courtroom. But this one meant more than advancing or falling in the standings. It changed the structure of baseball.

The Supreme Court of Wisconsin ruled that the Milwaukee Braves organization had the legal right to move the team to Atlanta.

The State of Wisconsin's legal team argued that the Braves organization violated antitrust principles. The court's decision authored by Justice Thomas Fairchild acknowledged the strength and meaning of antitrust laws but looked toward the danger of restrictions in the name of fairness. "It would be inconsistent with the very policy of an antitrust law for Wisconsin to insist that the Braves be returned without expansion, because such an outcome would maintain the monopoly at the expense of Atlanta, or communities elsewhere which might seek to have a team."

Further, Fairchild outlined a caveat for the Braves' management in determining their future aspirations. "What the circuit court decision says, as we view it, is that as long as it is economically feasible for a major-league team to have its home in Milwaukee, defendants must not use their monopoly power to deprive Milwaukee of a home team, but defendants were and still are free to choose whether the Braves should continue in Milwaukee or some new team should operate there."

Georgians reveled at the decision, which certified a new era for baseball. Milwaukee had been a prominent city in 19th-century baseball and later in the American Association from 1902 to 1952. After the Braves moved from Boston and began their Midwest tenure in 1953, Milwaukee's new major-league status meant it had to leave the AA. The league folded in 1962.

The court's ruling spread gloom ranging from disappointment to devastation across the Badger State. Milwaukeeans felt the incredible loss that Philadelphia did for the A's, Brooklyn for the Dodgers, and New York for the Giants.

The AL had added two teams in 1961—the Los Angeles Angels and the Washington Senators. This was the second iteration of the Senators. The first club had moved to Minnesota after the 1960 season and changed its moniker to Twins in honor of the state's Twin Cities—Minneapolis and St. Paul. There was no significant mourning period for baseball fans in the nation's capital.

The National League added the New York Mets and Houston Colt .45's in 1962. Atlanta's securing the Braves continued the migration factor in baseball. One city's loss was another's gain, an issue also addressed by the Supreme Court of Wisconsin: "It is clear that in the absence of the antitrust feature of defendants' agreement to remove the Braves (i.e., exercise of monopoly power and agreement in restraint of trade) the state would have no power to prevent or impede the removal of a business enterprise even though such removal injured the interest of the state in preserving business activity within its borders."

Translation: An organization can plant its flag elsewhere.

The Supreme Court of Wisconsin relied on the premise decided by the U.S. Supreme Court in 1922—baseball is not an interstate concern. There's a commonsense approach contravening this decision. Baseball teams travel to different states where their employees perform acts for income. The teams also generate revenue from these activities. In *Toolson v. New York Yankees*, the U.S. Supreme Court upheld the precept of the 1922 ruling. In essence, the Supreme Court of Wisconsin tossed the responsibility to Congress for legislation. "The type of decision involved in this case, in essence, whether to admit a new member in order to replace an existing member which desired to move to a new area, appears to be so much an incident of league operation as to fall within the exemption."

Four years after the ruling, Milwaukee became the new home for the Seattle Pilots, which only lasted the 1969 season before abandoning the Pacific Northwest. In acknowledgment of the American Association team that had been a bedrock franchise in the minor leagues for 50 years, the team's name changed to Brewers.

The court decision walloped Milwaukeeans, who had immediately embraced the Braves upon the move from Boston in 1953. Milwaukee County Municipal Stadium signaled a new era of ballparks that considered the increasing significance of cars. With the flight from urban areas to the suburbs, Milwaukee's decision makers responded with a state-of-the-art facility abutted by ample space for parking. Although the Braves' tenure had only been 13 years, it was a highly competitive period for the fans. The team never had a losing season. They won more than 90 games four times, the NL pennant twice, and the World Series once. They placed second in the NL standings five times.

Bob Buege recalled,

It never occurred to me that bringing them back could really happen. Once they moved the equipment and offices to Atlanta, there's no court that could make them come back. I first heard of a possible move during the All-Star Game of 1963. Bob Broeg of the *St. Louis Post-Dispatch* said that he had inside information that the Braves were leaving for Atlanta. I didn't believe it. The story seemed too far-fetched. They had been so successful in Milwaukee, so it didn't seem real that they could leave.

By 1964, it was pretty clear that they were leaving. People were starting to accept the inevitable. Kids just started to lose interest.

I went to maybe a dozen games or more each year with my dad. Lou Perini, the owner, had refused to televise the games. That changed in 1963 when he sold the team. There was a limited number of games on television. Until then, you went to the game or listened on the radio. Department stores put the broadcasts on the PA system. Milwaukee had several big stores including Gimbel's, Schuster's, and Chapman's.

The day that the Braves came to town for the first time in 1953, there was a parade set up. It took them to the Schroeder Hotel—the biggest hotel in the city. In the ballroom, there was a huge Christmas tree and every player got gifts. People wouldn't take their money. Dry cleaning. Groceries. Razors. The players got them for free. There was a car dealer that provided a new car for each player. Every business wanted to be associated with the Braves. Years after the team moved, players still talked about being invited into people's homes. They couldn't go anywhere without being idolized.

The Braves arrived on short notice. Most of them had no place to live, so a large number of them lived at the Hotel Wisconsin on North Old World Third Street. The breweries would give them something too. A pitcher would get a case of beer if he threw two shutout innings. A player who hit a home run would get a case. The players rented a room just to store the beer.

By the time the Pilots arrived from Seattle and became the Brewers in 1970, people had forgotten the Braves. Five years without your team is a long time. There was so much bitterness that made it easier to cut the cord. The thing that made it unique was the extent to which the people of Wisconsin fell in love with the Braves. That was unprecedented. I don't think any other city could compare with that.[8]

Rick Schabowski, treasurer of the Milwaukee Braves Historical Society, recalled,

It was very traumatic. I was 14 years old and the Braves were in Milwaukee my entire life. It was a golden era of baseball.

Many people called the new owners carpetbaggers because they were moving to Atlanta. Once they moved, baseball became more about business.

I really thought that it was done when the Wisconsin Supreme Court made its decision. All these appeals didn't matter because I think baseball wanted a team in Atlanta. You had nothing in the Southeast for Major League Baseball. It was virgin territory. Baltimore and Washington were the southernmost cities. Plus, you had great radio and television stations down there. Even if the team came back to Milwaukee, the fans might have been unforgiving because there was such animosity at that point.

It was a perfect blend in time for Milwaukee. We built a brand, and we had a state-of-the-art stadium. Everything fit into place. Winning year after year made it a no-brainer to be a fan. A lot of people are still Milwaukee Braves fans.

The other teams that moved out of their cities—A's, Browns, Dodgers, Giants—they had another team to turn to. There was a backup. When the Braves left Milwaukee, we didn't want to pursue a minor-league team again. The White Sox played a few home games here, and we made every effort to promote the games. We wanted to show that we're a major-league city.[9]

Kenn Olson remembers the Braves as a backdrop to his childhood in Menomonee Falls, where he played some form of baseball during spring and summer—Little League, pickup games, Wiffle ball. Like his classmates, Olson felt the emotional impact of the team's decision to vacate Milwaukee.

I was 14 years old when the Milwaukee Braves moved to Atlanta. All my life, I followed baseball. There were football and basketball too. But I didn't follow them with the same intensity. I was more angry than sad about the Braves moving. Having already announced during the start of the '65 season that they planned on moving was infuriating. I closely kept tabs on the situation. When Judge Elmer Roller decided in favor of the Braves, the city and fans were doomed.

I don't ever remember a time when a Braves game wasn't on the radio in our house. We would listen to Earl Gillespie and Blaine Walsh on WTMJ. Little Leaguers would join the "knothole club" for kids. Every Saturday home game, a bus would take us to the ballpark where we sat in the left-field bleachers. A couple of bucks could get you into the game with enough left for a program, hot dog, and a soda.[10]

———❦———

Indeed, July was a banner month for baseball.

The Koufax–Bunning duel, Astroturf's debut, and Wisconsin's losing battle to keep the Braves in Milwaukee gave fans high drama on and off the field. While they checked box scores, headlines, and sportscasts to update themselves, another story riveted the world: *Gemini 10*.

When John Young and Michael Collins readied for the launch, the mission's task list may have seemed repetitive to outside observers because the astronauts' predecessors in Project Gemini had executed the same actions—rendezvous and docking with an Agena spacecraft that NASA had launched before the mission. Space walks, too. But Young and Collins would perform these during one flight, which had not been done. Collins completed two space walks. Ed White and Gene Cernan had each accomplished one space walk on *Gemini 4* and *Gemini 9*.

To lighten the mood of this sobering task list, an unknown member of the crew put "photos of two voluptuous, wildly beautiful girls" into the equipment. Young and Collins discovered the photos while they were orbiting Earth and used them to decorate the capsule's interior.

It almost proved embarrassing.

Collins later recounted that he and Young discovered that the girls worked at the St. Louis Playboy Club as waitresses, otherwise known as "bunnies." A McDonnell engineer knew the girls and disclosed to them that their photos flew into space with the astronauts. And they were in Houston for the postflight press conference!

It could have been a public-relations disaster for NASA, which had promoted the astronauts as family men. "We were saved by a speedy phone call from Deke Slayton to some high McDonnell official, threatening I know not what form of ruin and damnation for all concerned. The girls never arrived."[11]

Young and Collins launched on July 18 and splashed down in the Atlantic Ocean three days later, finishing their journey about three miles

*Gemini 10* astronauts John Young and Michael Collins are aboard the recovery ship USS *Guadalcanal* after splashing down in the Atlantic Ocean. COURTESY OF NASA

from their intended target area in the Atlantic Ocean. Puerto Rico was about 400 miles southward.[12]

⸺ ⸺

As martini glasses clinked at cocktail parties and beer bottles at barbecues to celebrate the latest success for NASA, Frank Sinatra's "Fly Me to the Moon" emerged from hi-fi systems providing a sonic backdrop to conversations about NASA's latest achievement in its quest to surpass Russia in the Space Race.

Released in July, Sinatra's latest album was a pioneering work for the once skinny kid from Hoboken, New Jersey, who had sent bobbysoxers into a frenzy at New York's Paramount Theater in the 1940s.

*Sinatra at the Sands.*

It was the first live album for the star, now 50 and maturing into middle age after weathering two divorces and sustaining a movie career that suffered then rebounded with an Oscar-winning performance in *From Here to Eternity* in 1953.[13]

Many songs on this masterpiece recorded at the Sands Hotel and Casino in Las Vegas in early 1966 were instantly identifiable with him. When he sang a ballad, he made each audience member feel as if he were singing just to him or her. "One for My Baby" embodies this skill; he portrays a guy drinking in a bar and mourning a lost love never to be found again.

But Sinatra had the same effect on joy as he did on sadness. His optimism for romance shone with "Come Fly with Me," which beckons female listeners to trek with him to exotic places. Adding to the gargantuan list of the singer's output were "It Was a Very Good Year" and "You Make Me Feel So Young."

*Sinatra at the Sands* also provides humor in a comedy monologue poking fun at his upbringing in Hoboken, his early years in show business, and his pals Dean Martin and Sammy Davis Jr. Songs and stories prompted listeners to imagine being in the Copa Room, ordering drinks from buxom waitresses, and enjoying a live performance from a legendary vocalist.

Las Vegas prepared for another innovation in August. It redefined the city.

## CHAPTER EIGHT

# Hail, Caesars Palace! (August)

THE ODDS WERE AGAINST JAY SARNO. IT MATTERED AS MUCH TO HIM AS losing a $20 bill would matter to a Rockefeller.

On August 5, 1966, the 5'8" Sarno, whose weight fluctuated between 200 and 250 pounds, began his morning by jabbing his stomach with insulin, a daily happening, and anticipating the day ahead. A fear of poverty drove this rotund visionary who was about to set the gold standard for casinos and hotels in Las Vegas.

It was the debut date for his vision of a destination that would be formidable for tourists, fearsome for competitors. On his property, every lodger would be treated like royalty, whether he was a high-roller oil executive from Houston, a retired high-school vice principal from Kalamazoo, a used-car salesman from Buffalo, a mail carrier from Cedar Rapids, a bank manager from Joliet, or a landscaper from Seattle.

Caesars Palace.

Sarno did not invent the marriage of Las Vegas and gambling; Nevada had legalized blackjack, roulette, craps, et al. in 1931. Six months before he was assassinated in the Beverly Hills home of his girlfriend Virginia Hill, mafia chieftain Bugsy Siegel escalated the city's allure for hopeful dice tossers and self-perceived card sharks when he opened the Flamingo Hotel & Casino on the day after Christmas in 1946. It gave Las Vegas an informal Constitution for entertainment, elegance, and customer service. Others amended Siegel's concept; Sarno perfected it.

With a single-minded focus, Sarno spearheaded a new paradigm for the neon-rich metropolis that had become synonymous with fun by the mid-1960s. Caesars Palace would be accessible to all who wanted to indulge. Offerings would be unparalleled; competitors would pale in comparison to the excess that became the new norm under Sarno's watchful eye. The *Las Vegas Review-Journal* reported that the purchasing list for the three-day kickoff event included "two tons of filet mignon, 300 pounds of lump Maryland crabmeat, the world's largest Alaska King Crab, a dozen of the largest King Salmon available and the largest order of Ukrainian Caviar ever delivered to a single party."[1]

With a Roman theme conjuring visions of toga-clad emperors enjoying every desire sated, Caesars Palace had an expected list of 1,800 guests and 1,500 employees tending to them.

Sarno's daughter September recalled,

My father was a big fan of lots of variety on the table, which speaks to the Bacchanal restaurant with 11-course meals. He interacted with the guests, and he always believed that most people were living a life of existence, not a life of thrills. He kind of predicted the future because his competitors followed his model when he raised the bar.

His biggest challenge was getting the rooms finished at Caesars Palace because it wasn't a cookie-cutter type of building. A lot of it was breaking new ground for Las Vegas casinos in treating customers. The bureaucracy of the government was his biggest threat. He was a target of many people in the government and experienced a lot of anti-Semitism and bullying. But he wasn't a quiet, shy, reserved guy.[2]

Andy Williams and the Ritz Brothers inaugurated the entertainment at Caesars Palace; 500 veteran soldiers from Vietnam got a pass to a preview of Williams's performance on August 4, plus dinner.[3]

Building Caesars Palace was not a solo mission by any means. The Lone Ranger had Tonto. Batman had Robin. Jay Sarno had Stanley Mallin.

They had been roommates at the University of Missouri in the 1940s; Mallin's academic life took a three-year hiatus so he could serve in the army during World War II. After the surrenders by Germany and Japan, Mallin returned to the Show Me State to finish his studies and get his

Caesars Palace opened to the public on August 5, 1966. Jay Sarno escalated the standard of customer service in Las Vegas when he developed his idea of a destination where every guest would be treated like royalty.
COURTESY OF UNIVERSITY LIBRARIES, SPECIAL COLLECTIONS AND ARCHIVES, YOUNG ELECTRIC SIGN COMPANY CORPORATE RECORDS COLLECTION, UNIVERSITY OF NEVADA, LAS VEGAS

degree in business and public administration; he graduated in 1947 along with Sarno.

The duo began their postgraduate quest for work with Mallin's cousin, who worked in the tile business in Miami Beach. A chance meeting with a fraternity brother led to a revelation that changed their lives. Their pal's father-in-law built homes in Atlanta. They got lured with their tile contracting business and then learned from one of the workers about the Federal Housing Administration program, which allows banks to make loans for constructing apartments.

A 32-unit building was their first project. An eight-story building with 80 units followed, along with a doctors' building. Word spread in the South—doctors in Chattanooga and Jacksonville approached Sarno and Mallin about their needs for space. Motel construction became their next arena, which brought them to the attention of Morris Abram, a well-connected attorney who represented the Teamsters Union and offered to get them a loan for finishing their present motel project.

In an oral history for the Southern Nevada Jewish Heritage Project, Mallin recalled, "Then right after that we got invited on a junket to Las Vegas. We went. We got a bunch of guys from Atlanta. Went to the Flamingo. We thought, well, there isn't a decent hotel in this town, so maybe we can build a hotel or develop one. That's when we started to think about Caesars Palace. The Flamingo, the Riviera, the Stardust, nothing distinguished about them, nothing palatial. We thought we could do it better."[4]

Caesars Palace catered to the male gene controlling the appetites for food, sex, and entertainment. Everything was quality with an overarching Roman theme reinforcing the mission that guests are royalty deserving the best. With women dressed in toga-inspired uniforms boasting hem lines dangerously high on the leg, men felt like Caesar surrounded by members of the fairer sex whose mission was to serve, answer, and please.

The cartoon logo for Caesars Palace was a woman feeding grapes to a rotund, toga-clad man. It topped newspaper advertisements that differed from Caesars Palace's competition by personalizing it between the site's namesake and the customer. Tantalizing copy complemented the duo and a rendering of the hotel's exterior:

> I, CAESAR, INVITE YOU . . . TO AN ORGY OF EXCITEMENT . . . at my Palace of Pleasure . . . Caesars Palace! What's going on? Everything! High-powered action that'll jolt you into a new lease on life! Excitement that never quits! Luscious food! Feast . . . play . . . caper and cavort in Bacchanalian raptures of revelry! Join the lively ones . . . rub shoulders with the Jet-set, in the newest, most magnificent headquarters for the action faction! A live-wire family of entertainers with such stars as ANDY WILLIAMS . . . TONY BENNETT . . . WOODY ALLEN . . . ANTHONY NEWLEY . . . JACK BENNY . . . THE RITZ BROS.![5]

Dave Victorson, an entertainment executive at Caesars Palace, touted Williams as a paradigm setter for the new offering. Williams was reportedly not available in mid-July, the target date for the opening. So the debut got delayed. "We felt that it was well worth it to wait on Andy

Williams," declared the producer. "With Andy as our opening star for the theatre restaurant we have set a policy of bringing in the 'super star.'"[6]

Vision is one thing. Execution, quite another.

Sarno backed his royalty premise with replicas of classic sculptures and columns in front of the building. At the head of this massive undertaking was Stuart Mason, the assistant project manager who had worked in his family's construction business and moved to Las Vegas for the Caesars Palace job. It was a combined operation between Taylor Construction—the company owned by Mason's father that had already built the Riviera and the Tropicana—and another contractor named R. C. Johnson, who had been project manager for the latter casino and hotel.

Mason moved to Las Vegas in 1964 to begin working on Sarno's vision.

I remember it opening. Opening night we were in a suite with Jay Sarno and Nate Jacobson and some other people. And Jay had found this guy wandering around the casino and he was wearing a robe and some kind of screwy hat. And he brings him up to the suite. And the guy says that he is a forecaster of things to come. And he said that this is going to be the greatest success ever. And I remember we all said, you know, from your mouth to God's ears, it's okay.

I mean, they had spent all their money. They didn't have much operating capital left, if any. And it's been true. And I remember we all, I mean Jay Sarno was quite the showman. And I remember him taking that guy around and saying he is going to bless this place.

And you know what? I think he did. It worked. I think it was probably the first hotel that had a semblance of a theme and they carried that theme through even onto the stationery and so on. And the costuming and the stationery and the menus, whatever. It had a theme. It was the first hotel that did that.[7]

Originally named "Desert Palace" during the planning phase, Caesars Palace underscored a luxury image with scientific practicality, beginning with the oval shape that Sarno favored for its soothing effect. "Because the casino is shaped in an oval, people tend to relax and play longer," explained Sarno in a 1979 retrospective for the *Las Vegas Sun*. "And the casino's intimate feeling is no accident either; it is an optical illusion created by the twenty false columns encircling it."[8]

Further, Sarno insisted that the art and sculpture at Caesars Palace be optimal, with the highest-grade materials. It wasn't enough to have stately rooms, swank menus, and top-notch entertainment. Guests, in Sarno's view, needed constant reminders of opulence to make them feel like they deserved to be in such magnificence. In turn, splendor permeated this 14-story structure containing about 700 rooms.

Reproductions of great Roman statues fed the atmosphere of luxury. "The statuary that I used at Caesars was cut from the finest, purest, grade-A Carrera marble from Florence," revealed Sarno. "You know, with one statue, the 'Rape of the Sabines,' I had to argue like hell to get the sculptor to ship it to America. He feared that it would be damaged in transit. . . . There are also two of the finest pieces of art in the world situated near the coffee shop. These two friezes, depicting the battle of the Etruscan Hills, were made by the artist Teleki specifically for Caesars and yet hardly anyone knows of their great worth."[9]

Sarno had strong competition in the entertainment arena. Williams and the Ritz Brothers contended with Red Buttons at the Hotel Fremont, Waylon Jennings at the Golden Nugget, Jackie Mason at the Aladdin, Betty Grable starring in *Hello, Dolly* at the Riviera Hotel, Steve Lawrence and Eydie Gormé at the Sands, and Myron Cohen at the Flamingo.

Johnny Carson was an attraction as well, leveraging his fame as the host of *The Tonight Show* with appearances at the Sahara.

To prepare for their voyage, gamblers looking for an edge likely pored through the best seller *Beat the Dealer*—a 1962 book that had been reprinted in 1966—authored by Edward O. Thorp, a mathematician providing strategies and tactics for winning at blackjack. Thorp was a card counter, in common parlance.

He concluded that his approach, though sound, could not solely withstand the scrutiny of dealers and pit bosses. Some had developed a sixth sense when it came to card counters. Beating the casino required deception sourced in acting. "You can be the drunken cowboy from

Texas or the wildly animated lady from Taiwan who can't wait to get her next bet down," explained Thorp in his 2017 autobiography. "You can be Caspar Milquetoast, the nervous accountant from Indianapolis who has already lost too much down the street. Or Miss Spectacular, who draws all the attention to herself, not to how she bets and plays."[10]

Through card counters and competition, the stature of Caesars Palace has endured as other casinos were imploded to make room for a Las Vegas renaissance with newer, sleeker buildings, including the Venetian. The Dunes was gone in 1993; the Sands in 1996. The city bid farewell to the Aladdin in 1996, the El Rancho in 2000, the Desert Inn in 2001, and the Stardust in 2007.

Caesars Palace expanded. Its early-21st-century offerings dwarf what was available in 1966. But Sarno's vision remains strong as the foundation of excellence and opulence that welcomes every visitor.

---

Joe Resnick had a vision, too.

The Democratic congressman from New York's 28th District represented a section of the Catskill Mountains region, including Ellenville, and sought to serve the medical needs of his constituents. Resnick's influence drew President Johnson to dedicate the facility on August 19—Ellenville Community Hospital.

LBJ highlighted the importance of bipartisanship in his dedication speech to the crowd, which was estimated at 5,000. Senator Jacob Javits, an iconic Republican from New York, received the label of "a true progressive and a devoted American." But the hospital's construction received notice for its money source—the 1946 Hill–Burton Act provides financing and loans for the construction, maintenance, and updating of hospitals and other health-care facilities. The president explained that the new hospital cost more than $1 million to build; more than a third of the cost was absorbed by federal funds.

"Someone asked me one time what my political philosophy was," said Johnson. "And I said, 'Well, I am a free man first, an American second, a public servant third, and a Democrat fourth—in that order. . . . And in that order Senator [Joseph] Hill, a Democrat from Alabama, who has

President Lyndon Johnson talks with the staff of Ellenville Community Hospital at its opening. During his dedication speech, Johnson explained his political philosophy: "Well, I am a free man first, an American second, a public servant third, and a Democrat fourth—in that order." COURTESY OF LYNDON B. JOHNSON PRESIDENTIAL LIBRARY

done more for the health of the people of this country, I guess, than any single man, and former Senator and Justice [Harold] Burton, a Republican from Ohio, joined together to share this idea and to bring these hospitals all over our land."[11]

Ellenville was the last stop on a daylong presidential trek through New York State, beginning with Buffalo, then moving to Lake Erie, Syracuse, and finally the hospital. President Johnson and his wife, Lady Bird, stayed overnight at the Nevele Hotel in Ellenville.

It was a bipartisan trip. There were 12 congressmen from New York State—nine Democrats, three Republicans. New York governor Nelson Rockefeller, a Republican, joined the president in Buffalo, where he rode "in a 'We Love Lyndon' sign–studded caravan to Buffalo's Niagara Square."[12]

Johnson pioneered another milestone in August when the U.S. Senate confirmed his nomination of Constance Baker Motley to be a federal judge for the Southern District of New York. She was the first Black woman to serve on the federal bench, as the Manhattan borough president, and in the New York State Senate.[13] Four women had preceded her escalation to the hallowed position of federal judge: Sarah Hughes, Burnita Matthews, Florence Allen, Mary Donlon.

Motley had been nominated in January. But Senator James Eastland used his power as chairman of the U.S. Senate Committee on the Judiciary to keep Motley's nomination from going out of the committee to a vote. So she stayed in political limbo for seven months as the Mississippi senator launched unfounded accusations about her connections to communism.

Johnson, never shy about using political leverage, supposedly called Eastland's bluff. "Rumor has it that Johnson refused to send any other nominations for federal judgeships to the Senate until Eastland let my name out of the committee," wrote Motley in her 1998 autobiography.[14]

Constance Baker Motley was the first Black female judge on the federal judiciary. The U.S. Senate confirmed her by a voice vote on August 30, 1966. Motley was a key member of the NAACP legal team in the landmark U.S. Supreme Court case *Brown v. Board of Education of Topeka.*
COURTESY OF LYNDON B. JOHNSON PRESIDENTIAL LIBRARY

Johnson's selection of Motley in 1966 signaled hope for minorities and women during a turbulent decade for civil rights. A year later, Thurgood Marshall was confirmed as the first Black justice on the U.S. Supreme Court.

Motley was already synonymous with groundbreaking. Her legal career included being the head strategist on the team that overturned segregation in education with the 1954 U.S. Supreme Court decision in *Brown v. Board of Education of Topeka*.

On the federal bench, she would have a terrific impact on baseball through two landmark cases.

In the mid-1970s, Motley, herself a trailblazer, faced an extraordinary case that became a cornerstone of women's liberation.

Melissa Ludtke was a sports reporter for *Sports Illustrated* who wanted the same access to the locker room that her male colleagues received. Otherwise, they had an unfair advantage over her for stories that arose from pregame and postgame interviews. Baseball commissioner Bowie Kuhn refused to grant her the access. The fellow defendants—the New York Yankees and the American League—followed Kuhn's edict.

The lawsuit was a civil rights claim based on the denial of equal protection under the Fourteenth Amendment and the blocking of First Amendment rights giving the press freedom to report. An injunction against Kuhn's ban was sought.[15]

Ludtke recalled, "Judge Motley had little patience for this case. You could tell that she wanted to avoid writing a decision. So, she basically ordered the two sides to go back and talk. To me, it was an indication that she didn't want to resolve it. But when negotiations broke down, by then I have to say that I felt more assured because I did not think that baseball made a strong case. I watched the judge and listened to her exasperation as she tried to have a dialogue with the other side and found herself stuck having to give a ruling."[16]

Motley acknowledged the discomfort that men might feel if women were given a green light regarding the clubhouse. "Defendants say women reporters are excluded in order 1) to protect the privacy of those players who are undressed or who are in various stages of undressing and getting ready to shower; 2) to protect the image of baseball as a family sport; and 3) preservation of traditional notions of decency and propriety."[17]

But there was a salient legal issue that Kuhn et al. either dismissed or ignored.

Yankee Stadium had a business relationship with New York City because the land and its environs had been acquired by eminent domain. New York City leased Yankee Stadium to the team because there was a fear of the team moving from the Bronx.

So the Yankees' adherence to Kuhn made its involvement a state action, according to Motley. This brought it into conflict with federal law.

Motley ruled that the state action violated Ludtke's equal protection rights. She pointed out that the privacy issue was a nonstarter during the World Series, especially in the locker room of the winning team, when TV cameras broadcast the joyous celebrations capped by players pouring beer and champagne on each other. Millions of people watch the post-game shows; fans live vicariously through them. Making the clubhouse a men's club was not "substantially related" to the argument for privacy because equal protection superseded it.

Due process was also at issue. The Fourteenth Amendment guarantees the "liberty" to work, Motley highlighted with a string of cases as backup. But Kuhn's ban went against that bedrock principle; Motley declared that it "substantially and directly interferes" with Ludtke's right to compete against male colleagues. Her reporting would be shackled by the lack of access.

In 1993, Motley confronted the emotional, financial, and physical detachment that the Dodgers organization caused when it left Brooklyn after the 1957 season and began playing in Los Angeles. Restaurateurs established the Brooklyn Dodger Sports Bar and Restaurant in the late 1980s; LA's National League team and Major League Baseball joined forces to take them down on a trademark infringement case.

Motley scrutinized the restaurateurs' actions to determine whether they acted in good faith. She also highlighted the emotional fissure created by Dodgers owner Walter O'Malley transplanting the team across the continental United States. Her legal test was the standard "likelihood of confusion" paradigm.[18] The Dodgers and MLB believed that the restaurant not only traded on the team's goodwill but also confused patrons on whether it was associated with the team.

It was a David and Goliath situation. David won.

The Dodgers, according to Motley, had not used the Brooklyn association to any significant degree. Any usage was tenuous at best.

So the restaurateurs had a path to use the name. "At no time during their consideration of the 'Brooklyn Dodger' name did the individual defendants have any reason to believe that 'The Brooklyn Dodger' mark was being used by Los Angeles, and certainly not for restaurant or tavern services," ruled Motley.[19]

There was also the matter of good faith.

Motley acknowledged that the bar's owners "exercised all reasonable diligence to satisfy themselves that no one was using a 'Brooklyn Dodger' trademark for restaurant and tavern services, and that no one had filed a registration for this trademark for use in any other field."[20]

Major League Baseball did have a licensing agreement that included the Brooklyn Dodgers name for merchandise—T-shirts, jackets, mugs, and the like—but Motley noted that there was no agreement for restaurant and tavern services.[21]

---

In late August 1966, an urban anthem celebrating the season could be heard several times daily with the regularity of a metronome; such was the programming strategy of Top 40 radio. The Lovin' Spoonful's number-one hit "Summer in the City" describes the streets of an unnamed metropolis teeming with heat during the day and relieving the citizenry with coolness after sundown. It was part of an amazing breakthrough summer for the music industry underscored by Brian Wilson's auteur status solidifying with the Beach Boys album *Pet Sounds*.

Music journalist Stephen Davis called *Pet Sounds*, which boasted "Wouldn't It Be Nice" as its most popular song, a concept album about a relationship, presumably of the adolescent variety, and described it as having "the emotional impact of a shatteringly evocative novel."[22]

With a dash of mournfulness combined with a sprinkle of optimism and a smidge of self-loathing, "You Still Believe in Me" chronicles a young man's journey with his partner who stands by him despite his failings, perceived and otherwise. Wilson incorporated the band members' voices into the songs rather than using them as vehicles to express the lyrics.

Like a saxophone, piano, or guitar, voices can be modulated and adapted. Wilson unlocked that value, which other songwriters and producers either couldn't recognize to the same extent or simply ignored. It was Wilson's dedication, vision, and execution that made *Pet Sounds* a revolutionary album. "Brian saw our voices as another set of instruments, which he adjusted with unerring, autocratic whim, pushing us to achieve the closest thing possible to perfection," said fellow Beach Boy Mike Love.

———— ⚬⚬⚬ ————

Wilson's genius notwithstanding, Baltimore's baseball fans tuned to WBAL for sounds that were equally mellifluous—Chuck Thompson, Frank Messer, and Bill O'Donnell calling the Orioles games.

When August began, Baltimore's squad had a 13-game lead over the second-place Detroit Tigers. The O's played .500 ball for the month, ending with an 83–49 record. A stellar performance by Boog Powell during a road trip was a highlight. Against the Red Sox on August 15, the 230-pound, the 6'4" Oriole smashed three home runs, accounting for all the runs in Baltimore's 4–2 victory over the last-place hosts. The 11-inning game was the first win in Baltimore's three-game sweep.

Powell struck out against Jim Lonborg in his first at-bat, but knocked a two-out solo homer into Fenway Park's left-field stands at the top of the fourth inning. He followed with a single two innings later; Boston rebounded with a two-run effort in the bottom of the frame. Powell's second home run evened the score in the top of the ninth.

Frank Robinson walked to lead off the 11th. Powell's third round-tripper came against Boston reliever John Wyatt. Lonborg had pitched him outside, so Powell expected something different. "I figured they'd try to run the ball inside on me the last time, but the first pitch was outside again so I swung," reasoned the slugger, who hit .287 and went yard

34 times in 1966. "Hell, I just go up there and swing. I'm not looking for any particular pitch. I ain't that smart."[23]

Baltimore led second-place Detroit by 13½ games with a 78–41 record on August 16; it was a comfortable though not invulnerable lead.

As Orioles fans consumed journalists' retellings of Powell's exploits in Boston—the third time that the beefy batsman had a three-homer outing—UPI's Milton Richman reminded them of 1964, when the team neared 80 wins in mid-August, then lost more than half of the next 38 games. Baltimore finished the '64 campaign in third place.

In 1964, Hank Bauer had his first year as the Orioles' manager. Bauer, who won seven World Series championships as a player with the Yankees, knew that anything can happen in baseball. So he refused to acknowledge a potential downswing to the press, instead focusing on the competition. "That thought always crosses your mind," said Bauer. "I try not to think about it, though."[24]

But Richman figured that the competition in '66 would probably not catch the Birds anyway, much less eclipse them.

There was an aura of inevitability around Chesapeake Bay. Powell et al. ended the dog days of August at 83–49 and with a 12-game lead over the second-place Tigers. It was a pretty nice cushion.

The Orioles were about to soar even higher.

CHAPTER NINE

# Impossible Missions, Daydream Believers, and the Final Frontier (September)

WINNING THE '66 AMERICAN LEAGUE PENNANT WAS A FOREGONE CON-clusion for Baltimore's rooters at the beginning of September, even if it was not confirmed statistically.

The Orioles needed three weeks to make it official. Their opponent in the World Series had not been determined yet; three teams had a chance in the senior circuit. Pittsburgh and San Francisco were tied on the night of September 1; Los Angeles trailed by two games. Optimism and anxiety paired among the teams' followers in this pennant race, which inspired questions about the Dodgers' ability to repeat.

Television was an alternative for the fan bases of other AL teams, who were on a futile quest against the Orioles' inevitability, and for National League fans who needed a respite from the tension-filled pennant race.

*I Dream of Jeannie* manifested the heterosexual male fantasy—a beautiful genie granting her "master" his wish. Here, U.S. Air Force captain and NASA astronaut Tony Nelson has his *Stardust 1* mission aborted before orbiting when a rocket misfires, forcing his capsule to plunge into the ocean. He finds refuge on an island where he discovers a bottle, removes the stopper, and out comes a blonde, buxom genie. She accompanies him back to his home in Cocoa Beach, Florida, where her well-meaning intentions cause havoc and humor.

Larry Hagman played Captain (later Major) Nelson; Bill Daily played his best friend, Roger Healey; and Barbara Eden played Jeannie.

Screen Gems produced *I Dream of Jeannie* and *Bewitched*, an ABC sitcom relying on another female character with extraordinary powers. Jeannie blinked her eyes to make something happen; Samantha Stephens twitched her nose. *Jeannie* ran from 1965 to 1970 on NBC. *Bewitched* had a longer life, airing on ABC from 1964 to 1972.

Sidney Sheldon, Oscar-winning writer of *The Bachelor and the Bobby Soxer*, created *I Dream of Jeannie*. His daughter Mary Sheldon recalled,

First of all, it is an irresistible formula when you have a world that is prosaic and believable like the space program and add the level of fantasy. What makes it so delightful is the contrast between the real world and the fantasy. Papa was a wonderful writer, and the cast had marvelous chemistry. There was a blend of hard comedy with pratfalls and physical comedy combined with soft comedy in a romantic moment. That made it special.

My favorite moment happened in the first season. Papa wrote a part for my mother, who played a fortune teller. My papa's mother Natalie, my grandmother, was visiting from Chicago, and he wrote a part for her as a person at the séance. In the week leading to the shooting, he wrote a line, and she studied and researched and practiced. On the day of shooting, Queenie Leonard got grandma's line! Papa gave his mom a new line. She refused to do it and said, "My character would never say that." So he gave her back the old line!

Larry has gotten respect for his acting because of *Dallas*. I don't know about Barbara, but if she hadn't been the actress she was, people wouldn't have enjoyed it as much.

The astronauts adored *I Dream of Jeannie*. When Jeannie and Tony got married, we got flown to Cocoa Beach for the shooting of the episodes. I got to meet Buzz Aldrin. We went all over the NASA complex in Cocoa Beach; we sat in the simulator and crashed on the moon. They couldn't be nicer.

Papa could do a script in one day. He dictated scenes to his secretary. He wrote all day long. He was an introvert most of the time but loved hosting parties and going to them. He was a very sweet man and saw the world in an innocent way. Jeannie expressed that part of him.

———— ❧ ————

Another Barbara fascinated men in '66.

Where Barbara Eden's Jeannie was giddy, almost childlike, at serving her master, Barbara Bain's Cinnamon Carter on *Mission: Impossible* combined gorgeousness with sophistication, poise, and intelligence that made her equal to the men on the Impossible Missions Force team. With a ruler-straight nose and facial bone structure that could have plastic surgeons from Beverly Hills to Park Avenue using her as a template, Bain stood front and center as the women's liberation movement percolated.

Women fighting for equality in the workplace could tune their TV sets to CBS on September 17 for the show's premiere and watch a revelation: one of their own treated as a cornerstone with crucial skills that helped the team plan and execute a complex series of tasks requiring precision.

Impossible missions, hence the show's title. Desilu, the production company led by iconic comedienne Lucille Ball, produced this latest in a bonanza of espionage-themed TV shows. It's assumed that the IMF team works for a government agency, though it's unnamed. Instructions, usually by audiotape, at the beginning of the episode indicate that "the secretary" will disavow any knowledge of the team members if they are caught or killed.[1]

There was an undercurrent of the Cold War, but the IMF team also pursued domestic criminals. Lalo Schifrin's pulsating theme accompanied by an animated lighting of a dynamite fuse and action scenes from the episode became one of the most recognizable opening sequences in TV history.

Dan Briggs led the IMF team, populated by master of disguise Rollin Hand, electronics expert Barney Collier, and bodybuilder Willy Armitage. Steven Hill played Dan. He left after the first season; Peter Graves replaced him as the new team leader, Jim Phelps, and stayed in that role until the series went off the air in 1973.[2]

*Mission: Impossible* never disclosed the government agency that oversaw the Impossible Missions Force. When Paramount rebooted the premise as a movie franchise starring Tom Cruise in 1996, it was shown to be the Central Intelligence Agency headquartered in Langley, Virginia. COURTESY OF CENTRAL INTELLIGENCE AGENCY

Peter Lupus, a real-life bodybuilder, played Willy. Martin Landau's portrayal of Rollin relied on masks, accents, and state-of-the-art makeup. Landau and Bain were married.

Greg Morris played Barney, which was a breakthrough role for Black actors. Like Cosby on *I Spy*, he was treated as an equal member with neither fanfare nor social messaging. His presence alone dictated his value to the team.

Men noticed Cinnamon's contributions, too. Cinnamon's assignments required a terrific range from Bain, who made her character approachable. It was a tricky balance for the shapely blonde actress to portray Cinnamon as sexy but smart and entice viewers to embrace her as more than a sex symbol.

Attractiveness and acting did not solely distinguish the Chicago native, who had started her entertainment career as a dancer before modeling for *Vogue* and other top-selling magazines, then honed her craft under Lee Strasberg at the Actors Studio. For actors, the most important person on a set is the lighting director. *Mission: Impossible* creator Bruce Geller made a critical choice that emphasized this production angle.

Bain recalled,

> There are certain things that happened for me that couldn't be more fortunate. John Alton had written *Painting with Light*. Bruce brought him out of retirement to light the pilot episode. Nobody lit TV actresses like he lit me, so I was protected. He used old Hollywood glamour light. It was extraordinary. Nobody looks that good. Bruce said, "I don't want her ever to look less good than this." After that, every camera person on *Mission: Impossible* was shown that closeup. If we did a scene in a tunnel, he said, "I don't care if the guys are cross lit, do this with Barbara."
>
> Bruce actually had written the part for me, but he didn't tell me that. We were in an acting class that Martin was teaching. He had writers come to the class to see the actors' challenges. He also wrote Martin's part for him. When he had the role of the girl, he needed two qualities—smart and sexy. I had done quite a bit of guest starring on TV and played any number of dumb blondes up to that point. I had to up and audition six times. The last person to approve me was Lucille Ball.
>
> I was shaking in my boots. She was in this little bungalow on the Paramount lot. Lucy looked me up and down and said, "Looks okay to me."
>
> The thing that was wonderful was Bruce's estimation of me. He had seen me in acting class and told the writers, "Write anything. She can do it."
>
> Cinnamon was given a challenge every week, which was glorious. I was acknowledged. Every blonde wasn't dumb. It was an interesting time because women could choose to be in the workplace. Later, there was a big change in the culture when women had to work. *Mission: Impossible* was a breakthrough situation.
>
> We knew we were doing something really good, and we felt that during the pilot. Bruce was a meticulous person in every

way, and he had conceived so well what he had wanted to do. There was concern about every detail. He wrote the scripts in the beginning. Later, I only went to the writers once when I didn't know how to play a character within the character of Cinnamon. Before I opened my mouth, they knew why I was there.

But there was also a fear primarily because *Mission: Impossible* demanded your attention. The stories had layers like the Russian dolls. But the network executives were much more panicked that they would lose southern affiliates because Greg and I were on the same piece of film. Nat King Cole had a show, and those stations wouldn't show it. Here we come along and we're working together.

It does speak for the times. The executives would come on the set and ask questions. Do Greg and Barbara have to sit together? Isn't it hard to light them? They kept coming all the time we were in production, but when the shows aired, nothing bad happened. Now they were big supporters.

Our show was considered more fantasy than reality. But there were things that were based on real life. I would get asked years later by people who worked for the CIA, "How did you know about the submarine? How did you know about the false town?"

Although Martin and I were a married couple, we had different representatives and different deals. Paramount, which produced the show, didn't understand that Martin and I had separate deals, and they tried to get at him through me. They released stories that I was recalcitrant and wouldn't come to the set and locked myself in my dressing room. (I'm claustrophobic, and the last thing I would ever do is shut myself in a room.)

It came to a flashpoint the night I received my third Emmy. Two days before, I had agreed to shoot a public service announcement for the American Cancer Society. Paramount knew about it because they were letting me use their hair and makeup people. Nevertheless, they contrived a forced wardrobe call for me and, when I couldn't comply (as I was keeping my obligation to shoot the PSA), they served me with a breach of contract suit as I was getting ready to go to the Emmys!

At the same time, they smeared Martin and me in the press, referring to us as "the Legend of the Landaus" and kept me from working for a year of lawyers and depositions. A year later, Digby Diehl of *TV Guide* came to us intending to do a hatchet job, but when he heard the facts, they printed the real story. Nevertheless, the old one has persisted, and it simply isn't true.[3]

———— ✥ ————

The 1960s spy mania begun by James Bond also influenced Saturday-morning animation.

*Cool McCool* premiered on NBC, featuring an unlikely hero in the title role—an inept yet debonair spy with an alliterative, hip-sounding name and crime fighting in his DNA. His father Harry McCool was a cop, shown in shorter segments with his partners, who are also his brothers—Tom and Dick. Batman creator Bob Kane teamed with Al Brodax for this espionage-themed contribution debuting on NBC's fall 1966 lineup.

CBS strategized its Saturday-morning lineup to take advantage of *Batman*'s success. Every show had a superhero theme. Lou Scheimer's company Filmation got tagged by programming guru Fred Silverman to develop a series about Superman, which was titled *The New Adventures of Superman*. Silverman had seen a seven-minute pilot that Scheimer and his partner Hal Sutherland created for the Buck Rogers character, so he knew what they could do.

It made sense because Superman was a perennial success. Most of the time, anyway.

Scheimer's program was the second major iteration of the kryptonian hero in 1966. *It's a Bird . . . It's a Plane . . . It's Superman* premiered on Broadway in late March and closed three and a half months later. The musical was a verified flop on the stage. But the play wasn't dead forever. There was a 1975 TV special; subsequent revivals followed. Jean Louisa Kelly played Lois Lane in the 2007 version in Los Angeles: "There are so many adjectives for her! Smart, beautiful, independent, sexy, pragmatic but romantic. Lois is the 'Perfect Woman'—of course she wants the 'Perfect Man'!"[4]

Erika Scheimer saw how her father tackled the challenge of tapping a new vein in a world-famous franchise and surpassed his humble beginnings to become an animation legend.

My dad grew up poor in the slums of Pittsburgh. He was 14 when his dad died. His mom died when he was 22. He went to Carnegie Tech, now Carnegie Mellon, and walked to classes with Andy Warhol!

Hal Sutherland partnered with him to begin Filmation in 1962. They did corporate training films and other little jobs they could produce at home or in the back of Hal's station wagon at first. Outside of writing the script, Hal could direct and animate. My dad could do layout.

Later, Norm Prescott joined them. The logo of a spinning circle with their name was a solution to the question of whose name should go on top. Norm and my dad were able to assuage their egos this way. It made the shows memorable.

They found out that CBS was looking into Saturday-morning cartoons. Fred Silverman was in charge of daytime programming. A CBS executive wanted to visit the studio, but there was only the two of them. So they called up all their friends and had them pretend to work there. One of those people was Ted Knight. He ran around saying, "There's trouble at the lab!" He wanted to make sure it sounded like a busy studio. The executive saw this and said, "You guys run a tight ship here."

Filmation landed the Superman show in 1966. It was the first cartoon for the studio and the first show that Silverman ever bought. Everyone was on pins and needles. The very ironic thing is that I hated cartoons early on. I was watching old Randolph Scott movies. But my dad always put me on the phone with Silverman after a cartoon was broadcast. I was only six years old, so I would tell him how much I liked it.

He worked morning, noon, and night. He really loved what he did, and he was so happy to have work. Besides animation, they also did training films for companies. He really cared about the kids watching the shows and how the stories would affect them. There was a lot of criticism in the late 1960s about TV's effect on kids. The Children's Action Group started a movement. So, *Fat Albert and the Cosby Kids* became an educational show.

CBS wanted a good show that had prosocial messages. Dad got in touch with a college professor because he wanted to have the imprimatur of academia. That's when he met Dr. Gordon Berry from UCLA.

Dad was thrilled because Gordon was Black. It was so appropriate because the show dealt with Black teenagers. Gordon was instrumental in driving the stories and making sure that the messages were in the scripts. It became a model for other shows.

When the animators went on strike in the 1970s, he walked with them even though he was management. He never forgot where he came from.[5]

---

CBS's "Super Saturday" lineup aired for three hours: *Mighty Mouse & The Mighty Heroes, Underdog, Frankenstein Jr. and the Impossibles, Space Ghost and Dino Boy, The New Adventures of Superman,* and *The Lone Ranger.*

*Batman*'s influence on network executives was evident. But it had an added component to its popularity. A Batman film, also titled *Batman,* graced movie screens with four villains battling the Caped Crusaders: the Joker, the Riddler, the Penguin, and Catwoman.

Part of *Batman*'s success was Neal Hefti, an ASCAP Music Writers Hall of Fame member who won a Grammy for the theme song and later wrote the theme song and musical accompaniment to scene transitions in *The Odd Couple* movie and TV series.

Hefti's body of work for 1960s Hollywood showcases a talent for matching the era's varied musical tastes to the story. *Sex and the Single Girl, How to Murder Your Wife, Barefoot in the Park,* and *Boeing Boeing* were among his contributions for filmmakers.

It was a good bet to find Hefti lifting a Scripto pencil from its perch behind his right ear before jotting the notes and chords for Hollywood's latest offerings. "Everything my father wrote was golden," says Paul Hefti, a musician who carries on his dad's musical legacy with new arrangements and interpretations.

He was working on a couple of films when Bill Dozier approached him to write a theme song for a new television series, *Batman*. In interviews, he admitted that *Batman* was the toughest piece of music he had ever attempted, and that many versions were ripped up and thrown into the wastebasket.

In 1958, my father composed, arranged, and produced the LP release "BASIE," which won Best Jazz Performance, Group and Best Performance by a Dance Band at the First Annual Grammy Awards. Though none of those Grammys were awarded to him, Grammy success was soon to be his with the 1966 Best Instrumental Theme for *Batman*—a proud and cherished day for our family.[6]

---

ABC attempted to duplicate the success of *Batman* with *The Green Hornet* starring Van Williams in the title role. Also produced by William Dozier, this straightforward approach to a well-known character didn't quite have the sting of the campy show with colorful sets. *The Green Hornet* functioned primarily as a half-hour detective show and lasted one season.

The Green Hornet character dated back to 1936, debuting on radio as part of a renowned character's story line. Britt Reid is the grandnephew of John Reid, aka the Lone Ranger. As publisher of the *Daily Sentinel* in an unnamed metropolis, he has power and influence along with wealth presumably begun with an inheritance from his crime-fighting ancestor. The elder Reid owned a silver mine, which was the source for his famed silver bullets. So it can be presumed that either the mine or the wealth derived from its sale was handed down to subsequent generations of Reids.

Updated for the 1960s, Reid owned a TV station (DSTV) and enjoyed a rich bachelor lifestyle with a modern pad to match. His social status allowed him to investigate crimes without arousing suspicion and pursue criminals as his alter ego clad in an overcoat, hat, and mask.

Bruce Lee took on the role of Kato, Reid's valet and sidekick. Although Lee didn't get much dialogue, *The Green Hornet* gave him a platform to introduce martial arts to a mass audience during the fight scenes and begin his journey to worldwide stardom, only to die prematurely in 1973 at 32 years old.

The Green Hornet's car—Black Beauty—was a 1965 Chrysler Imperial reformatted by custom car builder Dean Jeffries. His son Kevin Jeffries remembers,

> For *The Green Hornet*, my dad built two versions of Black Beauty. He hired my grandfather, a retired truck driver, to drive one and promote the show.
>
> Designing and building custom cars was a job that required long hours, sunrise to sunset. He had this really creative side. It started when he went into the army during World War II and he was assigned to design maps. This old German guy told him how to pinstripe. It progressed from there, and he started pinstriping cars after World War II. My grandparents moved to California when my dad and his sisters were young, about six or seven years old. One of the neighbors was a race car guy named Rutherford. He got my dad hooked into the racing scene, cleaning parts of cars.
>
> He was very approachable 90 percent of the time. You could walk into his shop and strike up a conversation. He enjoyed the challenge of designing from the frame up and making the car unique from what others had done. At car shows, he always pointed out when someone had designed something different. He passed up the opportunity to design the Batmobile because he was involved in other projects.
>
> I think every guy's dream is to have a hot rod. It's something we can all relate to. There were other designers who were also pioneers, and we should give a lot of credit to them because they set the standards. Gene Winfield, Bill Hines, and Larry Watson were doing things that nobody else was doing. They didn't have the high technology of today. My dad and these guys started the industry of custom cars, and now it's widespread.[7]

Jeffries's other famed creation in 1966 was a modified Pontiac GTO for a new NBC show set around a quartet of young singers with a misspelled name for a band in a nod to the Beatles. Jeffries's "Monkeemobile" was a popular-culture mark for NBC's *The Monkees*. Peter Tork, Davy Jones, Michael Nesmith, and Mickey Dolenz combined comedy inspired by the Marx Brothers with guitars, drums, and a keyboard. They did not know each other before the show. Acting auditions were required.

The Beatles had just ended their last American concert tour in August. Their popularity was as steadfast as Big Ben, which gave Screen Gems, the television division of Columbia Pictures, an opportunity for another foursome. Screen Gems produced *The Monkees*, and its sister company Colgems released the song "Last Train to Clarksville" a month before the show's premiere on September 12 in a brilliant strategy to create publicity.[8]

Don Kirshner was the musical guru who selected the songs. At least initially.

Even though Kirshner had a knack for producing hits and the Monkees topped the charts, they wanted to split from him. Their success with Kirshner was confirmed by Top 40 radio disc jockeys playing the songs and record stores selling out of their albums.[9]

Going their own way proved unprofitable if not disastrous.

Monkeemania was gargantuan but brief. The Monkees had a two-year window of icon status with a weekly platform of millions of viewers; *The Monkees* went off the air in 1968. But its legacy is undeniable with chart-topping hits that have become fixtures on oldies radio stations: "Daydream Believer," "Pleasant Valley Sunday," "I'm a Believer," "A Little Bit Me, A Little Bit You."[10]

*The Monkees* entertained. *Star Trek* inspired. NBC placed this new drama created by Gene Roddenberry on the fall 1966 schedule, taking advantage of the popular space theme but adding a futuristic bent. *Star Trek* featured the crew of the USS *Enterprise*, a 23rd-century spaceship with a five-year mission to travel throughout the galaxies and learn from their civilizations. Earth is part of a group of planetary members called the Federation. "We deal with human conflicts against a science-fiction background," explained William Shatner, who played Captain James Tiberius Kirk.[11]

Created by Gene Roddenberry, *Star Trek* portrayed the crew of a 23rd-century starship on a five-year mission to explore "strange new worlds." William Shatner played Captain James T. Kirk of the USS *Enterprise*. Part of Kirk's backstory was his birthplace in Riverside, Iowa. COURTESY OF CITY OF RIVERSIDE, IOWA

Roddenberry furthered the point, underscoring his foundation of two rationales in conjunction with an interview for the show's premiere. "One, to show that science-fiction is an incredibly rich body of literature as yet untapped by the medium of television. And two, to show that sci-fi can be more than the Monster that gobbled up Tokyo or Cleveland. This is the distorted view most Americans have, thanks to cheap, [unimaginative] films. They have been playing to a 15-year-old mentality. I say to hell with that. I refuse to believe an audience is that stupid. Doesn't it make sense to give them something that truly stimulates their imaginations?"[12]

It did.

In the first-season episode "A City on the Edge of Forever," largely regarded as the best of the series, Kirk goes through a time portal—Guardian of Forever—with Science Officer Spock to find Dr. Leonard "Bones" McCoy, who jumped through it in an unintentional, drug-induced craze. Kirk and Spock land in 1930s Chicago and meet Edith Keeler, a pacifist who Mother Teresa would applaud; Keeler sees only the good in people and dedicates herself to helping the downtrodden.

Spock configures tubes and wires to work in conjunction with his tricorder—an all-purpose, hand-held device with terrific computing power and news archives—that lets him and Kirk see the change in the time line caused by McCoy. After he saves Edith in a traffic accident, she will persuade President Roosevelt to delay entering World War II, which allows Nazi Germany to be victorious. The time, date, and location of the accident are undetermined.

"Jim, Edith Keeler must die," explains Spock to his superior officer, who has fallen in love with Edith. If she doesn't, then millions more will die and fascism will reign. When Kirk and Spock reunite with McCoy, Keeler crosses the street to investigate. As a car heads down the street, McCoy starts to rush toward her; Kirk grasps him so that Edith can die and restore the original time line. "Do you know what you just did?!" exclaims McCoy. "He knows, doctor," says Spock. "He knows."

"A City on the Edge of Forever" illustrates an emotion-laden triangle of sacrifice, hope, and tragedy. Provocative stories requiring philosophical contemplation became a *Star Trek* staple.

*Star Trek* showcased inventions that seemed preposterous to 1966 audiences but became reality 30 years later. A flat screen for communicating by video is recognizable as the paradigm for early-21st-century television sets. Pocket-sized walkie-talkies that opened with a turn of the wrist had the same design as the popular flip phones of the 1990s and 2000s.

Spock was an alien with a human mother and Vulcan father from the planet Vulcan; his exhortation to live long and prosper was accompanied by the Vulcan salute borrowed from the kohanim—the ancient Jewish priesthood. You make a "V" by separating your fingers: pinky and ring from middle and index.

Leonard Nimoy played Spock and took the salute from his Jewish background. Shatner, too, was Jewish.

Spock's pointy ears, bowl-type haircut, and logical approach to the *Enterprise*'s ventures distanced the character from the crew. Where their responses led to exclamations of worry, Spock observed the situation and offered cold reactions. In a 2000 interview, Nimoy revealed that he got a "brilliant note" from the director in the first episode. Spock has only one word in a scene revolving around the USS *Enterprise* being in peril: "Fascinating."

When a conflict arises, there's a natural tendency to exclaim. But the director advised Nimoy, "Be different. Be the scientist. Be detached. See it as something that's a curiosity rather than a threat."

Nimoy adjusted his delivery to be monotone and restrained. They quickly became Spock hallmarks. Nimoy explained, "A big chunk of the character was born right there."[13]

NBC aired *Star Trek* for three seasons, then launched a mid-1970s animated series followed by the first of six movies with the original cast.[14]

Marc Rayman, a mission manager and chief engineer at NASA's Jet Propulsion Laboratory, reflected on *Star Trek*:

In 1966, space exploration was already illustrating the fascinating, exciting, even inspiring peaceful power of science and engineering. *Star Trek* extrapolated that beyond what one can imagine but with a sense of reality. It depicted an appealing picture that people like me wanted to live in. The U.S. and Russia were sending astronauts into orbit, but *Star Trek*'s characters visited new planets and new solar systems brimming with life. They had bright, clean, spacious ships with people we liked.

Even if you weren't interested in science and engineering, it depicted many positive aspects of a future. Not only was space exploration starting, but there was the fear of nuclear weapons and the power of war. But this gave people promise and hope. There is this bright, clean future. It at least allowed you to see a positive future. I think that appealed to a lot of people as well.[15]

*Star Trek* premiered on September 8; science-fiction fans coupled their imaginations of the future with NASA's achievements in the present.

East Coast office workers were on their second cup of coffee, and West Coasters were wiping the sleep out of their eyes when *Gemini 11* splashed down just before 10:00 A.M. Eastern. Launching on September 12—four days after NBC introduced Captain Kirk and his *Enterprise* crew—astronauts Pete Conrad and Richard Gordon took 44 laps around the Earth and ended their three-day voyage with a textbook splashdown in the Atlantic Ocean. Their descent from the heavens brought ear-to-ear smiles and pent-up exhalation to NASA's Mission Control team in Houston and its counterpart at Florida's Cape Kennedy; Conrad and Gordon landed just two miles from the target area.

When they climbed aboard the recovery ship USS *Guam*, NASA's latest space voyagers got cheers and ovations. Gordon underscored the importance of the flight when he mentioned the record-setting altitude: "This old world really looks good from the deck of this carrier. But I'll tell you something else again—it really looks great from 750 miles."[16]

*Gemini 11* marked another success when Conrad and Gordon joined with an Agena target craft. It warranted prestige and progress for the United States in the Space Race with Russia.

Not only was the maneuver a dry run for actions that would be needed on the three-man Apollo flights readying for moon landings; it was also the first time that NASA brought two spacecraft together, otherwise known as rendezvous and docking. They also connected the two in a different manner—using a specially designed rope that was 100 feet long. *New York Times* space reporter John Noble Wilford explained: "The maneuver's main goal was to practice formation flying with a tether, which could mean a large saving in maneuvering fuel."

Gordon also became the fourth NASA "spacewalker" on the flight when he left the spacecraft connected by a tether as well.

These ventures outside the spacecraft were opportunities for astronauts to learn about limitations of body movement if they needed to repair a capsule or other spacecraft on future missions. There was a second rendezvous and docking before the duo headed home.[17]

Astronauts Pete Conrad and Dick Gordon flew in *Gemini 11* and achieved the first docking of a capsule with an Agena target vehicle. Gordon had two "space walks" lasting a total of 2 hours and 41 minutes. COURTESY OF NASA

Baltimore delighted in the September 23 newspaper stories about the Orioles' latest victory—a 6–1 drubbing of the Kansas City A's that gave the O's a three-game sweep of the series, their 94th victory of the season, and the AL pennant.

Jim Palmer's stellar complete-game performance scattered five Kansas City hits, struck out eight, and walked two. The hurler went 15–10 in 1966.

Winning the AL flag validated Orioles owner Jerry Hoffberger, who considered the team not to be an investment for his bank book—at least not solely—but a reflection of his passion, loyalty, and civic responsibility. "I didn't buy this club to get my name in the newspapers, only to win," declared Hoffberger during spring training. "I made money in Baltimore and now I want to give the people a pennant."[18]

Hank Bauer contrasted his previous glories as a player. "And none of those Yankee pennants meant as much to me as this one," said the Baltimore skipper. "It's different when you're the manager."[19]

Baltimore basked. Los Angeles, not so much.

After stampeding their way to a 13–2 record in the first half of the month, the Dodgers went 7–7. With the suddenness of a Malibu rip current, fans in LA, Pittsburgh, and San Francisco went through the mathematical possibilities that could lead each team to the pennant.

Los Angeles led the NL with a one-and-a-half-game lead over Pittsburgh.

San Francisco occupied third place, trailing their Southern California rivals by three games.

The 1966 NL pennant race was an epic battle.

And an exhausting one.

## CHAPTER TEN

# Bird Is the Word
# (October)

WITH NO GAME ON THE SCHEDULE FOR OCTOBER 1, LA HAD A ONE-DAY break before closing out the season with a doubleheader the next day against Philadelphia. Pittsburgh and San Francisco had three games remaining—against each other.

|          |       |
|----------|-------|
| Dodgers  | 94–66 |
| Pirates  | 92–67 |
| Giants   | 90–68 |

The Giants had a path if the Dodgers fell to the Phillies in the October 2 doubleheader. Sweeping the Pirates would give the Giants a 93–68 record. There would need to be a makeup game from the Giants–Reds contest that was rained out on August 10.[1] If the Giants then beat the Reds, there would be a Dodgers-Giants playoff.

The Giants took both games of a doubleheader against the Pirates at Forbes Field on October 1; they were rained out the day before, prompting the addition of a game to the one already scheduled.

Juan Marichal pitched a complete game in the first contest, a 5–4 victory. Bobby Bolin followed with a one-hitter; San Francisco won 2–0. Bill Mazeroski got the only Pittsburgh hit—a two-out single in the bottom of the second.

Rain returned in the third inning, causing a 40-minute interruption. The Giants got their two runs in the top of the eighth. Pirates right-hander Tommie Sisk had limited them to six hits until Hal Lanier led off with a single and moved to second base on Sisk's error.

When the Pirates rearranged their infielders for a bunt, which was likely with a weak-hitting pitcher at the plate—Bolin finished 1966 with a .171 batting average—Giants manager Herman Franks analyzed the defense for vulnerabilities.

There were several ways that a bunt could be fielded for at least one out and perhaps a double play. Bob Bailey and Donn Clendenon had the third-base and first-base territories covered if Bolin bunted the ball down either foul line. If there was enough time, either infielder could toss to shortstop Gene Alley, who'd be responsible for second base.

Second baseman Mazeroski would take Clendenon's place at first base to catch any throws. If a bunt didn't get too far, Pirates backstop Jim Pagliaroni would field the ball and decide the optimum play.

San Francisco's skipper saw an opportunity that would have been counterintuitive to risk-averse skippers when the first and third basemen anticipate a bunt and move toward the batter. "That leaves the middle open. Whenever I see their infielders running around like that, I have my man hit away."[2]

Bolin advanced his cause with a double to score Lanier; Tito Fuentes's infield single put Bolin on third base, and Tom Haller's sacrifice fly to Jesús Alou in center field scored him for the second and final run.

Losing both games put Pittsburgh out of contention.

San Francisco stood two games behind Los Angeles but still had a chance to tie or win the National League pennant. Each team had played 160 games. The Dodgers had a doubleheader against the Phillies on October 2. A victory in either game would give Southern California another NL title.

If the Dodgers lost both games and the Giants won the next game against the Pirates, the Giants would have the makeup game against the Reds. A win would tie the Giants with their longtime rivals and create déjà vu for another best-of-three playoffs, having done it in 1951 and again in 1962.[3]

The Giants won the third game of the series, giving them a sweep against the Pirates.

But the Dodgers split their doubleheader in Philadelphia, losing the first game and winning the second to avoid a playoff.

―――∞∞∞―――

## World Series, Game One (Dodger Stadium, October 5)

The Dodgers fared against the Orioles in Game One about as well as Gilligan and the castaways trying to get off the island. Their battle for the NL flag was demanding, leading Maury Wills to state, "It appeared we might not have recovered fully from winning the pennant—from all the excitement and then the relief."[4]

Both starting pitchers left the game early. Final score: 5–2.

The visitors from the mid-Atlantic region vaulted to a three-run lead in the top of the first. Frank Robinson bashed a one-out home run with Russ Snyder on first base, having drawn a walk. Brooks Robinson followed with a solo homer.

Boog Powell, who had his second-highest batting average in 1966, fouled out with a pop fly caught by Dodger veteran Jim Gilliam at third base. Curt Blefary's single extended Baltimore's hopes; Davey Johnson's strikeout ended them.

The Dodgers responded quickly, with Wills drawing a walk and stealing second base. Wills had led the NL in stolen bases from 1960 to 1965 and the majors three times during this period. In 1966, he ranked third in the senior circuit behind Lou Brock of the Cardinals and Sonny Jackson of the Astros.

Dave McNally dampened LA's aspirations of scoring by retiring the next three Dodgers: Willie Davis's infield popout followed by Lou Johnson flying to Snyder in center field and Tommy Davis grounding out to O's third baseman Brooks Robinson.

Baltimore escalated their lead by a run in the second inning. Don Drysdale walked Andy Etchebarren, who moved ahead to second base on McNally's sacrifice bunt. After Luis Aparicio's fly ball to right fielder Johnson for the second out, Snyder banged a single to score Etchebarren and wound up in scoring position on Tommy Davis's throw to Dodgers catcher John Roseboro from left field.

Frank Robinson's presence at the plate inspired the Baltimore fan base to envision more runs, a logical prospect given the slugger's American League–leading .316 batting average and 49 home runs, topping the majors.

But Drysdale managed to get the fearsome Robinson out on a fly ball to Tommy Davis in left field.

Down 4–0, LA's lads got a shot of adrenaline when Jim Lefebvre bashed a solo home run in the bottom of the second off McNally, who had given up 22 homers in 34 games during the regular season.[5] It was the only homer that the Dodgers hit in the '66 World Series.

Wes Parker swatted the ball for a double and Jim Gilliam walked, but the home team didn't capitalize on it. Roseboro's lineout to Snyder in center field was the first out. Parker had a big lead off second base, and he returned; Alston absolved Parker of any second-guessing from fickle-minded fans. "But don't blame Wes," said LA's skipper, then in his 13th of 23 years managing the Dodgers. "He couldn't do both—take a lead and tag up—and it looked like the ball was going to fall in, so the lead seemed proper."[6]

Alston pulled his right-handed ace for pinch-hitter Dick Stuart, who hit a fly ball to Frank Robinson for the second out; Parker moved to third base. But with runners at the corners, McNally came through and struck out Wills.

Replacing Drysdale was a result of "control trouble," said Alston.[7] Admitted Drysdale, "I've got no excuses. If they had hit my good pitches, I would have a case. But all they hit was my mistakes. When you send up high, fat pitches to hitters like the Robinsons, you are asking for a kick in the rear."[8]

Joe Moeller took over the mound for the Dodgers in the Orioles' third inning, retiring Brooks Robinson and Powell on grounders; Blefary popped out to Wills.

Los Angeles mounted a rally in the bottom of the third, but not through their bats. After Willie Davis popped out to Aparicio, keen eyes and patience resulted in three consecutive walks to Johnson, Tommy Davis, and Jim Lefebvre. Not wanting to risk a dent in the three-run cushion, Orioles manager Hank Bauer went to Moe Drabowsky for relief efforts.

It was okay for a moment. Then it wasn't.

Drabowsky struck out Parker—the first of 11 whiffs for the right-hander—but walked home a run when he faced Gilliam to make the score 4–2. As the hearts of Orioles fans beat with worry and those of Dodgers fans did so with hopefulness, Roseboro popped out to his counterpart when Etchebarren snared the ball on its descent.

Baltimore added a run to make the score 5–2 in the top of the fourth. Davey Johnson began with a double and moved 90 feet on Etchebarren's grounder to Lefebvre at second base. Drabowsky drew a walk and became the catalyst for the fifth run; Aparicio's ground ball to Wills forced out Drabowsky at second but gave Johnson enough leeway to score.

Alston sent Jim Barbieri to pinch-hit for Moeller. It was for naught. Drabowsky struck out the side—Moeller, Wills, and Willie Davis. He repeated in the top of the fifth with whiffs of Johnson, Tommy Davis, and Lefebvre.

Six straight strikeouts had not been accomplished in the World Series since Reds hurler Hod Eller against the Chicago White Sox in 1919. His total of 11 set a new record for relief pitchers; Giants hurler Jess Barnes racked up 10 in Game Six of the 1921 World Series between the Giants and the Yankees.

Drabowsky got his eighth strikeout in the bottom of the seventh—Covington pinch-hitting for Bob Miller. Wills's walk and Willie Davis's single created a bit of momentum for the LA ball club. It was short-lived. Johnson fouled out to Brooks Robinson, and Tommy Davis's 4–6 ground ball accounted for the third out.

In the bottom of the eighth, Parker struck out for the second time in the game and gave Drabowsky his ninth "K." Roseboro and Fairly were number 10 and 11 in the bottom of the ninth.

Drabowsky had begun his major-league career in 1956 with the Chicago Cubs. He had gone up and down from the majors to the minors again and again before arriving in Maryland's port city. Bauer saw a liability in Drabowsky's lack of stamina and turned it into an asset. "Before this year, Moe had always been a starter," explained Bauer. "He used to run out of gas after six or seven innings and start throwing the long ball. So we made a long reliever out of him."[9]

Drabowsky had a 2.81 ERA in '66, playing in 96 innings across 44 games. He started three of them.

The Trinity College alumnus, who had pitched a no-hitter against Wesleyan College in his younger days, had a second career as a stockbroker. Analyzing investment performance in a cushy office with a nameplate adorning the desk is a sedate assignment compared to the physical toll demanded by athletic competition at the highest levels. And it almost went that way for Drabowsky, who admitted, "I suppose if Baltimore hadn't drafted me I might have retired. But when I had a chance to go with a club that could win the pennant, I changed my mind."[10]

There was also the impact of Bauer's decision to move him from the ranks of starting pitchers. "This was the first season I've ever known I was going to be strictly a relief pitcher all year," explained Drabowsky. "It's had a settling effect on me. I should have gone to the bullpen three or four years ago."[11]

Beth Morris and Laura Nevell are Drabowsky's two surviving children. Beth recalled,

On October 5, 1959, my parents lost their first child to leukemia. Debra was two months old. So when he wins that game in the World Series on the same date in 1966, that was really an emotional day. It was kind of like an angel on his shoulder.

My parents never photographed Debra from the front lest the flash hurt her tender eyes, so there's sadly no photograph of her face.

We lived in an apartment in Pikesville behind a Howard Johnson's. My maternal grandmother watched us that day because my mom went to Los Angeles with my dad. We didn't have a TV set. A neighbor lent us one so my grandmother could watch the game. My dad's parents watched from their living room in Connecticut.[12]

Little did they know that they'd see Moe set a World Series record.

Drabowsky's afternoon outing in Game One might have had a touch of miracle after all. The romance of baseball comes from stories, not statistics. Reflectiveness, not just records. If people can believe that the Red Sox endured a curse causing a championship drought of 86 years because the team sold Babe Ruth to the Yankees, then sentimentalists can also believe, rightfully so, that somewhere beyond the earthly realm, Debra was watching her father. And smiling.

---

## WORLD SERIES, GAME TWO (DODGER STADIUM, OCTOBER 6)

Baseball fans watching Sandy Koufax pitch in 1966 were like classical music aficionados watching Zubin Mehta conduct the Los Angeles Philharmonic. Awestruck.

Koufax started 41 games in 1966, which led his major-league brethren. So did his figures of 27 complete games, 5 shutouts, 323 strikeouts, 1.73 ERA, and 27 victories against 9 losses. There was every reason for fans to be optimistic for Game Two, matching the veteran lefty against rookie right-hander Jim Palmer, who went 15–10 in the regular season.

LA was a seasoned ball club with formidable assets: home-field advantage, best pitcher in baseball, resilience, and experience in high-pressure games. The Dodgers had lost the first two games of the 1965 World Series to the Minnesota Twins, rebounded to win the next three, lost Game Six, and finished with a 2–0 victory in Game Seven to take the championship. It was a Koufax masterpiece: a three-hitter with 10 strikeouts and three walks.

Koufax went 2–1 in his three World Series starts against the Twins, though superstitious folks anticipating a second consecutive title in '66 noted that the sole loss came in Game Two.

Brooks Robinson was optimistic despite the fireballer's prowess: "I'm fully confident that we can score three runs off Koufax and beat him."[13]

Palmer and Koufax kept their oppositions in zeroes, until a disastrous sequence in the top of the fifth that had Dodgers fans questioning one of the team's most prodigious players and perhaps their own loyalties.

Powell led off with the Orioles' second hit of the game, a single followed by Johnson's foul out to Roseboro. Paul Blair's smack to center field evaded the glove of Willie Davis, who lost the ball in the LA sunshine. Dropping the ball put Powell on third and Blair on second.

Jimmy Piersall of the Angels, nearing the end of his career, defended Davis: "The fact that other fly balls were caught out there doesn't mean a thing. Balls come at you from all angles, but no two are the same. Willie is a good outfielder. It's obvious he lost those balls in the sun."[14]

Davis erred twice in the next at-bat; Etchebarren got to third base as Baltimore's runners scored when the sun interfered with Davis tracking the ball into his glove, then caused him to drop it. His throw to Gilliam to tag out Blair was wild.

Approximately 3,000 miles from Davis's foibles in the Dodger Stadium outfield, Columbia University engineering major Barry Mednick watched his beloved Dodgers on TV with about 30 guys in a general room in his dormitory. What he saw made him wince. What he heard made him wince further. "There were a couple of Baltimore fans behind me, and someone said drop it, and Davis did."[15]

Koufax struck out Palmer for the second out, then Aparicio hit a double to score Etchebarren and put the O's up 3–0.

Frank Robinson's triple and Powell's single caused the fourth run for the visiting team in the top of the sixth.

An inning later, Ron Perranoski substituted for Koufax. The Orioles went three up, three down. Any relaxation for the Dodgers fan base was temporary. In the top of the eighth, Baltimore added two runs. Perranoski walked Frank Robinson, who moved to second base on Brooks Robinson's single and to third on Powell's sacrifice bunt. Davey Johnson's single brought both Robinsons across home plate to make the score 6–0, where it stayed for the remainder of the game.

Blair, the Orioles' center fielder, tried to enlighten the press on Davis's travails in the Chavez Ravine outfield. "If it gets in the sun, there's nothing you can do about it. You just put up your glove and hope it falls in.

"This park is worse than a lot of others. The screen behind home plate gives off a funny glare. It's kind of like a gold glare I've never seen before."[16]

Orioles skipper Hank Bauer offered condolences as well: "I feel sorry for Willie. I was an outfielder, and when the ball gets in a certain spot in the sun, you're helpless."[17]

Fairly, Gilliam, and Perranoski also made errors.

Palmer had tempered the Dodgers lineup with a four-hit outing as the Orioles prepared for a cross-country flight home full of momentum.

---

## WORLD SERIES, GAME THREE (MEMORIAL STADIUM, OCTOBER 8)

Wally Bunker started Game Three for the O's. Claude Osteen was the Dodgers' hurler. A solid performer, Osteen ended 1966 with a 17–14 record and 2.85 ERA. Bunker began his six-hitter and the quest for Baltimore's third victory by striking out Wills and Parker. Willie Davis's fly ball to left fielder Blefary sent the Dodgers to the field.

Baltimore also went three up, three down, including Frank Robinson's strikeout. It was a nail-biting afternoon—the only score came in the bottom of the fifth on a Paul Blair solo clout. Bunker allowed Johnson to go 2-for-4. Wills, Parker, Fairly, and Tommy Davis in a pinch-hitting role each got a hit.

The Orioles only got three hits off Osteen, including Blair's blast— Powell hit a one-out single in the bottom of the second, Aparicio led off the Orioles' fourth with a single.

This second shutout for the Birds marked 24 innings since a Dodger had crossed home plate. Bunker's complete-game effort yielded six strikeouts.

Osteen was gracious toward his counterpart and Blair. "Yes, that's the breaks of the game, but when a guy outpitches you, he deserves to win."[18]

Bunker's performance would have been recognizable in 1964, when he led the majors with a .792 winning percentage. His record was 19–5 with 29 games started and 12 complete games. In 1966, he went 10–6 but threw three complete games in 24 starts.

Bauer compared the Orioles' success to their performance during the summer, when they dominated their competition. In June, they went 25–8. Their July record was 19–10. Still, Bauer was hesitant to predict an outcome, preferring to stay calm but positive. "There's a possibility it might only go four. I'd have to say I'm a little bit encouraged, more than I was when this thing started."[19]

—∞∞∞—

## WORLD SERIES, GAME FOUR (MEMORIAL STADIUM, OCTOBER 9)
Four was the magic number.

Dave McNally and Don Drysdale each hurled a four-hitter in Game Four.

In storybook fashion, Frank Robinson, who Reds management had intimated was over the hill, banged a one-out home run in the bottom of the fourth to win the game and the Series for the Orioles.

The Dodgers had been in the postseason 10 of the last 20 seasons and won two of the last three World Series. The Orioles had a solid team, but it didn't seem possible that they could sweep the Dodgers, much less record three shutouts. Devastated, they were on the other side of dominance. "Suddenly it was all over," said catcher John Roseboro. "We sat in the dressing room thinking about how the Yankees must have felt when we won the World Series four straight from them. Again, I can't say we choked. The team hadn't choked in the tough fight for the pennant. Our lack of attack caught up to us. Our pitching could have gotten us back into it, but you can't win when you are shut out over three straight games."[20]

Indeed, Baltimore's pitching staff was the cornerstone of the championship team, nicknamed the "Baby Birds" for their youth. Dave McNally was three weeks shy of his 24th birthday. Wally Bunker was 21. At 20, Jim Palmer wasn't even old enough to vote—his birthday is October 15. Thirty-one-year-old Moe Drabowsky was the veteran.

Also dubbed the "Kiddie Korps" by the press, the Orioles surprised baseball's self-aggrandizing pundits, armchair experts, and beer-swilling barflies predicting another championship for Southern California.

McNally corrected those who believed the pitching staff to be subpar, at least compared to their competition. "Sure our staff lacked complete games during the season, but we could have finished a lot of those games," argued the star hurler. "Hank continually went to the bullpen when we had a three or four-run lead in the middle innings. You can't blame him. We have a great bullpen. But it was wrongly interpreted that the starters weren't good."[21]

There was a bit of sweet revenge for the man dubbed too old by his former employer.

"I wanted to have a good year especially to show the people in the front office there that I wasn't washed up, and I wanted to show them by having a good year," said the slugger who bashed 49 home runs to lead the majors and batted an AL-leading .316.

"And I wanted to show the people, the officials, the City of Baltimore they were getting a guy who still could play baseball."[22]

Message received. Mission accomplished.

Willie Davis had a redemption of sorts too. After Robinson's one-out bash, Brooks Robinson grounded to third baseman John Kennedy for the second out. Powell came to the plate, and the hefty slugger crushed a ball toward the other side of Memorial Stadium's center-field fence. Davis timed a jump to snare the ball.

Baltimore's victory was not secure with a one-run margin going into the ninth. LA rebounded. Alston plucked Al Ferrara from the Dodgers bench to pinch-hit for Drysdale; Ferrara singled, then got pulled for pinch-runner Nate Oliver. Orioles fans could hear their hearts beat as McNally walked Wills.

It was a tense and fearful moment for the city as Willie Davis strode to the plate. Batting .284 in 1966, Davis had the skill to punch a hit and score Ferrara. With the count 1–1, McNally tossed a slow curve; Davis smacked a line drive to Robinson in right field.

A sigh of relief could be heard among the Orioles fans, who dominated the Memorial Stadium crowd of 54,458. Up next, Lou Johnson. Dodgers radio announcer Vin Scully described the scene: "And as Johnson comes up to the plate, [Orioles pitching coach] Harry Brecheen goes walking out to the [mound] to make sure number one McNally remembers how to pitch to him and also to make sure he has enough left. Whatever Brecheen asked McNally, he nods yes."[23]

Johnson got into his batting stance; McNally did the same for his pitching posture. Scoreless, LA faced the ominous thought of being swept by the O's and suffering a third straight shutout. "You talk about a hungry ball club," said Scully. "They are down to their last bite."

As if on cue, the sun started to come out. McNally got a strike on Johnson, who swung at the pitch "breaking down and away." Another swing and miss on a breaking ball followed. Strike two. The third swing connected, sending the ball to right-center field where Paul Blair felt it settle into his glove's webbing as if it were a bird returning to the nest.

Blair's catch ended the game and set off a volcanic eruption of joy on 33rd Street. "I thought all the way, hurry up and get here," exclaimed Blair after the game.

McNally attributed his success to his curve ball and fast ball.

Bauer revealed that he thought about using a relief pitcher for the first time when Johnson came to bat. "I was a little afraid of Johnson, and Cat went out and asked him how he felt and said [he was alright]. We went to breaking balls with Johnson. I think if he would have got on base, I'd have brought in Stu Miller to pitch to Tommy Davis."[24]

Robinson's game-winning home run capped a wonderful season, marked by winning the Triple Crown—leading the AL in home runs, RBIs, and batting average. His 49 round-trippers topped the majors. He also won the World Series MVP Award.

For Orioles batboy Bob Scherr, being a part of this magical season on a day-to-day basis for home games gave him the best vantage point in Memorial Stadium for Frank Robinson's power, Brooks Robinson's fielding, and Hank Bauer's management of a young but exemplary ball club. He went to LA for the first two games at Dodger Stadium. "The whole thing stands out because when we got on the plane at Baltimore, there were thousands of fans sending us off," recalled Scherr.

We flew home, and we didn't get home till 1:00 A.M. Again, thousands of fans were at the airport.

In LA, 10 players and I were in the audience at Bob Hope's TV show. He acknowledged us and had us stand up. When we got to LA, we were greeted by Gene Autry. He owned the hotel where we stayed.

But probably the biggest experience was a joke that the Orioles played on me. Eddie Watt said that he went to school with Ann-Margret in Idaho and got her tickets to one of the games. Back then, she was a couple of years older than me and single. We're on the team bus to Dodger Stadium for the first game, and Eddie says, "I should fix Bobby up with Ann-Margret." They're all cheering, "Yeah, fix him up!" I'm 17, so this becomes more important than the game.

We're on the field for batting practice when Eddie comes up to me and points out Ann in the stands. He says that he's going down there to say hello. He was talking to a woman, but I was vain and refused to wear my glasses, so I couldn't see if it was Ann-Margret. They both wave to me. It turns out, they were kidding.

There were other celebrities. I met Milton Berle, Frank Sinatra, and Mia Farrow. They were in the stands right behind me.[25]

---

Baltimore's upset proved that mighty teams are fallible, as are so-called experts who offer proclamations with self-righteousness. Doubters were quieted. Naysayers were silenced. There was a respect, grudging in some quarters, given to this group of players who had slain giants on baseball's biggest platform.

But at least one member of the Los Angeles press had a different take. Melvin Durslag of the *Herald Examiner* posited that the Dodgers should get credited with losing the World Series rather than the Orioles winning it. The team's exhaustion preceding the World Series had no impact on the scribe.

Indeed, Durslag made a declaration that Ebenezer Scrooge might have made if he were a sportswriter before three ghosts showed him the impact of a life without comportment, generosity, and respect. "But dispensing with all the proprieties, we are here to announce that the watery performance of Los Angeles in the World Series was totally repulsive and must take its place among the all-time pratfalls of sports."

It's a brutal take.

True, the Orioles held the Dodgers to a measly .142 batting average. But the O's batted .200. Blair's blast was his only hit in six at-bats; Curt

Blefary batted .255 during the year but went 1-for-13 against the Dodgers. Etchebarren's contributions were more significant on defense—he had a .221 average in '66, but his World Series output was .083.

Baltimore was not a dominant club. But that didn't matter.

Despite the carrying-on of Durslag and other pundits who thought the AL champs had pitchers who were good but not great and hitters who were proficient but not fearsome, the fact remained that the Orioles played good baseball. After the loss, Drysdale acknowledged the AL squad's talent: "They didn't make any mistakes, not one. It's just one of those things. They had the pitching, hitting and defense when it counted, and we didn't."[26]

Durslag and other detractors also ignored the highly significant factor of exhaustion. The Dodgers captured the NL flag on the last day of the

Maury Wills steals second base in Game Four of the 1966 World Series. It was one of the few bright moments for the Los Angeles Dodgers, who got swept by the Baltimore Orioles in four games. During the offseason, the Dodgers traded Wills to the Pirates. COURTESY OF LOS ANGELES HERALD EXAMINER COLLECTION/LOS ANGELES PUBLIC LIBRARY

season. Wes Parker recalled, "We had to play a doubleheader on Sunday because of a rainout on Saturday. Drysdale pitched, so it surprised me that Alston started him on two days' rest in Game One of the World Series."[27]

Eddie Watt, a rookie pitcher who went 9–7 for the Orioles in '66, credits Hank Bauer and a hands-off approach of managing. "Bauer never interfered," says Watt of the skipper who was wounded twice in the Pacific Theater during World War II. "He never asked you to do something that you couldn't do. He respected everyone unless you were a wiseass young kid, if you conducted yourself as a professional, as someone who belonged in the big leagues and could play without harming the ball club."[28]

Frank Robinson winning the Triple Crown Award in 1966 made it appropriate, perhaps even poetic, that his solo home run provided the slim but sufficient one-run margin to beat the Dodgers.

Frank Robinson belts a solo home run in Game Four of the 1966 World Series to give the Orioles a 1–0 victory and a sweep of the Dodgers. In 1966, Robinson won the Triple Crown, American League MVP Award, and World Series MVP Award.
COURTESY OF LOS ANGELES HERALD EXAMINER COLLECTION/LOS ANGELES PUBLIC LIBRARY

Jim Gates was the head librarian at the National Baseball Hall of Fame and Museum for more than 20 years, which often put him in the company of the game's elite players who visited for Hall of Fame inductions, either as honorees or supporters. One of those players was Paul Blair.

A lifelong Orioles fan, Gates got an inside view from one of his heroes.

> I had a nice dinner talk with Paul Blair many years ago, and he said that was the one thing that changed. He said that going into spring training, the team thought they were good and had a chance for the pennant. However, after the first 15 minutes of Frank Robinson entering the clubhouse, everyone was convinced that they were going to crush the opposition and take the pennant. It was that simple. His impact was immediate. He convinced everyone and provided the confidence needed.
>
> As a fan, although I was very hopeful that the Orioles could win, this was their first World Series, and the Dodgers were the more experienced postseason team. As such, I had no illusions of winning the championship, but after the Orioles took the first two games, I became very optimistic and realized that the O's could do it.[29]

For Pacific Palisades native and lifelong Dodgers fan James Nahigian, the World Series loss was devastating.

> It was one of the major disappointments in my life for the Dodgers to be as good as they were and have the best pitching staff ever assembled, but lose like that. But there was the biggest thrill in how we watched the series.
>
> At Palisades Elementary School, Dr. Donald Macri was the coolest teacher in fifth grade. He brought his own TV in. This was unprecedented for the kids. He would let us watch some of the game. At recess and lunch, he came out with a radio and sat with the boys at the lunch table.

The next day, you're hoping they rebound for Game Two. But that became wishful thinking. The Dodgers just didn't hit. To me, the biggest disappointment was Koufax not getting it done in Game Two. It was tragic having to watch that game and Willie Davis's three errors. I just remember the major disappointment was the Dodgers couldn't score.[30]

For 13-year-old Bob Trostler, conversations with his fellow students at John Muir Junior High School in Burbank reflected the conventional wisdom that the Dodgers would win the World Series. Easily.

Going into the '66 World Series, it seemed that everybody in LA thought the Dodgers would blow the Orioles out of the water. They had an outstanding record, but we thought the NL was a superior league. I felt embarrassed by the Dodgers' performance.

There was no doubt in my mind that when the World Series was over, the Orioles were the better team.

I was stunned at how inept the Dodgers were at the plate. What the hell happened to these guys? It was just horrible. Still is.[31]

For 16-year-old Gregg Pericich, a student at Fermin Lasuen, a Catholic high school, there was an abundance of newspapers in Southern California, allowing the San Pedro teenager to absorb news about the Dodgers: *Los Angeles Times*, *Los Angeles Herald Examiner*, *San Pedro News-Pilot*, *Long Beach Press-Telegram*, *Hollywood Citizen-News*.

I bought the *Times* at Busy Bee Market, which was on Walker Avenue, between 24th Street and 25th Street. There were newspaper stands out front. I usually read the front page on the way home and devoured the sports page over breakfast.

My first game at Dodger Stadium was the team's first home game in 1962. Back then, you dressed up to go to the games. You didn't have the paraphernalia that they have now. Maybe buttons and hats.

I was surprised the Dodgers got swept. To see them lose four games to Baltimore was tough. But we swept the Yankees in 1963. By 1966, the Yankees had fallen apart. My favorite Dodgers were Sandy Koufax, Tommy Davis, and Lou Johnson. It was good to see Johnson come up after so many years in the minor leagues.

Being a Dodger fan in that World Series, you had a lot of disappointment.[32]

⸺◦∞◦⸺

Baltimore's victory was unexpected. A sweep, unthinkable. The Dodgers were about to suffer another seismic loss as California faced an upheaval on the political front.

# CHAPTER ELEVEN

# Splashdown (November)

RONALD REAGAN LOOKED LIKE A LEADER.

The 55-year-old actor followed a tradition of performance embedded in politics, perhaps beginning with Cicero, the Roman statesman prized as a stellar orator during Julius Caesar's reign. With a leading-man pedigree in his movie career, Reagan knew how to project an image of authority. He had the assets of knowledge, both innate and honed. When to pause. Which words to emphasize. How to position his body and moderate his vocal intonations.

To the extent that politics is theatrical, he proved it with a landslide gubernatorial victory against Governor Pat Brown on November 8, 1966.

Brown had aimed for a third consecutive term as California's governor. Disappointment pervaded the Embassy Room in LA's Ambassador Hotel, where the governor's supporters had gathered in anticipation of a triumph. The *Los Angeles Herald Examiner* reported that Reagan had outpaced Brown by nearly 560,000 votes when the concession call was made. Following the paradigm of urging the losing party to move forward, the Democratic state chairman said that the aim should be to "begin now to rebuild for the future."[1]

Reagan and Brown had spoken at the Pacific Gas & Electric Company Auditorium in San Francisco a few days before the election. It defined the policy and image differences between the candidates. Brown came across as a scowling high-school principal. The governor's approach gave the attendees questions to ask themselves in a rather general, vague manner. A solid strategy, it aimed at minimizing Reagan's gravitas and

Ronald and Nancy Reagan celebrate on Election Night 1966. Reagan, a former actor, defeated California governor Pat Brown with more than 57 percent of the vote. Reagan served two terms as governor and later won two presidential elections. COURTESY OF NATIONAL ARCHIVES

potential. "What has Ronald Reagan ever done for the state of California in his entire life other than make a motion picture? *Bedtime for Bonzo*, or *Ladies on Probation*, or *The Last Stand of Custer*?"[2]

Moreover, Brown inquired about Reagan's plans should he win. Looking and sounding like an optimistic, challenging, and disciplined football coach, Reagan responded. Forcefully.

"I'm quite sure that perhaps I'll make mistakes in that office," said the first-time candidate.

> But they'll be the mistakes that you can understand. They'll be the mistakes of trying to improve efficiency and productivity, trying to cut overhead and waste and streamline and put modern business practices into the running of this government.

I'll go out and try and I'll bludgeon companies like your own to try and get even on a leave of absence basis. Men and women who are qualified to come in and take over some of the administrative positions.

And some of the administrative positions I just won't go out and get anyone for because I don't think they're necessary. They were created as rewards for political favors and we're not going to give that kind of reward.

Partisanship is going to end on November eighth if we're elected. And we're going to set up a government for all of the people.

I know that many of you are Democrats and I offer to you a government not based on any narrow partisan concept, but a government that's based on the idea of all of the people of this state having a voice in their own destiny. Some control in running their own affairs. Yes, and in spending their own money because I believe we can have economy in government if we have a governor who believes in economy and who believes that costs can be cut.[3]

Reagan hardly went from acting into politics willy-nilly. His political beliefs about smaller government, a stronger military, and lower taxes had formed his lodestar.

To leverage his position as host of *General Electric Theater*, a drama anthology TV show on CBS in the 1950s, the sponsor tapped Reagan to give motivational speeches to GE employees. There were hints of conservative messaging, including the endorsement of business and free markets. Medicare's emergence as a viable plan in the early 1960s led Reagan to join forces with the American Medical Association and record a message highlighting the socialist tenets of the landmark health insurance legislation that Congress eventually passed in 1965.

Reagan had gained a national spotlight on his political heft with the speech "A Time for Choosing" endorsing 1964 GOP presidential candidate Barry Goldwater. Even though Goldwater lost to Lyndon Johnson, the speech solidified Reagan as a substantial political figure on the right.

Plus, fellow actor and Republican George Murphy had been elected as a U.S. senator from California in 1964, which gave bona fides indirectly to Reagan and other entertainers pursuing politics beyond campaigning and fund-raising for candidates.

The victory continued the momentum that the Reagan team had ignited in June when it secured the Republican nomination with a devastating defeat of San Francisco mayor George Christopher.

Former vice president Richard Nixon, who Brown had defeated four years earlier, forecast the victory and blamed Brown's strategy of labeling the Reagan philosophy as extremist: "I certainly won't fault Mr. Reagan on his campaign strategy because from all the reports that I have received, the question which is left in California now is the size of the Reagan majority when he wins and the number of the candidates at the state level who will win."[4]

Reagan's victory contrasted with the social disruption taking place across the country, particularly in the Golden State. He benefited from his stances that might have seemed staid for younger voters, but appealed to their parents who wanted the peace and prosperity attached to the Eisenhower presidency of the 1950s.

Reagan represented an antidote for Californians looking for an alternative to the progressive movement that might have been steeped in noble causes, such as equal justice, but often led to violent acts.

California's changing demographics provided fodder for Reagan, who targeted disappointed voters. Some weren't even Republican. "After two postwar decades of prosperity and high employment, most White voters no longer regarded government as an economic saviour," explained Reagan biographer Iwan Morgan. "Instead they wanted it to preserve societal order in the face of urban crime, student protest, counter-cultural lifestyles on University of California campuses, and ghetto unrest."[5]

Such was the strength of his appeal to Republicans and their opposition to the ideals of President Johnson's "Great Society" programs—which Reagan deemed as bordering if not balancing on socialism—that questions arose immediately about potential abandonment of the governor's mansion for a presidential campaign in two years.

Reagan's victory indicated a growing strength for Republicans across the country.

In Massachusetts, Edward Brooke became the first Black candidate elected to the Senate in almost 100 years. It had been the same time frame for a Republican getting elected to the governorship in Arkansas. Winthrop Rockefeller did it while his brother, New York's governor Nelson Rockefeller, gained a second term in Albany. Future vice president Spiro Agnew became Maryland's chief executive.[6]

Refusing to commit himself one way or the other after his victory in '66, a hallmark of potential but unconfirmed candidates in presidential politics, Reagan promised nothing but his service to the Republican Party. "It's a theoretical question because it leads into the area of the strategy of politics," said the former Warner Bros. star. "What the situation will be two years hence no one knows. It is possible that there could be circumstances that would lead that way simply to avoid, say, a devisive [sic] struggle—for the good of the party and the good of the people."[7]

Reagan's eight-year tenure in Sacramento was a time of massive national strife.

Vietnam War protests. Riots. The assassinations of Robert F. Kennedy and Martin Luther King Jr. The Kent State University protest where four students were killed by Ohio National Guardsmen. Managing the incredible responsibility of an increasingly complex political, social, and financial state during this time gave Reagan the credibility needed to move forward with his political agenda in Sacramento and a career beyond it.

Reagan won the 1980 and 1984 presidential elections.

A week after Reagan's victory in California, NASA celebrated its latest achievement.

When the capsule housing Jim Lovell and Buzz Aldrin smacked against the waves of the Atlantic Ocean 700 miles from Florida's Cape Kennedy on November 15, 1966, Project Gemini ended. It was a textbook finish to NASA's fifth Gemini flight of 1966, reportedly within four miles of its target area.

Jim Lovell and Buzz Aldrin go over the mission plan for *Gemini 12*. It was Lovell's second flight and Aldrin's first. Aldrin had three "space walks" on his rookie flight.
COURTESY OF NASA

Lovell and Aldrin extended the roster of NASA's successes with their four-day flight, gaining knowledge that they could hand to engineers and fellow astronauts for the Apollo missions and moon landings. There was an immense amount of information for NASA's staff to analyze thanks to the designs and executions of Project Gemini's missions and the one-man flights preceding them in Project Mercury.

NASA's Manned Spacecraft Center director, Dr. Robert Gilruth, explained Gemini's importance as he ticked off the list of topics they needed to master. "To go to the moon, we had to learn to operate in space. We had to learn how to maneuver with . . . precision, rendezvous, dock, light off large propulsion systems in space, and work outside the spacecraft in the hard vacuum of outer space. . . . We had to learn how man could go for long durations in the weightless environment and we had to learn how one made precise landings from orbit. This is where the Gemini program came in."[8]

One immensely bright spot was the space walk. NASA added footholds and handholds to the space capsule's exterior, which made it easier for Aldrin to maneuver during his three excursions. An adjustment in astronaut training became a key factor in the success as well. Aldrin committed to underwater training, which included maneuvering in his space suit to simulate the environment of working outside the craft.

One of Aldrin's three space walks lasted a little more than two hours, earning the accolade "milestone accomplishment" from Gilruth.[9] Aldrin set a new record—no astronaut had three space walks on one flight before him.

Aldrin was a pioneer before getting into space. Part of the third group of NASA astronauts—also known as "the Fourteen"—Aldrin was the first to have a doctoral degree in his credentials. His doctorate of science in astronautics from MIT rested on top of 66 combat missions during the Korean War as an air force pilot and a BS in engineering from West Point.

Lovell was a navy man.

He didn't make it through the selection process for the initial group of astronauts known as the Mercury Seven; NASA sidelined him because of a minor liver problem and excess bilirubin. The Mercury medical team had included an examination described by Lovell as treating the prospective astronauts like guinea pigs with a "physical [that] was nothing like anybody had ever heard of before."

In a 1999 oral history compiled for NASA, Lovell recalled,

> Well, I got back to the squadron. Got transferred down to Oceana [Virginia]. And I was going through, you know, training people at this time. I was an instructor. And in *Aviation Week*, there was a little article: "NASA Wants To Select Some More Astronauts." And so, before I knew it, the Navy called me down again and said, "Do you want to be in another selection?" They didn't know that I was kicked out because of a physical. And I said, "Sure." And so, I put my name in again, and I was selected to—again to go for the physical. This time at Brooks Air Force

Base [Texas]. Air Force physical. Much more practical. Much more, you know, looking at what's wrong and what's right. And I had no problems passing it.[10]

Lovell was in the second group of astronauts, which NASA labeled the New Nine.

The week after they splashed down, Lovell and Aldrin met with President Johnson at his ranch in Texas for a ceremony honoring the duo and other notables in space and aviation. It was a glorious moment for the 36th president, who had used his considerable political weight when he was Senate majority leader to help President Eisenhower create NASA in the wake of Russia's launching the first satellite in 1957. *Sputnik 1*. As vice president, Johnson had also been the liaison between the space program and President Kennedy.[11]

There was optimism in the air. A couple of weeks before the launch, Dr. Edward Teller, the famed atomic scientist who had worked on the Manhattan Project and developed the hydrogen bomb, said that America would have manned moon landings "within two years." But he said that the Space Race with Russia was not the underlying issue. It was critical to stay on the moon and use it as a way station for a launch to Mars.[12]

To use a baseball analogy, *Gemini 12* was the latest victory in a massive winning streak. Johnson warned that the upcoming Apollo missions would have more dangers; optimists, in his view, needed to take a beat and balance their outlook with caution. A prime reason: the Saturn booster rockets. These were bigger than the counterparts—Agena, Titan, and Atlas—used in Project Mercury and Project Gemini.

Johnson noted, "The Apollo program which follows is much more complicated. It has more elements of as yet unproven capability. And it will use the larger Saturn boosters developed especially for our civilian manned flight program.

"The months ahead will not be easy as we reach toward the moon. We must broaden and extend our know-how on the increased power of these mighty new boosters. But with Gemini as the forerunner, I am confident that we will overcome the difficulties and achieve another success."[13]

Aeronautics scored another milestone on November 18 when the X-15 rocket plane piloted by Air Force major William J. Knight broke a speed record—4,159 miles an hour.[14]

*Gemini 12* turned a major corner for NASA. A *Washington Post* editorial praised the global impact of America's leadership in space exploration and foreshadowed the words that Neil Armstrong uttered on July 20, 1969, when he became the first man to walk on the moon. "But this is not a triumph for Americans alone. It is one of those historic triumphs for mankind."

Although the thought of a flag bearing a hammer and sickle planted on the moon was unthinkable to many Americans and their freedom-loving allies, the editorial further emphasized that scientific pursuits, knowledge, and accomplishments cross political, social, and economic boundaries. It would be great to have astronauts placing Old Glory on the surface of the natural satellite that has mystified earthlings for thousands of years. But that was exactly the point that the *Post* editorial made: "[The] glories of each people are the glories of all."[15]

In the *New York Times*, an editorial coinciding with the launch of *Gemini 12* lauded the achievements of Project Gemini and *Lunar Orbiter 2*. While respectfully acknowledging "the important Soviet contributions" in space exploration, it highlighted America's research as responsible for "most of what men now know about the moon and about the possibilities and problems of manned space flight." NASA's successes caused Russia's decrease in manned missions, according to the *Times*.[16]

With their successes in *Gemini 12*, Lovell and Aldrin prompted a new round of conversations about the space race and boosted the national confidence that Americans were winning it. Russia hadn't sent a cosmonaut into space since Pavel Belyayev in March 1965.

---

Talk about current events at America's upcoming Thanksgiving dinners would likely be populated by space-related conversations. Kids rejoiced at their heroes' accomplishments but had another outlet to complement the TV coverage and newspaper stories. Literature further empowered their dreams of being space voyagers and following the path of Aldrin, Lovell, et al.

Science fiction flourished in the 1960s because of the achievements in the "new ocean," as President Kennedy had described it. Robert A. Heinlein was a legendary author in the field; *The Moon Is a Harsh Mistress* debuted in 1966 and delighted sci-fi fans. But Heinlein's literary contributions went beyond storytelling. He changed the business of the genre.

John Tilden, president of the Heinlein Society, explained,

Heinlein was the first sci-fi author to go mainstream. He was the first grand master among science-fiction writers and one of the few that had military experience. Heinlein had served in the navy but was discharged because he contracted tuberculosis aboard a ship. He was glad to have served his country, but his medical pension was small and he needed something to pay the bills.

He was an engineer by trade. Even after starting his writing, he really wanted to contribute in World War II, so he worked in the Philadelphia Naval Yards as an engineer. We think he contributed to plastics research—formulating canopies for planes. His knowledge about the world informed his writing later on. There was an authenticity in his stories. If he gave you a trajectory or an orbit, the math worked.

Heinlein thought that he could write to make a living, so he pursued it. When he started to get the sales coming in for that, he didn't really have any other career. He had his strong views, and as the decades went on, the culture changed around him. In his early adult years, he was a left-leaning Democrat. He ran for California State Assembly unsuccessfully in 1938. Some of his views went into his speculative fiction, like the concepts of freedom, equality, and personal responsibility.

He said that three of his biggest books are on the subjects of freedom and personal responsibility—*The Moon Is a Harsh Mistress*, *Stranger in a Strange Land*, and *Starship Troopers*. That's why people find him appealing. There's a thread there about pulling yourself up by your bootstraps. Those themes resonated with a lot of people.

Heinlein's oft-mentioned peers were Isaac Asimov and Arthur C. Clarke. They are known in the science-fiction community as the "Big Three." I would put Ray Bradbury in there as well-deserving to be mentioned. If you look at the *Apollo 11* moon landing, CBS had Heinlein and Clarke as commentators. Clarke was quick to take credit for being a visionary. Heinlein was just excited it was finally happening.

The Big Three captured that zeitgeist of the country's fascination with space exploration. But there's an important high ground to the moon, politically speaking. You look at the commercialization of space in recent years with Elon Musk and Jeff Bezos. Heinlein's works inspired that theme. He said that we have to fund space exploration even if we have to do it ourselves. He still resonates.

Kids who were 10–15 in the 1950s wound up being engineers in the space program, inspired by the space stories written by Heinlein. The same dynamic happened with kids in the 1960s.[17]

Velocities and vectors of spacecraft, real and fictional, fascinated America's future space scientists. So did velocities and vectors of baseballs for Little Leaguers, especially those thrown by Sandy Koufax. They earned idolatry for the left-handed Brooklyn native who announced his retirement on November 18, 1966.

Koufax's declaration ignited an abundance of eulogies for a career that astonished foes and friends alike. Dodgers owner Walter O'Malley wondered aloud if Koufax would have broken more baseball records had he stayed. Cubs skipper Leo Durocher—a Dodgers coach during Koufax's tenure—mourned the Dodgers' chances to win another National League flag without their star southpaw. But the pitcher's manner attracted praise as well. Astros owner Roy Hofheinz emphasized, "We all admired Sandy's ability, courage, competitive heart and fine conduct on and off the field. He was a great tribute to our national pastime."[18]

Pitching was a grueling task for Koufax, who often soaked his left arm in ice after a game. And that was just part of his routine to maintain

his superiority. It would have felled a lesser man; Koufax was not super-human, but his stamina was stronger than most of his brethren.

Just five weeks shy of his 32nd birthday, he divulged the rationale at his press conference. "I'll tell you what made up my mind. Fifteen or 18 cortisone shots made up my mind, along with an upset stomach from taking medication and being half high out there on the mound because of pain pills."[19]

Further pitching efforts could exacerbate an already exhausted left arm. The risk was considerable. The Dodgers front office now had an impossible challenge—find a suitable hurler in the massive void. Dodgers general manager Buzzie Bavasi responded to this dilemma with the humor of a Borscht Belt comedian complemented by a dash of defeatism: "We are in the market for a Jewish lefthander who has arthritis and has pitched four no-hitters."[20]

Koufax had been a major-league pitcher since 1955, the year that the Dodgers secured their first World Series title in Brooklyn. But his excellence had not emerged until 1961, when he led the majors with 269 strikeouts.

In his last season, Koufax had the highest number of wins in his career—27—and topped the majors in that category as well as ERA, innings pitched, strikeouts, and games started.[21] His 317 strikeouts far outpaced Jim Bunning, who occupied the number-two slot with 252.

It capped a five-season run when he led the NL in ERA five times. The major leagues, thrice. During this stretch, he also led the majors in strikeouts four times.

So, the announcement from the lefty who set new standards of excellence, particularly in his final season, came as a disappointment, if not a shock, to baseball followers. All except his teammates. They knew the pain that Koufax was in and the incredible endurance required to prepare for a game and maintain his elbow after it. Koufax was not simply irreplaceable for his talent. His mental endurance was peerless. Still, his absence inspired a few tears. "He may have been the greatest of all time," said Dodgers manager Walter Alston. "I can't comment about those great pitchers before my time. . . . He not only had the stuff but the competitive spirit as well."[22]

his superiority. It would have felled a lesser man; Koufax was not super-human, but his stamina was stronger than most of his brethren.

Just five weeks shy of his 32nd birthday, he divulged the rationale at his press conference. "I'll tell you what made up my mind. Fifteen or 18 cortisone shots made up my mind, along with an upset stomach from taking medication and being half high out there on the mound because of pain pills."[19]

Further pitching efforts could exacerbate an already exhausted left arm. The risk was considerable. The Dodgers front office now had an impossible challenge—find a suitable hurler in the massive void. Dodgers general manager Buzzie Bavasi responded to this dilemma with the humor of a Borscht Belt comedian complemented by a dash of defeatism: "We are in the market for a Jewish lefthander who has arthritis and has pitched four no-hitters."[20]

Koufax had been a major-league pitcher since 1955, the year that the Dodgers secured their first World Series title in Brooklyn. But his excellence had not emerged until 1961, when he led the majors with 269 strikeouts.

In his last season, Koufax had the highest number of wins in his career—27—and topped the majors in that category as well as ERA, innings pitched, strikeouts, and games started.[21] His 317 strikeouts far outpaced Jim Bunning, who occupied the number-two slot with 252.

It capped a five-season run when he led the NL in ERA five times. The major leagues, thrice. During this stretch, he also led the majors in strikeouts four times.

So, the announcement from the lefty who set new standards of excellence, particularly in his final season, came as a disappointment, if not a shock, to baseball followers. All except his teammates. They knew the pain that Koufax was in and the incredible endurance required to prepare for a game and maintain his elbow after it. Koufax was not simply irreplaceable for his talent. His mental endurance was peerless. Still, his absence inspired a few tears. "He may have been the greatest of all time," said Dodgers manager Walter Alston. "I can't comment about those great pitchers before my time. . . . He not only had the stuff but the competitive spirit as well."[22]

By the time I got to the Dodgers as a rookie in 1964, everything had come together for Sandy. Most people remember him as throwing hard, but he had probably the best curveball I've ever seen. It was sensational. I had to learn a new way to catch, so I moved closer to the batters. That's an uncomfortable feeling because you could get hit with the bat on the swing or the backswing.

He had two ways of throwing the curve. If he was behind in the count, he wouldn't throw it as hard. The other was a two-strike pitch that he did throw hard.

One of the things that I learned early catching Sandy was where to sit. He wanted me to sit in the middle to see if he could pitch it there. Then I moved to the corners. When I got to the Angels and worked with Nolan Ryan, I told him what I learned from Sandy and Don about how to approach a hitter and the count. We always tried to get strike one on a down-and-away pitch.

We had a great team in the mid-1960s. Maury Wills was such an intense player. He was a great captain. We had a series against the Braves in 1965 at County Stadium when Maury got picked off. Joe Torre was playing first base. Joe blocked him off, and he was out. Maury came back to the dugout and he was in tears. He felt like he let the team down. County Stadium had a long walkway from the clubhouse to the field. He's running up and down the ramp. He says, "I'll never get picked off first base again like that." He tried again and cut Torre's pants off.

When Maury got back to the dugout after doing something great, he would look at everyone who congratulated him and thank them individually. He would comment that he appreciated it. He was very special.[25]

Koufax's announcement came a couple of days after his teammates concluded a goodwill tour of Japan with a 9–8–1 record against Japanese teams. Koufax and Drysdale did not go. Neither did Bill Singer or Don Sutton, who was in the army. Wills complained of a bad knee and left the trip early.[26]

It was a major controversy. Wills maintained that he was only supposed to play a few innings—three maximum—so he could nurse and exercise his right knee. But Alston kept Wills in the first game into the ninth inning until the ace baserunner asked to be replaced. Wills played in the second game and requested a reprieve in the eighth inning. In the third game, Wills's "right leg buckled and twisted as [he] rounded third base."

Wills had injured his right leg at the end of spring training. His output showed how the injury and other maladies in the '66 campaign stifled him. Although Wills was an everyday player with 143 games, he went from leading the majors in '65 with 94 stolen bases to 38 thieveries in '66.

He told the *Los Angeles Herald Examiner* in an exclusive interview that his conscience was clear. It appeared in the November 11 edition of the paper. "I regret nothing I've done," said Wills. "I chose the lesser of two evils, to leave and get ready for 1967 or stay and wreck my entire future."

A phone call to O'Malley interrupted a party at the Dodgers owner's abode with a guest list including Major League Baseball commissioner William Eckert. Wills disclosed that his departure from Japan created tension with the front office. "Mr. O'Malley obviously did not like what I said, and told me very firmly and precisely that he would not permit my departure, that he expected more of me than this."[27]

If there was any doubt that Wills gave a 100 percent effort, *Herald Examiner* scribe Bob Hunter dispelled it: "I have seen his right thigh absolutely raw, with half-dollar size chunks of skin actually pulled out in a nightly ritual when yards of adhesive tape had to be removed."[28]

Gossipers debated about whether O'Malley would jettison his 34-year-old speedster. Dodgers general manager Buzzie Bavasi attempted to pacify the fan base six days after the *Herald Examiner*'s exclusive and maintained that both sides had reason to be disturbed by the situation. But he also emphasized that he was "bothered" by Wills taking refuge in Honolulu rather than coming back to LA to get treated. Wills did it to avoid the press.

Bavasi was in the middle of this mess. Wills was a beloved Dodger. It was growing to be a public-relations disaster, but he signaled the sobriety of Wills's actions, despite the intention to protect his viability for '67. "He has jeopardized himself in the eyes of the ownership of the club, that is apparent."[29]

Nearly two weeks later, what had begun as simmering tensions increased to a boil.

The baserunner who had set a record in 1962 with 104 stolen bases, who had led the NL in that category six consecutive seasons and the major leagues three seasons, who had inspired Dodger Stadium crowds to chant "Go! Go! Go!" when he was on base, and who had inspired kids to be his avatar in Little League games and backyard Wiffle ball contests found himself stranded. Dodgers management made him available to other teams.

Except for one season, Wills had been with the Dodgers organization since 1951, when he was an 18-year-old rookie with the Hornell club in the Pennsylvania–Ontario–New York (PONY) League. He was promoted to LA from the Dodgers' PCL club in Spokane in June 1959.

Wills preferred to go to the Angels, a natural fit for a player already synonymous with baseball in Southern California. But he also posited that retirement could be alluring.[30]

Other news increased worries in the environs of Chavez Ravine. The Dodgers traded Tommy Davis to the Mets. Davis, MLB's leading batsman for average in 1962 and 1963, went with Derrell Griffith for Ron Hunt and Jim Hickman.

Carol Davis added a bit of levity regarding her husband's situation when she proclaimed, "Tell the people Tommy didn't leave Japan, that he stayed there all the time."[31]

The nucleus of a great team was fractured. Irreparably. An iconic pitcher retired. A solid batsman headed to a NL foe. An aging though formidable baserunner would likely exit as well, taking with him institutional knowledge of how to evade pickoff moves from opposing pitchers and beat catchers' throws throughout the NL.

It was a tough time to be a Dodgers fan.

CHAPTER TWELVE

# Joy to the World (December)

It's said that a picture is worth a thousand words. But when Americans saw the latest photographs of the moon in the December 1 editions of the *Reno Evening Gazette, Couer d'Alene Press, Peoria Journal Star, Decatur Daily, Gettysburg Times*, and hundreds of other newspapers, they were likely speechless.

The Crater of Copernicus photos were part of NASA's reconnaissance mission to find a site for the first moon landing. It's situated in the Sea of Storms and named after the 16th-century astronomer Nicolaus Copernicus, who posited that the universe was heliocentric—planets revolved around the sun. It was a radical departure from the accepted view that Earth occupies the universe's center.

There was a new chapter to be explored in the theories about the genesis and evolution of the moon revealed by the photographs of the crater, belonging to a category described as "rayed" and having an estimated age of 500 million years or thereabouts. "The 'rays' or bright streaks that radiate from the craters under noon-time illumination, are strikingly similar to features that have radiated from the craters formed by underground nuclear explosions on earth [*sic*]," reported the *New York Times.*[1]

Amateur astronomers could see the crater—which was reported to be "60 miles across and about two miles deep"—from their backyards approximately 240,000 miles away "with a pair of binoculars on a good night."[2] NASA's photos were taken from the *Lunar Orbiter 2* spacecraft somewhat closer, a distance around 28 miles from the moon.

In addition to the Crater of Copernicus photo, NASA also had another breakthrough in December 1966 with this first full-disk image of Earth from a geostationary orbit. It was taken from the ATS-1 satellite. COURTESY OF NASA

The Copernicus photo was, at the time, considered to be "the picture of the century." Dr. Martin J. Swetnick, a scientist in the lunar orbiter program, proclaimed, "It is the finest picture ever obtained by man of Copernicus. It provides new information to scientists which certainly will lead to better understanding of the processes and structure of the moon."[3]

NASA had launched *Lunar Orbiter 2* about three weeks before Americans sat looking at the photos with their jaws agape at kitchen tables, on commuter trains, and in college dorms. Between November 18 and November 26, while the rest of the country was immersed in the chaos of preparing, enjoying, and recovering from Thanksgiving celebrations, NASA engineers calculated the spacecraft's trajectory. Protractors and slide rules in hand, they anticipated an outcome both revelatory and inspirational.

Even die-hard anti-NASA advocates arguing that tax dollars would be better spent on social programs would have to admit that the sheer beauty of what *Apollo 11* astronaut Buzz Aldrin would later call "magnificent desolation" during his walk on the moon was, indeed, breathtaking. Nevertheless, their arguments persisted.

While the latest photographs of the moon caused exhilaration for NASA endorsers, both political and civilian, NASA's chief, Dr. James E. Webb, went on defense at the National League of Cities conference in Las Vegas. On December 5, in an address that was explanatory but not specific, Webb countered the 3,500 civil servants attending this gathering at the Dunes. His speech emphasized that the value of space exploration went beyond bragging rights of getting to the moon ahead of the Russians and before the 1970 deadline set by President Kennedy. He estimated that research would yield benefits worth $83 billion. His projected cost for getting a man to the moon was nearly $23 billion.

Further, Webb charged the mayors, city councilmen, and their governmental brethren to prove the value of the urban programs they espoused.[4]

Webb's fellow NASA executive Dr. George E. Mueller used his platform for an audience ready to be inspired at the Achievement Rewards for College Scientists. On the same day in Los Angeles, Mueller underscored the rhetoric that NASA's astronauts, engineers, and analysts daily unlock mysteries that hadn't been conceived yet. NASA's value touches all parts of life, not just research for research's sake.

"Space exploration in its broadest meaning and in all of its ramifications has become a powerful force . . . socially, economically, politically, and even morally. . . . It is the creator of new technologies, new techniques, and new methods of management. It has great significance for our national security. It is a stimulus for our economic and national growth. It is a catalyst to the achievement of the goals of our society. And it provides us with the dimensions of a great challenge—to explore space for the benefit of all mankind."

NASA finished the *Lunar Orbiter 2* mission with a bounty of 211 photos capturing 1.6 million square miles of the moon, about 10 times the size of California. Both the near and far sides were chronicled;

NASA redirected the craft for data collection concerning the moon's effect on gravity. Ten months later, it purposely crashed "on the far side of the Moon to prevent communications interference on future missions."[5]

---

It was another victory for NASA, ending a year of success highlighted by the five Gemini missions. In the sports world, the Miami Dolphins rarely had cause to celebrate a victory in their inaugural season in 1966. A week before Christmas, the nascent team in the American Football League won for just the third time and ended their first year with a 3–11 record. But South Florida's sports fans had reason to cheer beyond the scoreboard.

Its AFL status gave Miami a groundbreaking foothold in football at the professional level. By the mid-1960s, the sun-soaked city had emerged as an alluring American metropolis favored by tourists for the balmy weather, access to the South Atlantic Ocean, and several miles of beaches. Snowbirds from the Northeast and Mid-Atlantic delighted in annual treks southward for vacations.

Miami had become a cultural icon thanks to the entertainment industry. *Moon over Miami* premiered in the summer of 1941, starring Betty Grable and Don Ameche. Having rebounded from a career slump, Frank Sinatra used his incredible clout to host *Welcome Home Elvis* on ABC—part of the Hoboken-born singer's four specials sponsored by Timex in the 1959–1960 television season—at the Fontainebleau, a Miami Beach hotel symbolizing luxury.[6] ABC also featured the Fontainebleau in the private-eye show *Surfside Six*, which ran from 1960 to 1962 and gave Miami weekly exposure to millions of Americans.[7]

Baseball fans had the Miami Marlins of the International League from 1956 to 1960. But the Dolphins took the city's sports lineage to a national level with the AFL berth in '66, reviving Miami's link to professional football that had previously lasted one season—1946—with the Miami Seahawks in the All-America Football Conference.

Danny Thomas was one of the Dolphins' founders. He had delighted millions with his performances, forged a prosperous career as a TV producer—including *The Dick Van Dyke Show*—and contributed his terrific fame to a cause that helped thousands of families in medical crisis.

A successful nightclub entertainer, Thomas, a Lebanese American born Amos Kairouz in 1912, had built a burgeoning film career that included a remake of *The Jazz Singer* before striking television gold with the family sitcom *Make Room for Daddy*. It took advantage of the nightclub vocation by placing Thomas's character, Danny Williams, as a Manhattan-based headliner at the Copa Club. After four years on ABC from 1953 to 1957, the show got canceled.

CBS figured that *Make Room for Daddy* had a longer life span even if its competitor thought otherwise. So the network that birthed *I Love Lucy* and *What's My Line?* picked up the show, retitled it *The Danny Thomas Show*, and kept it on the prime-time schedule until 1964.

Thomas's production company struck gold with Andy Griffith, a North Carolina comedian who had made his mark with folksy, down-home humor. *The Danny Thomas Show* introduced Andy Griffith's trademark character Sheriff Andy Taylor in a backdoor pilot, which typically offers the lead character and perhaps others from an established show introducing new characters in a story line meant to test audience reaction for a potential new show. Here, the sheriff catches Danny Williams speeding in Mayberry, North Carolina, on a trip heading back home to New York.

Because of his obstinacy in refusing to pay the fine, Williams is jailed. By the end of the story, he comes to respect the sheriff.

It set the tone for *The Andy Griffith Show*, which ran for eight years on CBS and spun off a favorite character into his own show; Jim Nabors starred as the titular character in *Gomer Pyle U.S.M.C.* for five years. *The Andy Griffith Show* ended in 1968; *Gomer Pyle*, the year after. In the last year of *TAGS*, new characters were introduced to get the audience familiar with them for an upcoming spinoff. *Mayberry R.F.D.* aired for three seasons and also featured characters that had been in the supporting cast of the seminal show.

A friendship with Joe Robbie, another successful American with Lebanese heritage, became the doorway to Thomas's experience in professional sports. Robbie needed partners for his idea to own an AFL expansion team in Miami. Lamar Hunt had spearheaded the efforts to create a league to compete with the National Football League, which had been founded in 1920.

Hunt, an oil man, from his perch atop the AFL's hierarchy, demanded approval, which Robbie and Thomas strived to get. In his autobiography, published a few months before he died in 1991, Thomas wrote that Hunt wanted him to be a majority owner at the 51 percent level. The entertainer countered with a proposal that he and Robbie could lead a group of investors to get that percentage. "I was a pro-football owner, though Joe Robbie was the real managing partner," declared Thomas. "For me, it was like being a kid turned loose in a candy store." Hunt owned the Dallas Texans.

There had been reports of Thomas owning as much as 30 percent of the team. In 1991, he stated, "Well, I sold out all my shares in the Dolphins—all except three percent, which I returned to Joe Robbie, with the proviso that the earnings be donated to the St. Jude Hospital in perpetuity. In addition, Joe donated a lot of money on his own and became a member of our board of directors. I remained a minority owner of the Dolphins and received a diamond-studded championship ring—as did the coaches and the players—the two times the Dolphins won the Super Bowl."[8]

It is part of show business lore that Thomas made a promise to God when he was young and struggling financially. If he became successful, he'd make sure to help others in need. And so was born his dedication that manifested in St. Jude's Children's Hospital in Memphis.

Besides his investments in football and television, Thomas had another source of his pride in 1966: *That Girl* premiered, starring his daughter, Marlo, as aspiring actress Ann Marie. It ran for five seasons on ABC.

———— ∞ ————

A year that began with strife for New Yorkers ended on a positive note, as is wont to happen when the holiday season descends upon the island of Manhattan and its environs with all the subtlety of galloping horses in the third race at Belmont.

Mayor Lindsay had no honeymoon period after getting sworn in as New York's 103rd mayor in January '66; the city's transit workers commenced their walkout on New Year's Day, paralyzing the city. But by December, the strike and its resolution were long forgotten. Once again, tourists and natives would trek to Midtown and visit Rockefeller Center to see the Christmas tree, walk down Fifth Avenue to window shop, enjoy the holiday spectacular featuring the Rockettes at Radio City Music Hall, and attend Christmas parties given by employers and clients alike. Their calendars would be filled with holiday shopping, vacation plans, and Christmas cards.

Chanukah began on December 7, a particularly somber day marking the 25th anniversary of the bombing of Pearl Harbor. The aura of holiday time has the power to make mourning potent but temporary.

Mayor Lindsay's contribution to holiday culture in 1966 began a tradition every bit as strong as the Macy's Thanksgiving Day Parade, which is the unofficial line of demarcation separating the calmness of autumn from the frenzy of Christmastime. It was a preposterous idea conceived by a TV executive, but it kept stride with the year's other groundbreaking events in popular culture.

*The Yule Log.*

WPIX was the home for this three-and-a-half-hour special consisting of burning logs in a fireplace set against holiday music. Gracie Mansion, the mayor's residence, supplied the fireplace. WPIX belonged to a category of TV and radio stations using call letters to signify a slogan or other indicator. The *Daily News*, a prominent New York City newspaper that began in 1919 and enjoyed the slogan "New York's Picture Newspaper," founded WPIX—Channel 11—in 1948 and used the call letters as a shorthand to honor the paper's mantra.[9]

Filming a fireplace and putting it on a loop may have seemed ridiculous. There would be no opportunity for the sales team to sell airtime to sponsors, a cardinal sin in commercially supported television.

But entertainment executives had made blunders in the past.

When Desi Arnaz and Lucille Ball proposed *I Love Lucy* to CBS, they got rejected by the network. Desi wanted to film with three cameras, which had only been done occasionally on quiz shows. CBS thought it was too expensive, so Desi and Lucy agreed to absorb the cost as long as they owned the show. *I Love Lucy* became a CBS blockbuster and later a programming staple in syndication for decades.

Decca Records rejected the Beatles because the decision makers felt that guitar groups were not going to be popular for much longer.

Burt Reynolds often told interviewers and audiences a story about being on *Gunsmoke* while Clint Eastwood starred on *Rawhide* in the 1960s. A Universal Television executive fired the TV actors in his office, telling Reynolds he couldn't act and Eastwood that his large Adam's apple was distracting viewers, along with a chipped tooth and a slow way of talking. Reynolds and Eastwood became box-office icons in the 1970s and 1980s.

WPIX general manager Fred Thrower had the inkling that *The Yule Log* would appeal to folks without a fireplace, which is a hallmark of the holiday season according to Christmas cards and Christmas movies. But there was another benefit—it fostered an identity for the station. After 1966, *The Yule Log* became a holiday institution. When New Yorkers talked about Christmas movies and TV specials in years and decades to come, *The Yule Log* would be a matter of civic pride if the conversations took place with people from other cities.

Thrower's memorandum on November 2 laid out the strategy. With a break in the station's college basketball schedule and the roller derby show vulnerable on Christmas Eve, there was an opportunity for what Thrower called the "WPIX Christmas Card."

His paradigm set the tone for all future incarnations: a few minutes of film on a fireplace looped for however long the show lasted. "The television set actually becomes a fireplace and since Christmas Eve is a time for decorating the tree after the children have gone to bed the overall presentation should be most appreciated and effective. And since we would be cancelling all programs and commercials, it is startling enough to gain attention."[10]

For music, they used the library at WPIX-FM, also owned by the *Daily News*.

In 1990, WPIX did not air *The Yule Log*, which had expanded to several more hours and used new films of fireplaces since Thrower's idea

New York City mayor John Lindsay allowed WPIX-TV to film a fireplace in Gracie Mansion for *The Yule Log*. Premiering on Christmas Eve 1966, this holiday special became an annual favorite for New Yorkers.
COURTESY OF NEW YORK CITY DEPARTMENT OF RECORDS AND INFORMATION SERVICES

became a reality. This hiatus lasted 11 years, to the dismay of those who found comfort in turning on Channel 11.

After the 9/11 attacks that brought down the Twin Towers in 2001, WPIX revived the special programming. It was a salve for the Greater New York area.

Rolando Pujol was the archivist at WPIX who found original footage of the 1966 *Yule Log* special that was thought to be long lost.

Back in October 2014, WPIX received a phone call from the family of Kay Arnold. She had just died. Arnold, an actress and TV producer and the aunt of the actor Tom Arnold, was the widow of Bill Cooper, who produced and filmed both versions of *The Yule Log*.

He was a PIX executive and a gifted documentary producer who had retired from WPIX in the mid-1980s and died shortly thereafter. He was also close friends with Fred Thrower, the station manager who conceived of *The Yule Log* in 1966, inspired by a Coca-

Cola commercial featuring Santa Claus by a fireplace and the idea that apartment-bound New Yorkers, devoid of fireplaces, might appreciate a televised one set to beautiful Christmas music. (He considered a ticker with lyrics too, but that idea was abandoned.)

Arnold's family was clearing out the Cooper/Arnold house in Paramus, New Jersey, and wanted to let us know that there was a significant amount of tape and film from WPIX that Cooper had collected in his home. There were reels and cassettes everywhere, in the basement and especially in the garage.

It was overwhelming in a good way—an archivist's dream discovery. So much analog treasure to explore. In the almost 30 years that had passed since Cooper's death, his widow had hung on to his legacy. And now it was at risk of being dumped.

Almost two years later, on a steamy night in July 2016, I was in the depths of the News Building, deep below East 42nd Street, examining videotapes in search of vintage news reports about the GOP presidential candidate Donald Trump. I was working with the PBS series *Frontline*, which was licensing the footage for an upcoming episode, "The Choice 2016."

These tapes were in the same room where we were storing a significant portion of the Bill Cooper material we had salvaged.

It was after 11 P.M., and I was about ready to call it a night when I passed a film can at eye level that had a label on it that said "Orig PIX Fireplace." It was scrawled on, and a little hard to read.

I froze. I immediately and ever so carefully pulled the can from the pile of canisters it was tucked into, opened it, and found three small rolls of 16-millimeter film. One of them was labeled *Yule Log*. It was about two minutes of film.

The footage began with an establishing shot of the Gracie Mansion fireplace that zooms in to a close-up of the flames, film that loops about every seven seconds. The camera zooms out to show the fireplace in its entirety again.

This was the master film that was the basis for the original fireplace. In its inaugural broadcast the evening of December 24, 1966, this footage played for three hours.[11]

*The Yule Log* was a holiday-laden oasis for New Yorkers in 1966. As the year moved into the home stretch, news followers couldn't escape the daily reports from Southeast Asia and the staggering number of young soldiers dying. By the end of the conflict in Vietnam in 1975, U.S. forces had sustained 58,220 casualties.[12] Endorsement for the war came from an unlikely source in 1966: Cardinal Francis Spellman, New York City's archbishop.

During a Christmas trip to South Vietnam—the 21st Christmas that he spent with soldiers abroad—Spellman shared Pope Paul VI's sentiments that the holiday truce would extend beyond December 25 when he visited 5,000 American troops for midnight mass at a supply base.[13]

But his trip also yielded a statement that some found puzzling coming from a man of the cloth: "[America's forces are] the defense, protection, and salvation not only of our country but, I believe, of civilization itself. I have no words to express the satisfaction and the gratitude I feel for what you have done and are doing for our country."[14]

There was no mistake in his verbiage. He echoed this sentiment in other statements, which were seen as unwarranted attacks by a powerful clergy member.

The Vatican did not comment, but the *New York Times* cited displeasure at the holy headquarters of Catholicism according to its sources.[15] Responding to Spellman's statements, the *Times* ran an editorial lacing into its city's leading Catholic. "What is different this time is that the Cardinal's action is also regarded as an embarrassment to the Vatican," declared the paper of record. "Pope Paul VI has been carrying on a campaign for a negotiated peace in Vietnam and has made it clear he would be happy to see a settlement based on something less than a victory for the American position."[16]

On New Year's Eve, Americans prepared to welcome 1967 as the Earth neared completion of its yearly revolution around the sun. Introspection, reflection, and resolutions emerged once again. To take their minds off their self-imposed restrictions for the upcoming year, celebrants conversed about the past one.

Spy genre buffs assessed the latest entry—Dean Martin in his second of four portrayals of Matt Helm. *Murderers' Row* debuted a few days before Christmas.

Comic-book fans talked about *Batman* revolutionizing television with its pop-art sensibilities.

Space buffs basked in NASA's Gemini missions pushing America toward the Apollo missions.

Gamblers praised a new paradigm of luxury defined by Caesars Palace.

Political insiders and observers assessed Ronald Reagan reinvigorating the Republican Party with his election to California's governorship.

Women found a voice of empowerment for their tribe in Nancy Sinatra's "These Boots Are Made for Walkin'."

Baseball fans reminded themselves of the unpredictability in sports evidenced by the Orioles sweeping the Dodgers in the World Series.

Black Americans reveled in the increasing momentum of social progress during 1966. Robert Culp and Bill Cosby did not address Cosby's race on *I Spy* or off the air, preferring instead to let story lines, dialogue, and character interactions indicate that Kelly Robinson and Alexander Scott were equal. During the show's three-year run from 1965 to 1968, Cosby won an Emmy Award each year.

Gregory Morris's portrayal of electronics expert Barney Collier on *Mission: Impossible* and Nichelle Nichols's presence as Communications Officer Nyota Uhura on the deck of *Star Trek*'s USS *Enterprise* were Goliath-size leaps supplementing the civil rights movement. In a last-season episode of *The Dick Van Dyke Show*, Godfrey Cambridge played an FBI agent using the Petries' home for a stakeout targeting a neighbor.

Robert Weaver becoming the first Black cabinet member further emphasized a new era for employers, public service and private sector alike.

There's an expression that some have deemed a curse while others proclaim it to be a wish of bountiful fortune. It would not be unusual to hear these words given as a toast belonging in the latter category as the clock struck midnight to initiate 1967: "May you live in interesting times."

In response, it would be unsurprising to hear a corollary citing the title of a Bob Dylan song that had become an anthem combining mid-1960s despair, caution, and hope.

"The times, they are a-changing."

# Appendix

## *"Drabowsky on the Mound"*

### David Krell

In November '53, the Browns
ended their time in St. Lou.
They moved to Baltimore and became the Orioles;
'54 marked their debut.

O'Malley abandoned Brooklyn after the '57 season
and suffered many a slander.
LA welcomed Dodger Blue to a region
that was sunnier and seemed grander.

The Dodgers swept the Yankees in '63
and won the World Series again in '65.
1966 would be more of the same;
they'd win in game four or five.

The outlook was not bright for Baltimore,
everybody knows.
Conventional wisdom favored Los Angeles
against the beloved O's.

Tommy Davis had played in 100 games
and batted .313.
Willie Davis batted .284,
thanks to judgment that was keen.

Koufax won 27 games;
LA had the skill to win it all in '66.
Pundits respected Baltimore,
but they didn't show it in their picks.

Hank Bauer helmed the Orioles,
a veteran of World Series glory.
Seven titles as a player with the Yankees,
that was his great story.

Walter Alston managed the Dodgers,
who also won in '55 and '59.
Oddsmakers leaned toward his squad
when they set the betting line.

The reigning World Series champions
battled Pittsburgh and San Francisco to the end of the season.
They ultimately surpassed their formidable rivals,
and so it stood to reason.

Even though the Orioles clinched on September 22nd
and boasted wonderful exuberance,
they were green in postseason play,
so stated in many a deliverance.

Baltimore finished '66 with a very nice cushion;
the rest of the AL stood far below.
Nine games behind was the nearest squad—
the dynamic Twins led by Tony O.

Game One: Baltimore racked up three runs
in the top of the first inning.
The Dodgers' fans were taken aback
but did not give up on winning.

Don Drysdale was their pitcher
on this October 5th afternoon.
His right arm was powerful;
an apt metaphor would be a typhoon.

Bauer sent up Dave McNally,
who would turn 24 at the end of October.
The young Orioles had a chance to win the series
if you analyzed it sober.

Baltimore went up 4–0 in the second,
when Snyder got an RBI single.
It looked like Christmas came early for the O's,
but they didn't need Kris Kringle.

Lefebvre knocked a solo home run,
the only LA round-tripper in the series.
Baltimore's offense was exemplary so far;
it prompted several queries.

But McNally walked three straight Dodgers;
it happened in the bottom of the third.
With bases loaded and one out,
Bauer replaced this baby bird.

He called on a journeyman from the bullpen
to take over the pitching.
His name was Moe Drabowsky,
and what he did was simply bewitching.

Drabowsky broke in with the Cubs in '56
and stayed for five years.
He played for the Braves, Reds, and A's
in the next stage of his career.

He came to Baltimore in the offseason,
 no longer a starter but a reliever.
In Game One, the Dodgers suffered greatly;
 Drabowsky was as sharp as a new cleaver.

 The first batter he faced was Parker,
 who struck out against the righty.
 But Dodgers were at every base;
 their opportunities seemed mighty.

Drabowsky walked Gilliam,
 which brought home the second LA run.
 Roseboro fouled out to Etchebarren,
 and so Baltimore's worry was done.

 With speed, precision, and control
 upon the ball that he dispatched,
 the righthander struck out 11,
a World Series relief record anyone has yet to match.

 The Orioles tallied another run,
 and the score stayed five to two.
 They swept the Dodgers in four games;
 it was quite the baseball coup.

Drabowsky did not have a Hall of Fame career,
 though he had a Hall of Fame day.
 But there's a sentimental postscript to Game One
 that I hope you will convey.

The Drabowskys had a daughter who suffered from leukemia;
 it took her life.
Her name was Deborah, and she was two months old.
 It was a time of immeasurable strife.

She died on October 5, 1959,
seven years before Game One to the date.
When Drabowsky dominated the Dodgers
and undeniably owned home plate.

Facing the NL champs could be compared
to Sisyphus and his boulder.
But if you believe in heaven,
then Moe Drabowsky had an angel on his shoulder.

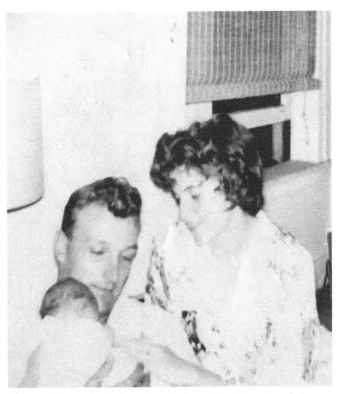

Moe and Elisabeth Drabowsky with their infant daughter, Debra.
Debra died of leukemia when she was two months old. COURTESY
OF ELISABETH DRABOWSKY

# Notes

## Chapter One

1. Williams played in 6 games in 1952 and 37 games in 1953.

2. Jim Elliot, "Officials Here Are Jubilant," *Baltimore Sun*, December 10, 1965, C1.

3. Lou Hatter, "'Tough, Really Tough'—Pappas," *Baltimore Sun*, December 10, 1965, C1.

4. Milt Pappas, interview with Gabriel Schechter, South Holland, Illinois, August 28, 1992, transcript in Milt Pappas File, Giamatti Research Center, National Baseball Hall of Fame and Museum, Cooperstown, New York.

5. Earl Lawson, "Robinson's Grin Hides Sadness over Trade," *Sporting News*, December 25, 1965, 11.

6. Frank Robinson with Al Silverman, *My Life Is Baseball* (Garden City, NY: Doubleday, 1968, 1975), 164. Citations refer to the 1975 version.

7. Lawson, "Robinson's Grin Hides Sadness over Trade."

8. Earl Lawson, "Reds Swap Robby—Get Hurler Pappas," *Sporting News*, December 18, 1965, 9.

9. "Robby Fined $250 in Hassle," Associated Press, *Dayton Daily News*, March 20, 1961, 1. In a 1970 *Sports Illustrated* article, Mark Kram recounted Robinson's contemporaneous version of the events at an all-night diner. Robinson and the cook "had been exchanging dark glowers." Robinson claimed that the cook pulled a knife "and made a motion as if he was going to slit my throat." At that point, he revealed the gun. Mark Kram, "Discord, Defied and Deified," *Sports Illustrated*, October 5, 1970, 26.

10. Morton Sharnik, "The Moody Tiger of the Reds," *Sports Illustrated*, June 17, 1963, 33.

11. Bob Scherr, telephone interview with author, October 6, 2020.

12. Scherr, telephone interview with author.

13. Bonnie Strangis, telephone interview with author, November 11, 2020.

14. Sam Strangis, telephone interview with author, November 11, 2020.

15. Deborah Dozier Potter, telephone interview with author, October 27, 2020.

16. William Dozier to Douglas Cramer, August 25, 1965, "To the Batpoles! An Ongoing Group Research Project into Batman '66!," https://tothebatpoles.libsyn .com/108-the-william-dozier-fanboy (accessed November 3, 2020).

17. Johanna Herwitz, telephone interview with author, October 31, 2020.

18. Adam West, "Adam West and Burt Ward Talk 'Batman' (1966)," YouTube, https://www.youtube.com/watch?v=3iWXFTR78Dg (accessed November 3, 2020).

19. Bob Kane to William Dozier, November 2, 1965 [*sic*], "To the Batpoles! An Ongoing Group Research Project into Batman '66!," https://tothebatpoles.libsyn .com/108-the-william-dozier-fanboy (accessed November 3, 2020).

20. Mark Racop, email to author, November 10, 2020.

21. William Dozier to Adam West, September 13, 1965, "To the Batpoles! An Ongoing Group Research Project into Batman '66!," https://tothebatpoles.libsyn .com/108-the-william-dozier-fanboy (accessed November 3, 2020).

22. Adam West with Jeff Rovin, *Back to the Batcave* (New York: Berkley Books, 1994), 58.

23. Annie Pilon, telephone interview with author, November 4, 2020.

24. Burgess Meredith, *So Far, So Good* (New York: Little, Brown, 1994), 260.

25. Mel Gussow, "Burgess Meredith, 89, Who Was at Ease Playing Good Guys and Villains, Dies," *New York Times*, September 11, 1997, B7.

26. "Robert Butler Discusses Guest Actors on 'Batman'—EMMYTVLEGENDS .ORG," https://www.youtube.com/watch?v=3n4-1XsSX8U (accessed November 14, 2020). Butler also directed the first appearance of Mr. Freeze and the two-episode pilot for *Star Trek*, which never aired. But *Star Trek* creator Gene Roddenberry later incorporated the footage into a two-episode story. Butler's outstanding roster of credits includes helming the pilots for *Hogan's Heroes*, *Hill Street Blues*, and *Remington Steele*.

27. John Antczak, "Actor Burgess Meredith Dies at 89," Associated Press, *San Bernardino County Sun*, September 11, 1997, A12.

28. Carroll Kilpatrick, "Weaver Is Named to Head Urban Dept.," *Washington Post*, January 14, 1966, A1.

29. Jack Eisen, "Senate Speedily Puts Approval on Weaver as 1st Urban Secretary," *Washington Post*, January 18, 1966, A2.

30. "Secretary Weaver," *Washington Post*, January 16, 1966, E6.

## CHAPTER TWO

1. Sherwood Schwartz, *Inside Gilligan's Island* (Jefferson, NC: McFarland, 1988; New York: St. Martin's, 1994), 13. Citation refers to the 1994 edition.

2. Lloyd Schwartz, telephone interview with author, January 5, 2022.

3. "Koufax, Big D Hint at $600,000 Deal," Associated Press, *San Bernardino Sun*, February 23, 1966, A12; Bob Hunter, "Will Sandy, Big D Make Plane?," *Los Angeles Herald Examiner*, February 23, 1966, E1.

4. Frank Finch, "Koufax, Drysdale Eye $1 Million Pact," *Los Angeles Times*, February 23, 1966, B1.

5. "Koufax, Big D Hint at $600,000 Deal."

6. Finch, "Koufax, Drysdale Eye $1 Million Pact."

7. Hunter, "Will Sandy, Big D Make Plane?"

8. "Koufax, Drysdale Want Equity with Identical Pay, Contracts," *San Bernardino Sun*, February 24, 1966, D1.

9. Don Drysdale with Bob Verdi, *Once a Bum, Always a Dodger: My Life in Baseball from Brooklyn to Los Angeles* (New York: St. Martin's, 1990), 123.

10. Sandy Koufax with Ed Linn, *Koufax* (New York: Viking, 1966), 271.

11. Koufax, *Koufax*, 258.

12. Drysdale, *Once a Bum*, 124–25.

13. Frank Finch, "Koufax, Drysdale Spurn Offer by Dodgers," *Los Angeles Times*, February 25, 1966, B1.

14. Finch, "Koufax, Drysdale Spurn Offer."

15. "Dodgers, Minus Three, Check into Camp Today," *Los Angeles Times*, February 26, 1966, A2.

16. Sid Ziff, "Bavasi Digs In," *Los Angeles Times*, February 28, 1966, B1.

17. Frank Finch, "Sandy, Drysdale Must Sign One-Year Pacts," *Los Angeles Times*, February 28, 1966, B1.

18. "Sherry's Tip Kept Sandy from Quitting in 1961," Associated Press, *Newark Star-Ledger*, January 20, 1972, 50.

19. Bill Roeder, "Dodgers Gamble on Drysdale, 19," *New York World-Telegram and The Sun*, April 4, 1956, 34.

20. Bill Roeder, "Rookie Drysdale Dodger Starter," *New York World-Telegram and The Sun*, April 10, 1956, 23.

21. Drysdale, *Once a Bum*, 67.

22. Wes Parker, telephone interview with author, February 14, 2021.

23. Joe Moeller, telephone interview with author, February 12, 2021.

24. Jeff Torborg, telephone interview with author, February 15, 2021.

25. "February 26, 1966 Launch of Apollo-Saturn 201," NASA, https://www.nasa.gov/content/apollo-saturn-201-launch (accessed May 4, 2022).

## CHAPTER THREE

1. Marvin Miller, *A Whole Different Ball Game: The Sports and Business of Baseball* (New York: Carol, 1991), 61.

2. Dick Young, "Stengel Name Associated with Game," *Orlando Evening Star*, March 9, 1966, 4C.

3. David R. Jones, "Creative Labor Man to Go to Bat for Ballplayers," *New York Times*, March 6, 1966, 32.

4. Marvin Miller, interview with Bill Veeck, *A View from the Bleachers with Bill Veeck*, part 1 of 2, 1982, https://mediaburn.org/video/bill-veeck-interviews-marvin-miller-1 (accessed June 24, 2021).

5. "Ballplayers Nominate Miller, Man of Steel," *Miami News*, March 6, 1966, 3C.

6. Victor Riesel, "Inside Labor—Ball Players United," *Shreveport Journal*, October 7, 1966, 6A.

7. Miller, *A Whole Different Ball Game*, 43.

8. Jim Trinkle, column, *Fort Worth Star-Telegram*, March 22, 1966, 21.

9. Edgar W. Ray, *The Grand Huckster: Houston's Judge Roy Hofheinz, Genius of the Astrodome* (Memphis, TN: Memphis State University Press, 1980), 343.

10. "Astroturf: A Decisive Weapon," Associated Press, *San Bernardino Sun*, March 21, 1966, 9.

11. "Astroturf: A Decisive Weapon."

12. Mike Rathet, "Astroturf Looks Good, but Presents Some Problems," Associated Press, *Daily Independent Journal* (San Rafael, CA), March 21, 1966, 32.

13. James Tuite, "Leo like Bouillabaisse," *Decatur Daily Review*, March 8, 1966, 6.

14. "In the Wake of the News," *Chicago Tribune*, March 8, 1966, 49.

15. "Durocher Instills New Spark," Associated Press, *Alton Evening Telegraph*, March 9, 1966, 17.

16. Leo Durocher with Ed Linn, *Nice Guys Finish Last* (New York: Simon & Schuster, 1975), 350.

17. Peter Golenbock, *Amazin': The Miraculous History of New York's Most Beloved Baseball Team* (New York: St. Martin's, 2002), 183.

18. Derek Jeter tallied 99.74 percent in 2020. As of the publication of this book, Mariano Rivera is the only player to reach 100 percent.

19. Bill Buchalter, "Ole Case in Hall of Fame: He's Exceptional Case, and Baseball Proves It," *Tampa Bay Times*, March 9, 1966, 1C.

20. Lou Niss, "Stengel Says Dodgers Have Chance to Win Flag," *Brooklyn Times-Union*, February 24, 1936, 9.

21. Steve Jacobson, "Casey Improves with Age—Just Like Mets," *Newsday*, March 5, 1966, 21.

22. Jacobson, "Casey Improves with Age."

23. Marvin Miles, "Gemini Pair Safe," *Los Angeles Times*, March 17, 1966, 1.

24. David Scott and Alexei Leonov, *Two Sides of the Moon: Our Story of the Cold War Space Race* (New York: St. Martin's, 2004), 169.

25. John Noble Wilford, "Gemini 8 Mishap Traced by NASA to Short Circuit," *New York Times*, March 20, 1966, 1.

26. The astronauts selected were Alan Shepard, Gus Grissom, John Glenn, Scott Carpenter, Wally Schirra, Gordon Cooper, and Deke Slayton. Because of a heart issue, NASA grounded Slayton. He became a top administrator at NASA. In 1975, NASA okayed him to fly on the joint U.S.-Russia Apollo-Soyuz mission. Armstrong and Buzz Aldrin flew in the *Apollo 11* mission and became the first astronauts to land on the moon. Scott and James Irwin landed in *Apollo 15*.

27. See died on February 28, 1966, with Charles Bassett in a NASA T-38 jet crash at the McDonnell Aircraft Building, Lambert Field, St. Louis. Scott, Bassett, and Aldrin were part of the group of astronauts labeled the New Fourteen, selected for Project Gemini and Project Apollo.

28. Evert Clark, "President Reaffirms Goal of Moon Landing in 60's," *New York Times*, March 17, 1966, 1.

29. *Apollo 7* flew from October 11 to 22, 1968, with the crew of Walt Cunningham, Donn Eisele, and Wally Schirra.

30. "Astros Figure Cost of Dodger Holdouts at about $200,000," Associated Press, *San Bernardino Sun*, March 21, 1966, 10.

31. Jim Murray, "Sandy Eager to Play, Waits for Buzzie's Call, but . . . ," *Los Angeles Times*, March 17, 1966, C1.

32. Maloney had an outstanding season in 1965. His 20–9 record for the Cincinnati Reds tied him for seventh in the majors with Bob Gibson and Mel Stottlemyre. He tied for fifth place in winning percentage with Stottlemyre and had the sixth-highest number of strikeouts.

33. "Dodger Duo Puts Down New Offer," United Press International, *Santa Maria Times* (Santa Maria, CA), March 30, 1966, 21.

34. Charles Maher, "Peace at Last! K&D Return to Fold: Sandy Signs for $120,000, Don $105,000," *Los Angeles Times*, March 31, 1966, B1.

35. "Two 100-Grand Pitchers: Sandy, Big D Are in the Fold," *Los Angeles Herald Examiner*, March 30, 1966, F1.

36. Bud Furillo, "Koufax Highest Paid Ever," *Los Angeles Herald Examiner*, March 31, 1966, D1.

37. Don Drysdale with Bob Verdi, *Once a Bum, Always a Dodger* (New York: St. Martin's, 1990), 130.

38. Connors was a first baseman for the Dodgers' minor league teams in Newport, Norfolk, Mobile, and Montreal. His tenure was 1940, 1942, and 1946–1950. He played in one game for the Brooklyn Dodgers in 1949. Connors was also a member of the 1951–1952 Los Angeles Angels—the triple-A team for the Chicago Cubs in the Pacific Coast League. He played in 66 games for the 1951 Cubs.

39. Maher, "Peace at Last!"

40. Maher, "Peace at Last!"

## CHAPTER FOUR

1. Hank Hollingworth, "New Home Will Help Angels," *Long Beach Press-Telegram*, April 20, 1966, C1.

2. Expansion was largely a result of the implosion of the Continental League, a proposed third league headed by Branch Rickey. The CL folded, but it led to AL franchises in the LA and Washington, DC, markets and NL franchises in New York and Houston.

3. Charlie Roberts, "Braves 'Take It All' as Hoopla Climaxes," *Atlanta Constitution*, April 12, 1966, 40.

4. Jesse Outlar, "Let's Get on with It," *Atlanta Constitution*, April 12, 1966, 39.

5. Charlie Roberts, "No Butterflies for Braves' Veterans," *Atlanta Constitution*, April 13, 1966, 43.

6. Charlie Roberts, "Willie's Wallop Surprised Him," *Atlanta Constitution*, April 13, 1966, 42.

7. Roberts, "Willie's Wallop Surprised Him."

8. Lester J. Biederman, "Stargell Gets Pirates Off to Swinging Start," *Pittsburgh Press*, April 13, 1966, 93.

9. "Braves to Face Anti-Trust Suit," United Press International, *Wisconsin State Journal*, January 26, 1966, 27.

10. "Georgia Court Orders Braves to Play in Atlanta, Regardless of Wisconsin," United Press International, *Sheboygan Press*, February 9, 1966, 37.

11. "Judge Rules Braves Must Return or NL Give Milwaukee 1967 Expansion Franchise," Associated Press, *Wisconsin State Journal*, April 14, 1966, 13.

12. Will McDonough, "Lonborg Changes Mind, O's Win in 13th, 5–4," *Boston Globe*, April 13, 1966, 51.

13. Frank Finch, "Fairly, Osteen Shoot Down Astros, 3–2," *Los Angeles Times*, April 13, 1966, C1.

14. Sally Field, interview, "A Look Back at Gidget," Light Source & Imagery, https://www.youtube.com/watch?v=3a6pDHKAtWE (accessed August 8, 2021).

15. Lynette Winter, email to author, June 2, 2022.

16. James Michener, *The Source* (New York: Random House, 1965; trade paperback edition, New York: Dial Press, 2014), 5. Citations refer to the Dial Press trade paperback edition.

17. Michener, *The Source*, 56.

18. *Cast a Giant Shadow*, directed by Melville Shavelson, Mirisch Corporation, 1966.

19. Sophia Loren starred in *Judith*, which had premiered in January. This movie revolved around the end of the British Mandate of Palestine, which was superseded by the 1947 United Nations resolution creating modern-day Israel. The title character is the Jewish wife of a German tank commander, who abandoned her and their son in World War II. He assists the Arabs in military planning. She helps the Jews find him and learn his plans. After Israel declared independence in 1948, Arabs attacked. The war lasted nearly 10 months. Israel was victorious.

## Chapter Five

1. The stadium was named Sportsman's Park until 1953 when the St. Louis Browns left for Baltimore and changed the team name to Orioles. There was a wooden Sportsman's Park on the site from 1867 to 1901, originally called Grand Avenue Ball Grounds, but newspapers sometimes dubbed it Grand Avenue Park in game accounts. The successor debuted in 1902; the location of the diamond changed from the northwest section to the southwest in 1909. The Cardinals began using the field in 1920.

2. Jim Elliot, "Frank's Belt Not His Best," *Baltimore Sun*, May 9, 1966, C1.

3. Mark Melonas, telephone interview with author, October 2, 2021.

4. "'Flintstone' as Spy Is Stone Age Bond," *Syracuse Post-Standard*, September 1, 1966, 12.

5. Margaret Harford, "Freddie Flintstone Succeeds as a Spy," *Los Angeles Times*, September 9, 1966, pt. 4, 10.

6. Robert Vaughn, "Robert Vaughn on Fans of Napoleon Solo and Illya Kuryakin—EMMYTVLEGENDS.ORG," https://www.youtube.com/watch?v=Y-3wMLipB0U, November 6, 2007 (accessed September 25, 2021).

7. Harry Haun, "Cross James Bond with Batman—and Voila," *Nashville Tennessean*, February 11, 1966, 18.

8. Clifford Terry, "Jet Age Catches Up with Film Tours," *Chicago Tribune*, February 6, 1966, G11.

9. Saul David, *The Industry: Life in the Hollywood Fast Lane* (New York: Times Books, 1981), 178.

10. These stories imagined Archie, Jughead, Veronica, Betty, and Reggie as agents working for P.O.P. (Protect Our Planet) and battling C.R.U.S.H. (Criminal Recruits United to Spread Havoc). R.I.V.E.R.D.A.L.E. stands for Really Impressive Vast Enterprise for Routing Dangerous Adversaries, Louts, Etc.

11. Vince Waldron, *The Dick Van Dyke Show: The Definitive History & Ultimate Viewer's Guide to Television's Most Enduring Comedy* (New York: Applause Theatre Books, 2001; originally published 1994), 136–37. In other tellings, Carl and Estelle Reiner returned home from an event. Robert Culp, "Robert Culp on the Creation of 'I Spy'—EMMYTVLEGENDS.ORG," November 6, 2007, https://www.youtube.com/watch?v=lh83ghG0BGc (accessed September 25, 2021).

12. Robert Culp, "Robert Culp—on Bill Cosby and 'I Spy,'" Archive of American Television, November 6, 2007, https://www.youtube.com/watch?v=z7up2M_cbKs (accessed September 25, 2021). In a 1968 lecture at UCLA, executive producer Sheldon Leonard said otherwise and proclaimed that the show appeared on every NBC station. Sheldon Leonard, lecture, University of California, Los Angeles, February 9, 1968, UCLA Communications Studies Archive, https://www.youtube.com/watch?v=3wfyUS-POm28 (accessed October 16, 2021).

13. Harold Stern, "He's Giving Up Laughs for a Series," *Baltimore Evening Sun*, January 4, 1965, 22.

14. Robert Culp, "Robert Culp on Co-starring with Bill Cosby on 'I Spy'—EMMYTV LEGENDS.ORG," November 6, 2007, https://www.youtube.com/watch?v=0l0ET-eBbL8 (accessed September 25, 2021).

Cosby had a massive impact on the entertainment industry. His accomplishments in *I Spy* widened the doorway for Black entertainers. In 1984, *The Cosby Show* premiered on NBC, became an immediate smash, and launched the network to the top of the Nielsen ratings for eight seasons. The family-oriented sitcom anchored NBC's Thursday-night lineup for eight seasons.

In the mid-2010s, sexual assault allegations by 60 women covering several years surfaced. Some alleged events dated back to the 1960s. The expiration of the statute of limitations in most cases prevented prosecution, but an accusation concerning an assault in 2004 was within the window.

A Pennsylvania jury convicted Cosby in 2018. The Pennsylvania Supreme Court overturned the conviction in 2021. Doha Madani, "60 Women Accused Bill Cosby. His Conviction Had Been Considered a Big Win for #MeToo," NBC News, July 1, 2021, https://www.nbcnews.com/news/us-news/60-women-accused-bill-cosby-his-conviction-had-been-considered-n1272864 (accessed June 27, 2022); David K. Li, "Bill Cosby Released after Assault Conviction Overturned by Pennsylvania Supreme Court," NBC News, June 30, 2021, https://www.nbcnews.com/news/us-news/bill-cosby-be-released-after-sexual-assault-conviction-overturned-pennsylvania-n1272748 (accessed June 27, 2022).

15. Jason Culp, telephone interview with author, October 4, 2021.

16. Bill Cosby, "Bill Cosby Remembers Robert Culp," Ruth Eckerd Hall, Clearwater, Florida, March 27, 2010, https://www.youtube.com/watch?v=Jc6r7f-SlTU (accessed September 25, 2021). Cosby told the audience the story about Kentucky native Reese putting his arm around Robinson before a ball game to show his Southern brethren that he accepted Robinson.

17. Culp and Cosby reunited in a 1987 episode on the latter's blockbuster sitcom *The Cosby Show*. In an homage to their former pairing, Culp's character was named Scott Kelly. They revisited their *I Spy* characters in the 1994 TV movie *I Spy Returns*. Kelly Robinson's son and Alexander Scott's daughter represented the next generation of spies in this story. *I Spy Returns* aired on CBS rather than the show's original network, NBC.

## CHAPTER SIX

1. Dick Van Dyke, *My Lucky Life in and out of Show Business: A Memoir* (New York: Crown Archetype, 2011), 73.

Carson succeeded Jack Paar as host of NBC's *The Tonight Show* a year later and stayed there for 30 years.

2. The castaways on *Gilligan's Island* didn't get rescued until a TV movie in the late 1970s. *My Favorite Martian* lacked a final episode with a resolution deciding whether Uncle Martin stays on Earth or returns home to Mars. NBC canceled *Star Trek* after three years, leaving fans to wonder what happened for the remainder of the USS *Enterprise*'s five-year mission.

3. Reiner had come full circle. Television folklore says that CBS didn't think a Jewish actor would be viable for the lead role in a series based on the *Head of the Family* pilot. In the final episode, Reiner appears as Alan Brady and says that he wants to play Rob in a TV version of Rob's memoir.

4. Dick Van Dyke, interview with Lee Goldberg, Santa Monica, California, Archive of American Television, January 8, 1998, https://www.youtube.com/watch?v=CG7j2f0q67g&t=57s (accessed October 16, 2021).

5. Sheldon Leonard, lecture, University of California, Los Angeles, February 9, 1968, UCLA Communications Studies Archive, https://www.youtube.com/watch?v=3wfyUSPOm28 (accessed October 16, 2021).

6. Rita Katleman, "Dick Van Dyke Aims at True-to-Life Flavor," *Ithaca Journal*, December 30, 1961, 19.

7. The mention of THRUSH pays homage to *The Man from U.N.C.L.E.* It's an interesting reference because *U.N.C.L.E.* aired on NBC and *The Dick Van Dyke Show* aired on CBS.

8. *The Dick Van Dyke Show*, Season 4, episode 20, "The Redcoats Are Coming," written by Bill Persky and Sam Denoff, directed by Jerry Paris, Calvada Productions, aired February 10, 1965, on CBS.

9. *Mary Tyler Moore: Love Is All Around*, CBS News, aired January 26, 2017, on CBS. The special's title is an homage to the title of the theme song for Moore's popular, eponymous 1970s sitcom *Mary Tyler Moore*, which also aired on CBS.

10. Bill Persky, *My Life Is a Situation Comedy* (Weston, CT: Mandevilla Press, 2012), 44.

11. Mary Tyler Moore, *After All* (New York: Putnam, 1995), 86.

12. *The Dick Van Dyke Show* won 15 Emmy Awards during its run, including three for Van Dyke and two for Moore. Reiner won three awards for writing. Persky and Denoff won two. John Rich and Jerry Paris each won an Emmy for directing. The show won for Outstanding Comedy Series three times.

13. Leonard, lecture.

14. *Change of Habit* was Elvis Presley's 31st and last movie.

15. Marie Law, "Two All-Time TV Favorites Will Be Reunited Sunday," *Jackson Sun* (Jackson, TN), April 11, 1969, 24.

16. Law, "Two All-Time TV Favorites."

17. Jerry Van Dyke appears as Stacey Petrie, Rob's brother. Bill Idelson plays Herman Glimscher, who had dated Sally. In the reunion, they were married. Besides the 2004 special, Reiner had appeared as Alan Brady twice. In a 1995 episode of NBC's *Mad about You*, Paul Reiser's character, documentary producer Paul Buchman, recruits him to be the narrator for a documentary about comedy. Reiner wrote the script for and voiced the title character of the 2003 CGI-animated special *The Alan Brady Show*. It aired on TV Land and featured the star, acidic as ever, battling with his young writers. Buddy, Sally, and Rob were briefly referenced.

18. Miranda was granted parole in 1972. But he broke the parole condition when he got arrested for gun possession. Prosecutors later declined to bring the case to court. In 1976, Miranda died from stab wounds in a bar fight.

19. Stafford and Cernan were the backup crew for the prime crew—Elliot See and Charles Bassett. NASA moved them up when See and Bassett died in a plane crash on February 28. It happened as all four pilots flew from Ellington Air Force Base in Texas to Lambert Field in St. Louis, each two-man crew in a T-38 plane. Their purpose for being in St. Louis was to train in simulations at McDonnell Aircraft for space rendezvous. Bad weather—rain, snow, fog, and limited visibility—forced the pilots to land by using instruments. See apparently tried to land the standard way, by visuals, despite the weather. NASA investigated and found that pilot error was "the primary cause, due to the pilots' inability to maintain visual reference for a landing." "55 Years Ago: Remembering Elliot See and Charles Bassett," NASA, March 1, 2021, https://www.nasa.gov/feature/55-years-ago-remembering-elliot-see-and-charles-bassett (accessed October 26, 2021).

20. John Noble Wilford, "Loose Shield Blocks Gemini Docking," *New York Times*, June 4, 1966, 1.

21. Eugene Cernan with Don Davis, *The Last Man on the Moon: Astronaut Eugene Cernan and America's Race in Space* (New York: St. Martin's, 1999), 123.

22. Cernan, *The Last Man on the Moon*, 124.

23. Cernan, *The Last Man on the Moon*, 125. Gene Kranz said that the astronauts' exhaustion prevented further discussion about an EVA to fix the shroud problem. "Sometimes you need luck. The program dodged a bullet when the crew waved off. They also saved me from eating crow. I was glad that I never had to follow through with my words

to [NASA flight director Chris] Kraft in the heat of the moment that this would be my last mission." Gene Kranz, *Failure Is Not an Option: Mission Control from Mercury to Apollo 13 and Beyond* (New York: Simon & Schuster, 2000; New York: Simon & Schuster Paperbacks, 2009), 186. Citation refers to the paperback edition.

24. Cernan, *The Last Man on the Moon*, 132–33.

25. John D. Pomfret, "President Hails Crew's Coolness," *New York Times*, June 7, 1966, 34.

26. Cernan, *The Last Man on the Moon*, 133.

27. Pomfret, "President Hails Crew's Coolness."

28. "Birds a Happy, Couageous [*sic*] Flock—Bauer: Praises Snyder, Etchebarren," *Salisbury Daily Times* (Salisbury, MD), 14. Bauer had managed the A's in 1961 and 1962. His tenure in Baltimore lasted four full seasons. He got fired midway through the 1968 season. In 1969, he managed the Oakland A's. But the A's owner fired him in September, after 149 games. It was Bauer's last season as a major-league manager.

29. Powell broke into the majors in 1961, playing four games for the Orioles. He became an everyday player the next year. Powell ended his career with the Dodgers in 1977, compiling a .266 career average and clocking 339 home runs.

## Chapter Seven

1. "Sportsman," "Live Tips and Topics," *Boston Globe*, March 25, 1939, 6.

2. As of the publication of this book in 2023, the closest is Tony Gwynn's .394 in 1994.

3. As of the publication of this book in 2023, the closest is Babe Ruth's .474 career on-base percentage.

4. "Negro Leaguers" is a term used here to describe players who were prevented from playing in the major leagues for their entire careers or a substantial part. Roy Campanella was inducted in 1969. He played with the Washington Elite Giants in 1937 and the Baltimore Elite Giants from 1938 to 1946. He also played a couple of seasons with Monterrey in the Mexican League. But he broke through the color line and had a 10-year career with the Brooklyn Dodgers. Jackie Robinson played one season with the Kansas City Monarchs and 10 seasons in a Dodgers uniform. Hank Aaron played about three months with the Indianapolis Clowns before the Boston Braves signed him in 1952. He played a couple of seasons in the Braves' minor-league system before beginning a 23-year career in the major leagues. A Puerto Rican native, Roberto Clemente was the first Latino player to get inducted. Usually there's a five-year wait after a player ends his career. Clemente's induction happened in 1973 because of a special election—he died in a plane crash off the Puerto Rico coast on New Year's Eve 1972. He was on a humanitarian mission to help earthquake victims in Nicaragua.

5. Casey Stengel, National Baseball Hall of Fame and Museum induction speech, July 25, 1966, Cooperstown, New York, Major League Baseball, https://www.youtube.com/watch?v=fQmODIPhNfc (accessed December 26, 2021).

6. Houston had incorporated the synthetic grass in the Astrodome infield during the season.

7. Ed Schuyler Jr., "Farrell Leads Astros to Win over the Phillies," Associated Press, *Kane Republican*, July 20, 1966, 5.

8. Bob Buege, telephone interview with author, January 3, 2022.

9. Rick Schabowski, telephone interview with author, January 5, 2022.

10. Kenn Olson, email message to author, January 3, 2022.

11. Michael Collins, *Carrying the Fire: An Astronaut's Journeys* (New York: Farrar, Straus & Giroux, 1974; 50th anniversary edition, New York: Farrar, Straus & Giroux, 2019), 252. Citation refers to the 2019 edition.

Slayton was one of the original seven astronauts in Project Mercury, selected in 1959. But NASA grounded him because of an irregular heartbeat, so he took on the position of chief of the astronaut office. NASA later cleared him to fly in Apollo-Soyuz, a joint mission between the United States and Russia in 1975.

12. Young flew on *Gemini 3*, *Gemini 10*, *Apollo 10*, and *Apollo 16*. He also flew on the first space shuttle flight in 1981 with Robert Crippen. He was NASA's chief of the astronaut office from 1974 to 1987. Collins flew on *Gemini 10* with Young and later on *Apollo 11* as the command module pilot. While he maneuvered *Columbia*—the module—around the moon, Buzz Aldrin and Neil Armstrong became the first astronauts to walk on the moon's surface on July 20, 1969.

13. Sinatra married actress Mia Farrow on July 19, 1966. She was 21. They divorced two years later. Sinatra married Barbara Marx—ex-wife of Zeppo Marx—in 1976 and remained married to her until his death in 1998.

## CHAPTER EIGHT

1. "Caesars Palace Feast Ready," *Las Vegas Review-Journal*, August 4, 1966, 25.

2. September Sarno, telephone interview with author, April 28, 2022.

3. "Casino Has $1 Million Party, Two Tons of Steak," Associated Press, *Reno Evening Gazette*, August 5, 1966, 11.

4. Stanley and Sandy Mallin, interview by Barbara Tabach, January 7, 2015, transcript, Southern Nevada Jewish Heritage Project, Oral History Research Center University of Nevada, Las Vegas.

5. Caesars Palace newspaper advertisement, *Los Angeles Times*, July 27, 1966, 28. The ad copy differed slightly in other newspapers.

6. "Andy in for Gala Opening," *Las Vegas Sun*, August 5, 1966, 16.

7. Stuart Mason, interview by Claytee D. White, November 9, 2006, transcript, Boyer Las Vegas Early History Project, Oral History Research Center, University of Nevada, Las Vegas.

8. George Stamos Jr., "The Great Resorts of Las Vegas: How They Began! Part 16 of a Continuing Series," *Las Vegas Sun Magazine*, October 14, 1979, 6.

9. Stamos, "The Great Resorts of Las Vegas."

10. Edward O. Thorp, *A Man for All Markets: From Las Vegas to Wall Street, How I Beat the Dealer and the Market* (New York: Random House, 2017), 108.

11. President Lyndon Johnson, "Dedication of the Ellenville Community Hospital," Ellenville, New York, August 19, 1966.

12. Richard McGowan, "LBJ Vows 4-Front War on Poverty," *New York Daily News*, August 20, 1966, C3.

13. The president initially targeted Motley for a different judicial assignment. In her autobiography, Motley wrote, "Originally, Johnson had planned to submit my name to the Senate for appointment to the U.S. Court of Appeals for the Second Circuit in New York City, filling the vacancy created by his appointment of Thurgood Marshall to the position of solicitor general of the United States. However, there was so much opposition on the court and among Wall Street lawyers to my appointment to that bench, which had never had a woman, that Johnson was forced to withdraw my name." Constance Baker Motley, *Equal Justice under Law* (New York: Farrar, Straus & Giroux, 1998), 212.

14. Motley, *Equal Justice under Law*, 215.

15. Ludtke v. Kuhn, 461 F. Supp. 86 (S.D.N.Y., September 25, 1978).

16. Melissa Ludtke, telephone interview with author, May 17, 2022.

17. *Ludtke*, 461 F. Supp. 86.

18. There are different versions of the test depending on the jurisdiction, but they all follow the same basic format of analysis based on several factors: strength of the plaintiff's trademark, similarity between the trademark used by the parties, proximity of the products, likelihood that plaintiffs will "bridge the gap," actual confusion, good faith or intent of the defendant, quality of defendant's services, and sophistication of services.

19. Major League Baseball Properties v. Sed Non Olet Denarius, Ltd., 817 F. Supp. 1103 (S.D.N.Y., April 6, 1993).

20. *Major League Baseball Properties*, 817 F. Supp. 1103.

21. *Major League Baseball Properties*, 817 F. Supp. 1103.

22. Stephen Davis, "Pet Sounds," *Rolling Stone*, June 22, 1972, https://www.rollingstone.com/music/music-album-reviews/pet-sounds-249007 (accessed March 13, 2022).

23. Neal Eskridge, "'I Just Swung,' Says Boog Powell," *Baltimore News-American*, August 16, 1966, 3C.

24. Milton Richman, "Orioles Blow Flag? Bauer Shuns the Thought," United Press International, *Baltimore News-American*, August 16, 1966, 3C.

## Chapter Nine

1. The 1996 movie *Mission: Impossible* starring Tom Cruise made it clear that the IMF team works for the Central Intelligence Agency.

2. Wally Cox played a safecracker named Terry Targo in the pilot, which focused on the IMF team getting nuclear missiles out of a hostile country. Graves reprised the Phelps character in the 1988–1990 sequel series. Bob Johnson's voice was on the audiotapes at the beginning of the episodes. As of the publication of this book, there have been eight movies starring Tom Cruise as IMF team leader Ethan Hunt.

3. Barbara Bain, telephone interview with author, January 10, 2022.

4. Jean Louisa Kelly, email to author, March 5, 2022.

5. Erika Scheimer, telephone interview with author, January 12, 2022.

6. Paul Hefti, telephone interview with author, January 10, 2022.

7. Kevin Jeffries, telephone interview with author, January 12, 2022.

8. Screen Gems and Colgems repeated this scheme with *The Partridge Family* in 1970, releasing "I Think I Love You" in the summer before the show's fall premiere.

9. There was a controversy in the beginning over whether the Monkees played their instruments and sang the lyrics. But the tours proved that they did.

10. Monkeemania persisted in subsequent decades. In 1986, they reunited for a concert tour with newfound interest thanks to MTV airing reruns. There was also a 1997 reunion TV special. In 2010, another reunion tour began with Jones, Tork, and Dolenz. The trio performed together until Jones's death from a heart attack in 2012. Nesmith joined Tork and Dolenz, then bowed out a couple of years later and rejoined Dolenz after Tork died in 2019. As of this book's publication, Dolenz is the last living Monkee, and the group has yet to be inducted into the Rock and Roll Hall of Fame.

11. Charles Witbeck, "'Star Trek' Is 'Adult Science-Fiction,'" *Fresno Bee*, September 11, 1966, TV8.

12. John Stanley, "A Trek through Deepest Space," Entertainment Section, *San Francisco Examiner*, September 4, 1966, 10.

13. Leonard Nimoy, interview with Karen Herman, Beverly Hills, California, November 2, 2000, Television Academy Foundation, Archive of American Television, https://www.youtube.com/watch?v=mogZP_fexfA (accessed January 19, 2022).

14. Roddenberry had shot two pilots for the original series with Jeffrey Hunter as USS *Enterprise* captain Christopher Pike, who is the character in the prequel series *Star Trek: Strange New Worlds*. As of this book's publication, there have been seven live-action spinoffs: *Star Trek: The Next Generation*, *Star Trek: Deep Space Nine*, *Star Trek: Voyager*, *Star Trek: Enterprise*, *Star Trek: Discovery*, *Star Trek: Picard*, and *Star Trek: Strange New Worlds*. *Star Trek: Lower Decks* and *Star Trek: Prodigy* are animated shows. Initially, *Star Trek: Enterprise* was titled *Enterprise*. It was also a prequel to the original show. *The Next Generation* cast starred in four films. A reboot brought the franchise back to films in 2009 with Chris Pine as Kirk and Zachary Quinto as Spock. There were two sequels as of the publication of this book in 2023.

15. Marc Rayman, telephone interview with author, January 25, 2022.

16. John Noble Wilford, "Computer Guides *Gemini*'s Re-Entry and Splashdown," *New York Times*, September 16, 1966, 1. Gordon approximated the number. It was reported to be 739 nautical miles and 850 statute miles.

17. Wilford, "Computer Guides."

18. John Steadman, "Happy Hoffberger: Leader of Baltimore Band," *Sporting News*, October 8, 1966.

19. Douglas Brown, "Amid Flag Fun, Orioles Remember Two 'Buddies,'" *Baltimore Evening Sun*, September 23, 1966. During Bauer's tenure, the Yankees won seven World Series championships.

## CHAPTER TEN

1. After the rainout, National League president Warren Giles decreed that the game wouldn't be rescheduled unless it would be a factor in deciding the pennant winner at the end of the season. Lou Smith, "Game Canceled Unless Necessary to Decide Flag," *Cincinnati Enquirer*, August 11, 1966, 29.

2. Charles Maher, "Sweep Keeps S.F. in Chase with Dodgers," *Los Angeles Times*, October 2, 1966, D1.

3. The Dodgers also had a two-of-three series in 1959 against the Milwaukee Braves. LA won the playoff in three games and defeated the White Sox in the World Series.

4. Charles Maher, "Day to Forget at Dodger Stadium," *Los Angeles Times*, October 6, 1996, B4; Allan Malamud, "Wills: 'Too Quiet,'" *Los Angeles Herald Examiner*, October 6, 1966, D8.

5. He appeared in 34 games but was the starting pitcher in 33.

6. Fred Neil, "Alston Remembers Moe," *Los Angeles Herald Examiner*, October 6, 1966, D2.

7. Neil, "Alston Remembers Moe."

8. Melvin Durslag, "Moe Just Another Jaster," *Los Angeles Herald Examiner*, October 6, 1966, D1.

9. Jack Disney, "O's Love Day Baseball," *Los Angeles Herald Examiner*, October 6, 1966, D4.

10. Douglas Brown, "It's Koufax-Palmer in 2d Series Game," *Baltimore Evening Sun*, October 6, 1966, A1.

11. John Hall, "Stunned Drabowsky Modest in Series Victory," *Los Angeles Times*, October 6, 1966, B1.

12. Beth Morris, telephone interview with author, March 2, 2022, and June 5, 2022.

13. Brooks Robinson, "Confident We Can Beat Koufax—Brooks," *Baltimore News-American*, October 6, 1966, 2D.

14. Frank Finch, "A Tragic Comedy: Dodgers Lose, 6–0," *Los Angeles Times*, October 7, 1966, B1.

15. Barry Mednick, telephone interview with author, January 13, 2022.

16. Jack Disney, "Ravine Holds No Terror for Orioles," *Los Angeles Herald Examiner*, October 7, 1966, B2.

17. Douglas Brown, "Birds Home Two-Up after Palmer's Record Shutout," *Baltimore Evening Sun*, October 7, 1966, B9.

18. Bob Myers, "Osteen Just Shrugs," Associated Press, *Los Angeles Herald Examiner*, October 9, 1966, E-8.

19. Lou Hatter, "Bauer Never Planned Hook," *Baltimore Sun*, October 9, 1966, A10.

20. John Roseboro with Bill Libby, *Glory Days with the Dodgers and Other Days with Others* (New York: Atheneum, 1978), 217.

21. Mitch Chortkoff, "How the Kiddie Korps Stopped L.A.," *Los Angeles Herald Examiner*, October 10, 1966, D2.

22. Mike Rathet, "Frank Robinson: His Ambitions Are Accomplished," Associated Press, *Hagerstown Morning Herald* (Hagerstown, MD), October 10, 1966, 15.

23. "1966 10 09 World Series Game 4 Orioles vs Dodgers Vin Scully Radio Broadcast," https://www.youtube.com/watch?v=X5vsv71qRBg (accessed February 26, 2022).

24. "1966 10 09 World Series Game 4."

25. Bob Scherr, telephone interview with author, October 6, 2020.

26. W. Lawrence Null, "Walt Alston Not Planning to Jump Off Any Bridges," *Baltimore Sun*, October 10, 1966, C5.

27. Wes Parker, telephone interview with author, February 14, 2021.

28. Eddie Watt, telephone interview with author, February 28, 2022.

29. Jim Gates, email to author, February 21, 2022.

30. James Nahigian, telephone interview with author, January 8, 2022.

31. Bob Trostler, telephone interview with author, January 11, 2022.

32. Gregg Pericich, telephone interview with author, January 8, 2022.

## CHAPTER ELEVEN

1. Jud Baker, "Reagan and Finch: Easy Win for GOP Pair," *Los Angeles Herald Examiner*, November 9, 1966, A3.

2. https://www.youtube.com/watch?v=442rW8QaRtA.

3. https://www.youtube.com/watch?v=442rW8QaRtA.

4. "Richard Nixon on 1966 Gubernatorial Race," KTVU-TV, Bay Area TV Archive, San Francisco State University, https://diva.sfsu.edu/collections/sfbatv/bundles/238898 (accessed May 28, 2022).

5. Iwan Morgan, *Reagan: American Icon* (New York: I. B. Tauris, 2016), 92.

6. Agnew later resigned the vice presidency in 1973 because of a tax fraud and corruption investigation.

7. De Van L. Shumway, "Landslide Gives Reagan Mandate for His Program," *Redlands Daily Facts*, November 10, 1966, 1.

8. Thomas O'Toole, "Gemini Scores Near-Bullseye," *Washington Post*, November 16, 1966, A1.

9. Rudy Abramson, "Final Gemini Mission Ends, Sets Stage for Apollo Project," *Los Angeles Times*, November 16, 1966, A1. Aldrin's total time outside the capsule was reported to be "about five hours and 38 minutes."

10. James A. Lovell Jr., interview by Ron Stone, May 25, 1999, Edited Oral History Transcript, NASA Johnson Space Center Oral History Project, NASA, Houston, https://historycollection.jsc.nasa.gov/JSCHistoryPortal/history/oral_histories/LovellJA/LovellJA_5-25-99.htm (accessed May 27, 2022).

11. NASA's Manned Spacecraft Center in Houston was renamed the Lyndon B. Johnson Space Center less than a month after Johnson's death in 1973.

12. "U.S. Man on Moon by '68 Predicted," *New York Times*, November 1, 1966, A8.

13. "Johnson Cautions on Moon Mission," *New York Times*, November 24, 1966, 36.

14. "X-15 Rocket Plane Sets Speed Record of 6 Times Sound," *New York Times*, November 18, 1966, 24.

15. "Gemini's Triumph," *Washington Post*, November 17, 1966, A22.

16. "Advances into Space," *New York Times*, November 12, 1966, 28.

17. John Tilden, telephone interview with author, April 21, 2022.

18. "O'Malley Praises Koufax," United Press International, *Los Angeles Herald Examiner*, November 19, 1966, C2.

19. Bob Hunter, "Sandy's Woe: 'Mental Torture,'" *Los Angeles Herald Examiner*, November 19, 1966, C1.

20. Melvin Durslag, "The Dilemma: Did Sandy Quit Too Soon?," *Los Angeles Herald Examiner*, November 20, 1966, E1.

21. Koufax tied with Jim Bunning and Jim Kaat. Each pitcher started 41 games in 1966.

22. "Alston: We Should Do Okay," Associated Press, *Los Angeles Herald Examiner*, November 24, 1966, G2.

23. Chic Feldman, "Tracewski Doubts Koufax Will Reconsider," *Scrantonian*, November 20, 1966, 55.

24. "Clemente Wins MVP Award," *Los Angeles Herald Examiner*, November 16, 1966, C1.

25. Jeff Torborg, telephone interview with author, May 28, 2022.

26. Alston acknowledged that Japanese players had improved their hitting since the Dodgers visited Japan in 1956. "Japan Losses Bother Manager Alston," Associated Press, *Los Angeles Herald Examiner*, November 13, 1966, E1.

27. Bob Hunter, "Maury's Own Story," *Los Angeles Herald Examiner*, November 11, 1966, C1.

28. Bob Hunter, "Wills Wants Chat with O'Malley," *Los Angeles Herald Examiner*, November 12, 1966, C2.

29. Bob Hunter, "Wills to Get Axe? Bavasi Doubts It," *Los Angeles Herald Examiner*, November 17, 1966, F1.

30. Bob Hunter, "Wills May Follow Koufax, Quit," *Los Angeles Herald Examiner*, November 30, 1966, G1.

31. Bob Hunter, "T. Davis Unsuspecting," *Los Angeles Herald Examiner*, November 30, 1966, G1. Davis also led the majors in hits and RBIs in 1962.

## CHAPTER TWELVE

1. "Orbiter 2 Transmits Spectacular Close-Up of Moon," *New York Times*, December 1, 1966, 1.

2. "Orbiter Takes 'Picture of the Century,'" United Press International, *Waco News-Tribune*, December 1, 1966, 1.

3. "Orbiter Takes 'Picture of the Century.'"

4. Webb said that there was an additional $15 billion in costs for associated projects. There had been an amount of $70 billion argued in some corners. He called that reflection of the program's expenses "inaccurate." Donald Janson, "Webb Backs Cost of Space Program," *New York Times*, December 6, 1966, 34.

5. *Lunar Orbiter 2*, NASA, https://solarsystem.nasa.gov/missions/lunar-orbiter-2/in-depth (accessed March 9, 2022).

6. This special marked Elvis Presley's first TV appearance since his two-year stint in the army finished. Presley had been stationed in West Germany.

7. Produced by Warner Bros., *Surfside Six* existed in the same fictional universe as three other private-eye shows starring young, attractive actors and actresses—*77 Sunset Strip* (set in Los Angeles), *Bourbon Street Beat* (set in New Orleans), and *Hawaiian Eye* (set in Honolulu).

8. Danny Thomas, with Bill Davidson, *Make Room for Danny* (New York: G. P. Putnam's Sons, 1991), 202–3. The Dolphins played in three consecutive Super Bowl games in the 1970s. They lost in 1972 and won the next two contests.

9. Other examples include WDVR-FM (Delaware Valley Radio), WJLA-TV (station owner Joseph L. Allbritton), WJNC-AM (Jacksonville, North Carolina), and WISC-TV (Wisconsin). WGN in Chicago had a similar paradigm to WPIX. The Tribune Company owned the radio station WDAP and changed the call letters to publicize the link to the *Chicago Tribune*. WGN stands for "World's Greatest Newspaper." The *Tribune* also used these call letters for its TV station, which also debuted in 1948.

10. Fred M. Thrower, memorandum to WPIX staff, November 2, 1966, reprinted, Mitch Thrower, "The Lost Memo That Sparked the Original WPIX Yule Log," December 25, 2019, https://medium.com/@mitchthrower/the-lost-memo-that-sparked-the-original-wpix-yule-log-7653779d0cb9 (last accessed April 10, 2022).

11. Rolando Pujol, email to author, May 30, 2022.

12. "Vietnam War U.S. Military Fatal Casualty Statistics," Military Records, National Archives, https://www.archives.gov/research/military/vietnam-war/casualty-statistics (accessed June 5, 2022).

13. "Spellman Celebrates Midnight Mass at Camranh Bay," *New York Times*, December 25, 1966, 3.

14. "Spellman Again Tells G.I.s in Vietnam They Are Defending Civilization," *New York Times*, December 27, 1966, 4.

15. "Spellman's View Decried in Rome," *New York Times*, December 28, 1966, 3.

16. John Cogley, "The Spellman Dispute," *New York Times*, December 29, 1966, 3.

# Bibliography

*Note:* This bibliography contains a sample of the tremendous scholarship regarding the events that I've chronicled.

Adelman, Tom. *Black and Blue: The Golden Arm, the Robinson Boys, and the 1966 World Series That Stunned America.* Boston: Little, Brown, 2006.

Alston, Walter, with Si Burick. *Alston and the Dodgers.* Garden City, NY: Doubleday, 1966.

Alston, Walter, with Jack Tobin. *A Year at a Time.* Waco, TX: Word Books, 1976.

*A.R.C.H.I.E. as The Man from R.I.V.E.R.D.A.L.E.* Mamaroneck, NY: Archie Comics, 2019. All stories in the anthology were previously published by Archie Comics in 1966–1967.

*Astronautics and Aeronautics, 1966: Chronology on Science, Technology, and Policy.* Text by Science and Technology Division, Library of Congress, Sponsored by NASA Historical Staff, Office of Policy, Scientific and Technical Information Division, NASA, 1967.

Barbree, Jay. *Neil Armstrong: A Life of Flight.* New York: Thomas Dunne, 2014.

*Batman vs. The Penguin.* New York: Signet, 1966. All stories in the anthology were previously published by National Periodicals Publications in 1952, 1953, 1954, 1956, 1963, and 1966.

Bavasi, Buzzie, with John Strege. *Off the Record.* Chicago: Contemporary Press, 1987.

Brooke, Edward W. *Bridging the Divide: My Life.* New Brunswick, NJ: Rutgers University Press, 2007.

Cernan, Eugene, and Don Davis. *The Last Man on the Moon: Astronaut Eugene Cernan and America's Race in Space.* New York: St. Martin's, 1999.

Collins, Michael. *Carrying the Fire: An Astronaut's Journey.* New York: Farrar, Straus & Giroux, 1974.

David, Saul. *The Industry: Life in the Hollywood Fast Lane.* New York: Times Books, 1981.

Drysdale, Don, with Bob Verdi. *Once a Bum, Always a Dodger: My Life in Baseball from Brooklyn to Los Angeles.* New York: St. Martin's, 1990.

Evans, Thomas W. *The Education of Ronald Reagan: The General Electric Years and the Untold Story of His Conversion to Conservatism.* New York: Columbia University Press, 2006.

Fleming, Ian. *Octopussy.* London: Jonathan Cape, 1966.

Hansen, James R. *First Man: The Life of Neil Armstrong.* New York: Simon & Schuster, 2005.

Henneman, Jim. *Baltimore Orioles: 60 Years of Orioles Magic.* San Rafael, CA: Insight Editions, 2015.

Johnson, Lyndon B. *The Vantage Point: Perspectives of the Presidency, 1963–1969.* New York: Holt, Rinehart & Winston, 1971.

Koufax, Sandy, with Ed Linn. *Koufax.* New York: Viking, 1966.

Krell, David. *1962: Baseball and America in the Time of JFK.* Lincoln: University of Nebraska Press, 2021.

Leahy, Michael. *The Last Innocents: The Collision of the Turbulent Sixties and the Los Angeles Dodgers.* New York: HarperCollins, 2016.

Leavy, Jane. *Sandy Koufax: A Lefty's Legacy.* New York: HarperCollins, 2002.

Leonard, Sheldon. *And the Show Goes On: Broadway and Hollywood Adventures.* New York: Limelight Editions, 1995.

Lifson, Hal. *Hal Lifson's 1966: A Personal View of the Coolest Year in Pop Culture History.* Dallas: Taylor Trade Publishing, 2003.

Love, Mike, with James S. Hirsch. *Good Vibrations: My Life as a Beach Boy.* New York: Blue Rider Press, 2016.

Mansfield, Irving, with Jean Libman Block. *Life with Jackie.* New York: Bantam, 1983.

McCue, Andy. *Mover & Shaker: Walter O'Malley, the Dodgers, & Baseball's Westward Expansion.* Lincoln: University of Nebraska Press, 2014.

Millikin, Mark R. *The Glory of the 1966 Orioles and Baltimore.* Haworth, NJ: St. Johann Press, 2006.

Moore, Mary Tyler. *After All.* New York: Putnam, 1995.

Morgan, Iwan. *Reagan: American Icon.* London: I. B. Tauris, 2016.

Motley, Constance Baker. *Equal Justice under Law.* New York: Farrar, Straus and Giroux, 1998.

Nimoy, Leonard. *I Am Spock.* New York: Hyperion, 1995.

Patterson, Ted. *The Baltimore Orioles: 40 Years of Magic from 33rd Street to Camden Yards.* Dallas: Taylor Publishing, 1994.

Persky, Bill. *My Life Is a Situation Comedy.* Weston, CT: Mandevilla Press, 2012.

Reiner, Carl. *My Anecdotal Life: A Memoir.* New York: St. Martin's, 2003.

Robinson, Brooks, with Fred Bauer. *Putting It All Together.* New York: Hawthorn, 1971.

Robinson, Brooks, and Jack Tobin. *Third Base Is My Home.* Waco, TX: Word Books, 1974.

Robinson, Frank, with Al Silverman. *My Life Is Baseball.* 1966; Garden City, NY: Doubleday, 1975.

Robinson, Frank, and Berry Stainback. *Extra Innings.* New York: McGraw Hill, 1988.

Roseboro, John, with Bill Libby. *Glory Days with the Dodgers and Other Days with Others.* New York: Atheneum, 1978.

Scheimer, Lou, with Andy Mangels. *Lou Scheimer: Creating the Filmation Generation.* New York: TwoMorrows Publishing, 2014.

Schwartz, David G. *Grandissimo: The First Emperor of Las Vegas—How Jay Sarno Won a Casino Empire, Lost It, and Inspired Modern Las Vegas.* Las Vegas: Winchester Books, 2013.

Scott, David, and Alexei Leonov, with Christine Mooney. *Two Sides of the Moon: Our Story of the Cold War Space Race.* New York: Thomas Dunne, 2004.

Shatner, William, with Chris Kreski. *Star Trek Memories*. New York: HarperCollins, 1993.

Steele, Patrick W. *Home of the Braves: The Battle for Baseball in Milwaukee*. Madison, WI: University of Wisconsin Press, 2018.

Stout, Glenn. *The Dodgers: 120 Years of Dodgers Baseball*. New York: Houghton Mifflin, 2004.

Susann, Jacqueline. *Valley of the Dolls*. New York: Bernard Geis Associates, 1966.

Thomas, Danny, with Bill Davidson. *Make Room for Danny*. New York: Putnam, 1991.

Thorp, Edward O. *Beat the Dealer: A Winning Strategy for the Game of Twenty-One*. New York: Random House, 1962.

Thorp, Edward O. *A Man for All Markets: From Las Vegas to Wall Street, How I Beat the Dealer and the Market*. New York: Random House, 2017.

Tiemann, Robert L. *Dodger Classics: Outstanding Games from Each of the Dodgers' 101 Seasons, 1883–1983*. St. Louis: Baseball Histories, 1983.

Van Dyke, Dick. *My Lucky Life in and out of Show Business: A Memoir*. New York: Crown Archetype, 2011.

Waldron, Vince. *The Official Dick Van Dyke Show Book: The Definitive History and Ultimate Viewer's Guide to Television's Most Enduring Comedy*. New York: Hyperion, 1994.

Weisman, Jon. *Brothers in Arms: Koufax, Kershaw, and the Dodgers' Extraordinary Pitching Tradition*. Chicago: Triumph Books, 2018.

Wills, Maury, and Mike Celizic. *On the Run: The Never Dull and Often Shocking Life of Maury Wills*. New York: Carroll & Graf, 1991.

Wills, Maury, and Don Freeman. *How to Steal a Pennant*. New York: Putnam, 1976.

Wills, Maury, and Steve Gardner. *It Pays to Steal*. Englewood Cliffs, NJ: Prentice-Hall, 1963.

Wilson, Doug. *Brooks: The Biography of Brooks Robinson*. New York: Thomas Dunne, 2014.

# INDEX

Note: Page numbers in *italics* refer to figures.

Boyle Heights, California, 24
Bragan, Bobby, 42
*Breakfast at Tiffany's*, 91
Brecheen, Harry, 157, 158
Brewer, Jim, 32
Brinegar, Paul, *21*
Broccoli, Cubby, 74
Brock, Lou, 149
Brodax, Al, 135
Bronson Canyon, 8
Bronson Cave, 8
Brooke, Edward, 169
Brooklyn Gladiators, 4
Brooks, Mel, 82
Brooks Air Force Base, 172
Brown, Pat, 165–66, 168
*Brown v. Board of Education of Topeka*, 105, 124
Brubeck, Dave, 2
Buege, Bob, 109–10
Buffalo, New York, 66, 115, 122
Bunker, Wally, 155
Bunning, Jim, 107, 176
Burbank, California, 163
Burton, Harold, 122
Busch Stadium, 71, 72
Busy Bee Market, 163
Butler, Robert, 15
Buttons, Red, 120
*Bye Bye Birdie*, 87

Caesar, Julius, 165
Caesar, Sid, 81
Caesars Palace: art, 120; comparison to other casinos,

118, 192; creation of, 115–17; debut, 116, 118–19; food, 116; marquee, *117*; original name, 119; oval shaped, 119–20; sex appeal, 118; uniforms for women, 118
California Angels, 154
California State Assembly, 174
Calvert, Cecil, 4, 7
Cambridge, Godfrey, 89, 192
Cannon, Dyan, 31
Cannon, Robert, 37
Cape Canaveral, Florida, 35
Cape Kennedy, Florida, 144, 169
Carnegie Tech (Carnegie Mellon), 136
Carney, Art, 13
Carpin, Frank, 66
Carroll, Leo G., 76
Carson, Johnny, 2–3, *3*, 87
Carty, Rico, 63
*Casino Royale* (novel), 74
*Casino Royale* (television), 74
*Cast a Giant Shadow*, 68–69
Catskill Mountains, 121–122
CBS, 20–21, 87–88, 92, 131, 136, 137, 167, 175, 185, 187–88
Cedar Rapids, Iowa, 115
Central Park West, 77
Cepeda, Orlando, 71
Cernan, Gene, 95–98, 112
Chandler, Happy, 44
Chaney, Lon, Jr., 14
*Change of Habit*, 92
Chanukah, 79, 187

Series, 149–50, 156–57, 160–61
Drysdale, Ginger, 26
Dual, 2
Dunes Hotel and Casino, 183. *See also* Las Vegas, Nevada
Durocher, Leo, 31, 41–44, 175
Durslag, Melvin, 159–60
Dutton, Cathy, 57–58
Dutton, Jack, 56–59
Dylan, Bob, 192

Earth, 181
East 42nd Place, 55
East 42nd Street, 190
Eastland, James, 123
Eastwood, Clint, *21*, 188
Ebbets, Charles, 105
*The Echoing Green*, 44
Eckert, William, 45, 179
Eden, Barbara, 129, 131
*The Ed Sullivan Show*, 11, 81, 89
Eisenhower, Dwight, 42, 172
El Camino College, 31
Ellenville Community Hospital, 121
Ellenville, New York, 121–22
Eller, Hod, 151
El Rancho Hotel and Casino, 121
Emmy Award, 82, 85, 91, 92, 134
Enunciation Church, 73
espionage in popular culture, 74–79, 192
Etchebarren, Andy, 149, 151, 153, 154, 159

Evans, Maurice, 13
Evers, Medgar, 105
*Everybody Loves Raymond*, 84

Face, Elroy, 63
Fairchild, Thomas, 107
Fairly, Ron, 65, 155
Farrell, Dick, 6
Farrow, Mia, 159
*Fat Albert and the Cosby Kids*, 137
FBI, 13, 89
Federal Housing Administration, 117
Fenway Park, 103, 127
Fermin Lausen High School, 163
Ferrara, Al, 157
Ferrari, 12
Field, Sally, 66
Fifth Amendment, 93
Fifth Avenue, 187
Filmation, 135–36
First Amendment, 124
Flamingo Hotel & Casino, 115, 118, 120
Fleming, Ian, 74, 98
Flint, Derek, 77
*The Flintstones*, 75
Florence, Italy, 120
Florsheim, 2
"Fly Me to the Moon," 113–14
Flynn, Doug, 45
Fonda, Henry, 14
Fontainebleau Hotel, 184
Forbes Field, 147
Fort Knox, 6

*Los Angeles Herald Examiner*,
24, 52, 159, 163, 165,
179
Los Angeles International
Airport, 27
Los Angeles Philharmonic, 153
*Los Angeles Times*, 48, 75, 163
*Lou Grant*, 92
Louise, Tina, *21*, 22, 23
*Louisiana Hayride*, 42
Love, Mike, 127
Lovell, Jim, 50, 169–73, *170*
Lovin' Spoonful, 81, 126
Ludtke, Melissa, 124–25
*Lunar Orbiter 2*, 173, 181–84
Lupus, Peter, 132

Mack, Connie, 46
MacPhail, Lee, 45
Macri, Donald, 162
Macy's Thanksgiving Day Parade,
187
Madison Avenue, 80
Magnavox, 81
Major League Baseball, 125
Major League Baseball Players
Association, 37. *See also*
Miller, Marvin
*Make Room for Daddy*, 186
Malcom X, 105
Malibu, California, 10, 26, 66
Malibu Creek State Park, 24
Mallin, Stanley, 116–18
Maloney, Jim, 44, 51
*The Man Called Flintstone*, 75

*The Man from R.I.V.E.R.D.A.L.E.*,
79
*The Man from U.N.C.L.E.*, 76–77
Manhattan Project, 172
Man in Space Soonest (MISS), 49
Marceau, Marcel, 48
March on Washington, 105
Marcus, David "Mickey," 68
Marichal, Juan, 44, 51, 147
Marie, Rose, 88, 92
Maris, Roger, 6
*The Marriage of a Young
Stockbroker*, 11
Marshall, Thurgood, 124
Martin, Dean, 75–76, 114, 192
Martin, Ross, *21*
Marx Brothers, 140
*Mary Poppins*, 91
*Mary Tyler Moore* (also known as
*The Mary Tyler Moore Show*),
92
*The Mary Tyler Moore Hour*, 92
Mason, Jackie, 120
Mason, Stuart, 119
Mathews, Eddie, 44, 63
Mathewson, Christy, 101
Matthews, Burnita, 123
*Maverick*, 13
Mayberry, North Carolina, 185
*Mayberry R.F.D.*, 185
May Company, 9
May, David, 9
Mays, Willie, 24, 43, 44, 53
Mazeroski, Bill, 147–48
McCarthy, Joseph, 15

Pittsburgh Pirates, 129, 146–48, 177

*Playboy*, 75

Playboy Club, 112

"Pleasant Valley Sunday," 140

Podres, Johnny, 31, 32

Poe, Edgar Allan, 7

Polo Grounds, 44

Pomona, New York, 16

Pontiac GTO, 139

Porter, Don, 66

*Post-Standard* (Syracuse, New York), 75

Powell, Boog, 5, 72, 99, 127–28, 149, 150, 153, 154, 155, 156

Prager, Joshua, 44

Preminger, Otto, 14

Prescott, Norm, 136

Presley, Elvis, 42, 92, 184

Preston Street, 73

Prima, Louis, 75

Princeton, 75

Procter & Gamble, 88

Project Gemini, 8, 47–50

Project Mercury, 49–50

Pryor, Richard, 81

Puerto Rico, 113

Pujol, Rolando, 189–91

Pyle, Ernie, 14

Quaker's Dippy Canoes corn chips, 79

Quartermaster (Q), 74–75. *See also* Bond, James

Radio City Music Hall, 187

"Rape of the Sabines" (statue), 120

Rayman, Marc, 143

RCA, 2

"Reach Out, I'll Be There," 81

Reagan, Nancy, *166*

Reagan, Ronald, 165–69, *166*

"Red Rubber Ball," 81

*The Red Skelton Show*, 22

Reese, Pee Wee, 84

Regan, Phil, 30

Reiner, Carl, 81–82, 87, 90, 92

Reiner, Rob, 81–82

*Reno Evening Gazette*, 181

Reno Silver Sox, 30

Resnick, Joe, 121

*Return of the Man from U.N.C.L.E.*, 77

Reynolds, Burt, 188

Rheingold, 47

*Rhoda*, 92

Rice University, 34

Richman, Milton, 128

Rich Uncle Pennybags, 25

Rickey, Branch, 27

*The Rifleman*, 13

Riviera Hotel & Casino, 118, 119, 120

Ritz Brothers, 116, 118

Robbie, Joe, 185–86

Roberts, Robin, 37, 66, 104

Robertson, Cliff, 13

Robin Hood, 13

Robinson, Brooks, 5, 149, 153, 154, 156, 158

# ABOUT THE AUTHOR

**David Krell** is the author of *1962: Baseball and America in the Time of JFK* and *Our Bums: The Brooklyn Dodgers in History, Memory, and Popular Culture*. He edited the anthologies *The New York Mets in Popular Culture* and *The New York Yankees in Popular Culture*. Krell often presents at Society for American Baseball Research conferences, the Cooperstown Symposium on Baseball and American Culture, and the Mid-Atlantic Nostalgia Convention. He's the chair of SABR's Northern New Jersey Chapter. He lives in Jersey City, New Jersey.

CPSIA information can be obtained
at www.ICGtesting.com
Printed in the USA
BVHW042226200523
664578BV00002B/45